Snakes

The de Kay snake.

Snakes

An Anthology
of Serpent Tales

EDITED BY Willee Lewis

FOREWORD BY George Plimpton

For Michael with best wishes from Willee Lewis

M. EVANS AND COMPANY, INC.
New York

M. EVANS AND COMPANY, INC.
216 East 49th Street
New York, New York 10017

Library of Congress
   Cataloging-in-Publication Data

Snakes : an anthology of serpent tales / edited by Willee Lewis
      p.   cm.
    ISBN 1-59077-008-0
      I. Snakes—Literary collections. 2. Snakes. I. Lewis, Willee.
PN6071.S49S58 2003
    808.8'0362796—dc21   2003043896

Book design and typesetting by Terry Bain

Printed in the United States of America

9 8 7 6 5 4 3 2 1

to Finlay

Contents

Folklore and Mythology

Foreword

I HAVE A FRIEND who fancied snakes and kept them when he was a young boy. His mother, a great beauty, was a member of high society in Chicago and on one occasion at a party in Lake Forest she wore one of her son's small boas as a bracelet around her wrist. I wasn't there to vouch for this, but her son told me the story a few times and I always believed him. The thought (the long arms with the thin coils of speckled yellow at the wrist) has been too much to dismiss from my mind. To my surprise my friend's mother is not unique. In her engaging introduction to this volume Willee Lewis writes of Alice Roosevelt Longworth who enlivened her Washington dinner parties by pulling a green garter snake out of her evening bag.

Willee Lewis is one of my great Washington friends. With her husband Finlay, their house is a gathering place for figures from media, political and the literary circles. Quite unlikely that Willee will ever greet her guests at the door with a boa encircling her wrist (or a larger species, around her thin waist), or provide entertainment at dinner by pulling a garter snake out of an evening bag. Indeed, she confesses she is "scared by the most innocent of snakes." But fortunately she has put her fears aside and gathered things reptilian for this delightful collection.

There is much here—the great classics (Arthur Conan Doyle's "The

Speckled Band," Rudyard Kipling's "Rikki-Tikki-Tavi," Roald Dahl's "The Green Mamba," John Steinbeck's "The Snake," Tom Wolfe's rattlesnake-house episode from *A Man in Full*).

Many of the contributors (Philip Bobbitt, Kate Lehrer, Susan Kinsolving, Joanne Leedom-Ackerman, Willie Morris, Emily Dickinson, Mary Lynn Kotz, Finlay Lewis, Randall Kenan, Gail Godwin) had childhood memories involving snakes, indeed moved enough by the experience to commit whatever happened at the time to verse or prose. Only a few turn out to be truly admiring of snakes (Virginia Adair, Mary Oliver, D. H. Lawrence, Stanley Kunitz, Rose Styron), others not (John Milton, Margaret Atwood, Michael Collier, Jim Lehrer, J. D. McClatchy, Winston Groom).

Some of the stories involve confrontations (Marie Ridder with her copperheads, James Corbett with a king cobra in a pitch-black bathroom. Dave Barry worries about being with a python on an airplane. Susan Eisenhower has a snake drop out of a tree onto her head.) One or two are truly chilling, even *X-Files*-ish: Ambrose Bierce's tale ("The Man and the Snake"), whose protagonist spots something alarming on the other side of the room. Theodore Roethke wants to be a snake. Paul Bowles actually turns into one. Ogden Nash suggests what it is to be eaten by a snake. Saint-Exupéry's snake eats an elephant. Kuki Gallmann describes her son Emanuele's giving mouth-to-mouth resuscitation to a spitting cobra (via a cocktail-glass straw!) and who, alas, is eventually killed by a puff adder.

A rich and varied collection to be sure.

Thanks to Willee I have a contribution in this volume, but I feel a little guilty about its presence among the others since my snake, indeed, is imaginary. She has permitted me to make amends by repeating a story told to me by Jim Fowler, the famous animal handler who is a familiar figure (invariably dressed in a safari jacket) on TV talk shows. The snake in this story was an eighteen-foot, 150-pound anaconda Jim was planning to bring to the Johnny Carson *Tonight Show.* He was with the snake in his room on the fourth floor of the Sheraton Universal in Burbank. Since the anaconda was covered with cedar chips and strips of newspaper from his carrying case, Jim undressed and draped the snake over his shoulders to take him into the shower to get him cleaned off. While he was swabbing him dry he thought he heard someone knocking on the door in the other room. With the snake still on his shoulders he went to answer it.

"It turned out no one was there," Jim told me. "False alarm. But just over the sill I noticed the newspaper. I had seen it on the way in—the complimentary copy they drop outside your door in the morning. So I thought I'd take a look at it. When I reached down for the paper, on my shoulder the anaconda shifted his weight forward, extending his neck for about six feet as a sort of counterbalance, which got me off balance—a lot of weight out there—and I half-stumbled out into the corridor."

"Oh, brother," I said.

Jim nodded. "I heard the door behind me click shut. So there I was—locked out in the hotel corridor with the anaconda."

Jim knows how to tell a story and he let the mental picture of his dilemma sink in before he continued.

"My hope," he said finally, "was to get to the elevator—the alarm button, or that someone would come out who wouldn't panic, who would get a bellhop up to the fourth floor so I could get back into my room. So I was on my way, slumped as low to the floor as I could get, crouched next to the wall, when suddenly the elevator door opened. Inside I heard this absolute barrage of giggling, and out they came into the corridor—a girls' basketball team! I discovered later that they had come in from out of town for a tournament. They stared at me in total disbelief."

"Looking at a naked man crouched against the wall with a snake!"

"Right. I heard a couple of screams," Jim said. "My mind was kind of flaked out at the time, so I couldn't tell if the basketball team ducked back into the elevator or if it disappeared around the corner."

"How was the anaconda reacting to all this?"

"The warm bath had heated up his metabolism. It was quite active on my shoulders. But by this time, the word eventually got downstairs that there were some terrible goings-on up on the fourth floor. Finally one of their hotel guys came up and I was able to get back in my room."

I don't recall that Jim ever told me if he mentioned the episode that night on the Johnny Carson talk show. What stayed in my mind for quite a while was the thought of a team member back in Carson City or Fresno trying to explain to her parents the highlights of her trip to California.

One of the reasons I'm delighted to get Jim's story into Willee's book, even if tucked away in the foreword, is the possibility that one day a member of that girls' basketball team will pick up this book in a bookstore (or perhaps a library) and when she comes across the explanation of that extraordinary scene in a Burbank hotel corridor her mind will be put to rest. There must have been a time when she (and the rest of the basketball team) must have doubted their senses. . . .

—*George Plimpton*

Introduction

Growing up in a small town in southern Indiana, I would routinely go blackberry picking with my mother in a ritual that linked her to the land, a natural outgrowth of her own rural girlhood. All of her life, she loved the idea of planting and of harvesting a garden, and our hours among the berry brambles were some of our happiest. But she was not without her phobias, and some of them, too, tied her back to her childhood. Basically, she had one overriding fear, a kind of terror that never left her. Mother was deathly frightened of snakes.

Lots of people share that fear, of course. But for mother it was a little more complicated because she knew from her years around the farm—and particularly its garden and barn—that snakes in that part of the country are harmless and in many ways a farmer's friend: they kill rodents, hold down the mosquito population and generally stay out of trouble. She knew all of that intellectually, but at an emotional level there remained that fear of a creature that slithered on the ground, had a forked tongue and eons ago was responsible for our paradise lost.

Time did not diminish her phobia. As a visiting grandmother, she would sit down with my son to explore books that had captured his imagination.

Unfortunately, one of those books was *The Encyclopedia of the Animal Kingdom*. She was literally incapable of looking at pictures that fascinated him of a tongue-flicking adder, button-eyed pit viper, coiled cobra or tiger rattler.

I acquired some of her queasiness, but along with the tendency to cringe came a certain curiosity. For instance, years later my son would ask me how a creature with no arms or legs could climb a tree. Sunday school Bible classes led to more advanced questions about good and evil, and how a serpent beguiled the first woman/first man into disobeying God.

And so something clicked for me after an evening several years ago. My husband and I joined a group of writers following a literary gala sponsored by the PEN/Faulkner Award for Fiction Foundation. We gathered around a table at the Jockey Club in the old Ritz-Carlton Hotel, and, after several rounds of drinks, the writers began telling stories. I urged George Plimpton to tell his story, "My Last Cobra," which had been published in *Harper's* magazine some time before. When the laughter subsided, other writers, including the late Willie Morris, chimed in with their own snake stories.

That evening planted the germ of an idea, of which this volume is the fulfillment.

In planning the book, I decided to seek out stories that would illuminate the hold that serpents have exerted through the ages on the human imagination—the primordial fears, religious insights, artistic inspirations, symbolic associations, mythological connections.

~

In the beginning or nearly so, there was a snake in the grass. Judging by the reactions of the first couple, the creature must have been a great storyteller, because they certainly fell for his line. The rest, one might say, is history. One thing is for certain: Adam and Eve's insubordination landed them, and the rest of us, in a lot of trouble. But that episode in the Garden of Eden also laid the foundation for a rich tradition of storytelling, one that embraces virtually all cultures in all times and places. Call it what you will—snake, serpent, viper, asp—that reptile described by Emily Dickinson as the "narrow fellow in the grass" has inspired, among others, poets, mythologists, writers, filmmakers, cultists and religious cranks. Perhaps more than any other creature's, the image of the serpent confronts us with intimations of our own mortality—think of all those poor devils who had the misfortune to gaze on

Medusa: They immediately became little better than stones on the beach. Medusa herself was a beautiful woman transfigured by a vengeful Athena who turned her lovely tresses into hideous, writhing vipers. Notions of the metaphysical and supernatural also merge with serpents. In the early civilizations that predate Mexican history, the myth of the Plumed Serpent came to represent the possibilities of rebirth in the form of Quetzalcoatl—*quetzal* meaning "bird" and *coatl* signifying "snake" in an ancient Aztecan language.

~

The image of a serpent can also convey a sense of beauty, both terrible and redemptive. Few literary passages are more arresting than Virgil's description, in the *Aeneid*, of those sea snakes stalking and ultimately destroying Laocoon, a priest, and his two sons; Laocoon's sin lay in warning his fellow citizens of Troy about Greeks bearing gifts and specifically an offering shaped in the form of a huge wooden horse. A little later, here's what they saw:

> When, dreadful to behold, from sea we spied
> Two serpents, rank'd abreast, the seas divide,
> And smoothly sweep along the swelling tide.
> Their flaming crests above the waves they show;
> Their bellies seem to burn the seas below;
> Their speckled tails advance to steer their course,
> And on the sounding shore the flying billows force.
> And now the strand, and now the plain they held;
> Their ardent eyes with bloody streaks were fill'd;
> Their nimble tongues they brandish'd as they came,
> And lick'd their hissing jaws, that sputter'd flame.

Coleridge offers a quite different literary experience in "The Rime of the Ancient Mariner":

> Beyond the shadow of the ship
> I watch'd the water-snakes:
> They mov'd in tracks of shining white;
> And when they rear'd, the elfish light
> Fell off in hoary flakes.

> Within the shadow of the ship
> I watch'd their rich attire:

Blue, glossy green, and velvet black
They coil'd and swam; and every track
Was a flash of golden fire.

O happy living things! no tongue
Their beauty might declare:
A spring of love gusht from my heart,
And I bless'd them unaware!
Sure my kind saint took pity on me,
And I bless'd them unaware.

The self-same moment I could pray;
And from my neck so free
The Albatross fell off, and sank
Like lead into the sea.

My hunch is that most people react to snakes as I do—with a flinch of horror. Even the most innocent garden snake can be unnerving. That common reaction helps to explain the power of literary passages that depict serpents as an instrument of punishment and death. Shakespeare prepares the audience for Cleopatra's suicide with a stage direction indicating that she is about to say something to a snake: "To an asp which she applies to her breast . . ." She then addresses the beast:

With thy sharp teeth this knot intrinsicate
Of life at once untie . . .

A few lines later, another stage direction: "Applies another asp to her arm." After which she dies.

Chaucer, writing two centuries earlier, had a somewhat different take on this, one of literature's most famous suicides. After describing how the queen rounded up all the serpents in the neighborhood and put them in a pit, Chaucer has her declare fidelity to the dead Anthony and then: " . . . (W)ith that word, naked, with full good heart,/ Among the serpents in the pit she (leapt)."

What could be more horrible than that? Surely Dante, in Canto XXIV of *The Inferno*, understood the hold such an image would have on the reader's imagination when he described a pit filled with "a frightening swarm" of serpents:

Amid this horde, cruel, grim and dense,
People were running, naked and terrified,
Without a hope of hiding or a chance

At heliotrope for safety. Their hands were tied
Behind their backs—with snakes, that thrust between
Where the legs meet, entwining tail and head

Into a knot in front. And look!—at one
Near us a serpent darted, and transfixed
Him at the point where neck and shoulders join.

This, we learn later, is where thieves wind up, including one "Who took adornments from the sacristy/For which another, falsely, was accused . . ."

Centuries later, novelist Harry Crews may have had Dante and *The Inferno* in mind in describing the denouement of *A Feast of Snakes* in which the central character, Joe Lon, goes crazy at a rattlesnake roundup in Georgia and starts shooting people with his twelve-gauge pump. When he exhausts his ammo, the other hunters take matters into their own hands. Grabbing Joe Lon, the mob acts with a common intent: "The gun went into the snake pit with him. He fell into the boiling snakes, went under and came up, like a swimmer breaking water. For the briefest instant, he gained his feet. Snakes hung from his face. . . ."

In moments of despair, snakes can deploy profound metaphorical power. After a bitter blowup with his daughter Goneril, Shakespeare's King Lear says to Albany, "How sharper than a serpent's tooth it is/To have a thankless child!"

Nor is it with cheerful intent that political speechwriters use snake metaphors. In a statement aired by the Qatar-based Al-Jazeera television network shortly after Christmas 2001, Osama bin Laden described that year's terrorist assault on September 11 as a "blessed attack that took place against the head of the snake, the United States. . . ." President Bush in the months that followed would reciprocate by likening al Qaeda to a snake and vowing to cut off its head, meaning bin Laden.

"This snake can crawl without its head and we need to be aware of that," said Dick Armey of Texas, the House majority leader at the time of the attacks.

Fortunately, Bush and Armey have targeted a single-headed monster, unlike those reptilian anomolies that are born with two heads.

Clearly, anybody who can claim credit for cleansing a country of snakes can expect to reap major rewards. In St. Patrick's case, it's sainthood. Myth has it that the early Christian missionary rid Ireland of all serpents. That is a dubious claim, to say the least, but St. Patrick certainly did have a lot to do with converting Ireland to Christianity and greatly shrinking its population of pagans, who, in the minds of many, were equated with snakes.

In fairness to reptiles, serpents have won a more positive image for themselves in the eyes of modern medicine. This comes about, in part at least, because of Aesculapius, the son of Apollo and the God of healing. He thought snakes were sacred. According to legend, Aesculapius would occasionally take the form of a serpent, and sick people who were visited by snakes in their dreams had reason to think that the god himself had come to their aid. Today, modern medicine has adopted the staff of Aesculapius with a coiled serpent wrapped around it as a symbol of what it is all about—of healing and health. And, indeed, the Bible takes a similar tack by describing how Moses brandished a brass serpent on a pole in order to heal the Israelites of snake bites.

This, of course, is the merest fraction of the compelling poetry and stories that I uncovered in gathering material for this volume.

My husband, a political reporter, reminds me that a story about Washington and those political "snakes in the grass"—and the connotations people attach to that species—should be included in this collection. But then that would be his book. However, I am reminded of the story of Alice Roosevelt Longworth, who loved to enliven particularly dull Washington dinner parties by reaching into her purse and pulling out her green garter snake—named Emily Spinach—to the horror of those assembled.

Another bit of American history worth mentioning concerns the famous Revolutionary War flag depicting a rattlesnake and the terse warning, "Don't Tread on Me." There were actually several different such flags, but they all combined the two main features: the snake and the words of deadly caution—delivered very much like the anticipatory rattle of the quintessential and ready-to-strike American snake.

Historians believe that Benjamin Franklin instilled the idea for the emblem in 1754, when he created a flag depicting a chopped-up rattlesnake. Franklin's message—underscored by the words, "Join or Die"—was aimed at inspiring colonial unity during the French and Indian War.

Other cultures have related to snakes in a more direct fashion. There was a snake tribe in Punjab where the local kinfolk would clothe and bury a dead serpent. The ritual would include placing a copper coin in its mouth and burning the body while performing an exotic ceremony—all to stymie the evil spirits. In India, snake charmers, however, are now becoming an endangered species, because of strict enforcement of wildlife laws and the efforts of animal rights activists.

And, in Venezuela, about 800 giant anacondas, the largest snake in the world, have been captured and released by graduate students in herpetology who have a passion for rescuing snakes from muddy lowland swamps to safe waters.

Throughout history snakes have had a knack for worming their way into positions of local importance, often because they were credited with possessing the key to good health, great wealth or sexual fertility. Thus the myth—it apparently endured well into the nineteenth century—that attached itself to the tomb of Mohammedan Sheikh Heridi, who was thought to have been transformed into a snake. The local medical practitioners would serve their patients by dispatching a particularly innocent and virtuous nude virgin to the Sheikh's cave to entice the resident serpent into making a house call to the ill.

Then there were the Psylli of Africa who felt that they had devised a sure-fire way of weeding out the bastard children in their midst. A youngster of questionable parentage would be exposed to a serpent on the theory that the creature would not harm a child of legitimate origins.

Thus, from the beginning of time, one impulse seems to have united most of humanity: Don't cross a snake. A rich dynasty in the Upper Nile felt it had reason to conclude that its material good fortune had nothing to do with hard work, thrift or low tax rates: it was all the doing of a particular serpent in a local well. The elders did what anybody else would have done under the circumstances. Once a year, they would appear with a young maiden in tow, all decked out in bridal finery—and pitch her in. Then they skipped a year—and promptly suffered the consequences of drought and pestilential famine.

The poetry and stories gathered in this book are evocative of the rich literature that owes its inspiration in some measure to the hold that serpents have on mankind's imagination. Because the field is so very vast—stretching from the revelations in Genesis to the fantasies of Harry Potter—I make no claims for this book but to say that its aim is to entertain and perhaps to enlighten the reader. This is not the kind of book that a scholar might produce, and it certainly should not be taken as exhaustive in its exploration of any theme or literary convention. It is simply intended to be a representative collection of serpent stories and poems—old and new.

The Sacred

Genesis

CHAPTER ONE

IN THE BEGINNING, God created the heaven and the earth.

2   And the earth was without form, and void; and darkness *was* upon the face of the deep. And the Spirit of God moved upon the face of the waters.

3   And God said, Let there be light; and there was light.

~

26   And God said, Let us make man in our image, after our likeness: and let them have dominion over the fish of the sea and over the fowl of the air, and over the cattle, and over all the earth, and over every creeping thing that creepeth upon the earth.

~

CHAPTER THREE

Now THE SERPENT was more subtle than any beast of the field which the
LORD GOD had made. And he said unto the woman, Yea, hath God
said, Ye shall not eat of every tree of the garden?

2   And the woman said unto the serpent. We may eat of the fruit of the
trees of the garden:

3   But of the fruit of the tree which *is* in the midst of the garden, God
hath said, Ye shall not eat of it, neither shall ye touch it, lest ye die.

4   And the serpent said unto the woman, Ye shall not surely die:

5   For God doth know that in the day ye eat thereof, then your eyes shall
be opened, and ye shall be as gods, knowing good and evil.

6   And when the woman saw that the tree *was* good for food, and that it
was pleasant to the eyes, and a tree to be desired to make *one* wise, she
took of the fruit thereof, and did eat, and gave also unto her husband
with her; and he did eat.

7   And the eyes of them both were opened, and they knew that they *were*
naked; and they sewed fig leaves together, and made themselves aprons.

8   And they heard the voice of the LORD GOD walking in the garden
in the cool of the day: and Adam and his wife hid themselves from
the presence of the LORD GOD amongst the trees of the garden.

9   And the LORD GOD called unto Adam, and said unto him, Where
art thou?

10   And he said, I heard thy voice in the garden, and I was afraid, because
I *was* naked; and I hid myself.

11   And he said, Who told thee that thou *wast* naked? Hast thou eaten of
the tree, whereof I commanded thee that thou shouldest not eat?

12   And the man said, The woman whom thou gavest *to be* with me, she
gave me of the tree, and I did eat.

13   And the LORD GOD said unto the woman. What *is* this *that* thou hast
done? And the woman said, The serpent beguiled me, and I did eat.

14   And the LORD GOD said unto the serpent, Because thou hast done
this, thou *art* cursed above all cattle, and above every beast of the field;
upon thy belly shalt thou go, and dust shalt thou eat all the days of
thy life . . .

Numbers

CHAPTER 21

6   And the Lord sent fiery serpents among the people, and they bit the people; and much people of Israel died.

7   Therefore, the people came to Moses, and said, We have sinned, for we have spoken against the Lord, and against thee; Pray unto the Lord, that he take away the serpents from us. And Moses prayed for the people.

8   And the Lord said unto Moses, Make thee a fiery serpent, and set it upon a pole: and it shall come to pass, that everyone that is bitten, when he looketh upon it, shall live.

9   And Moses made a serpent of brass, and put it upon a pole, and it came to pass, that if a serpent had bitten any man, when he beheld the serpent of brass, he lived.

~

Paradise Lost

BOOK NINE

John Milton

Thoughts, whither have he led me, with what sweet
Compulsion thus transported to forget
What hither brought us, hate, not love, nor hope
Of Paradise for Hell, hope here to taste
Of pleasure, but all pleasure to destroy,
Save what is in destroying, other joy
To me is lost. Then let me not let pass
Occasion which now smiles, behold alone
The Woman, opportune to all attempts,
Her Husband, for I view far round, not nigh,
Whose higher intellectual more I shun,
And strength, of courage hautie, and of limb
Heroic built, though of terrestrial mould,
Foe not informidable, exempt from wound,
I not; so much hath Hell debas'd, and paine
Infeebl'd me, to what I was in Heav'n.
Shee fair, divinely fair, fit Love for Gods,
Not terrible, though terrour be in Love
And beautie, not approacht by stronger hate,
Hate stronger, under shew of Love well feign'd,
The way which to her ruin now I tend.

So spake the Enemie of Mankind, enclos'd
In Serpent, Inmate bad, and toward EVE

Address'd his way, not with indented wave,
Prone on the ground, as since, but on his reare,
Circular base of rising foulds, that tour'd
Fould above fould a surging Maze, his Head
Crested aloft, and Carbuncle his Eyes;
With burnisht Neck of verdant Gold, erect
Amidst his circling Spires, that on the grass
Floted redundant: pleasing was his shape,
And lovely, never since of Serpent kind
Lovelier, not those that in ILLYRIA chang'd
HERMIONE and CADMUS, or the God
In EPIDAURUS; nor to which transformd
AMMONIAN JOVE, or CAPITOLINE was seen,
Hee with OLYMPIAS, this with her who bore
SCIPIO the height of ROME. With tract oblique
At first, as one who sought access, but feard
To interrupt, side-long he works his way.
As when a Ship by skilful Stearsman wrought
Nigh Rivers mouth or Foreland, where the Wind
Veres oft, as oft so steers, and shifts her Saile;
So varied hee, and of his tortuous Traine
Curld many a wanton wreath in sight of EVE,
To lure her Eye; shee busied heard the sound
Of rusling Leaves, but minded not, as us'd
To such disport before her through the Field,
From every Beast, more duteous at her call,
Then at CIRCEAN call the Herd disguis'd.
Hee boulder now, uncall'd before her stood;
But as in gaze admiring: Oft he bowd
His turret Crest, and sleek enamel'd Neck,
Fawning, and lick'd the ground whereon she trod.
His gentle dumb expression turnd at length
The Eye of EVE to mark his play; he glad
Of her attention gaind, with Serpent Tongue
Organic, or impulse of vocal Air,
His fraudulent temptation thus began . . .

Abraham and Isaac

Philip Bobbitt

MY FATHER WAS a large, handsome man who worked downtown. We lived then—in the 50s—in a house at the top of a long, broad lawn that sloped down to the street. In the back of that house, there was a rectangular yard of grass and behind it, a terrace that angled up to a stone wall. At the back of the yard, at the beginning of the terrace, there was a child's swingset that appeared before I have a memory of it not being there and disappeared one day when I was more enamored of baseball and other sports and so I have no memory of it being taken away either.

When this story occurs, I am about four. I am swinging on the flat, suspended seat attached to the swingset by chains, swaying and bucking to get the seat higher and make the arcs longer. I hear my father's car come up the long driveway from the street and move into the garage. He goes into the house by the kitchen door and then emerges to walk over to me. He has on a tan-colored suit, a white starched shirt and a light-colored tie. He approaches me and then stops and turns and walks back into the house, as if he'd forgotten something. And I am swinging higher and higher. He comes back out the door, still in his business suit, but holding a garden hoe slack in his right arm, like a carbine. I slow my swinging. The arc gets shorter. He comes closer to the swing. I'm almost stopped now. He raises the hoe above his head, now grasping the handle with both hands and then, without any strain or really much effort, brings the face of the hoe down quickly just in front of the swing past my face, just parallel to my knees and slices into the grass below. He reaches over, picks me up off the swing—my feet never touching the ground—and gently brings me back into the house. He puts me in his big, green, leather chair, takes off his coat and drapes it across the arm of a sofa. He tells me he'll be right back; he just wants to put away the hoe and dispose of the coral snake.

Austin, our hometown, lies in Travis County, which boasts the distinction of having all four types of poisonous snakes found in North America. At various times in the years to come I will encounter cottonmouths (water moccasins) swimming around a small boat from which I am fishing, rattlesnakes in the rocky shoals above the creek that runs through Fredericksburg where I spend summers playing baseball, copperheads on the grounds of the house I will buy when I return from New York to begin teaching at the university, but never again will I see a coral snake. Its venom is the deadliest of the four, and it belongs to the class of cobras, kraits and mambas whose toxins attack the neurological system. "Red on black, venom lack/red on yellow, kill a fellow" is the cowboy's rhyme that is meant to spare the more ubiquitous and benign species that are easily confused with the colorful, banded coral snakes who are usually nocturnal and are seldom seen.

My father, the least violent of all men, will never lose my blind trust. One day we will fail to save my mother from a savage predator—a cancer that consumes its host with such fury that it kills itself with her death—and one day Father also will move beyond the protection I want to cloak him with as he once cloaked me.

It is unlikely I will ever have another relationship with any person so total in its faith as the one I had with Father. But perhaps some day, this: that I shall give to a child of my own, if I ever have children, the same grounds for trust as Father always gave to me.

As the Angel of the Lord said to Abraham: "Your descendents shall be as many as there are stars in the heaven and grains of sand on the seashore. And they shall be blessed because of you."—Genesis 22, the sacrifice of Isaac.

God to the Serpent

Virginia Hamilton Adair

Beloved Snake, perhaps my finest blueprint,
How can I not take pride in your design?
Your passage without hoof or paw or shoe print
Revels in art's and nature's S-curve line.

No ears, no whiskers, fingers, legs, or teeth,
No cries, complaints, or curses from you start;
But silence shares your body in its sheath
Full-functioning with no superfluous part.

Men try to emulate your forked tongue,
Their prideful prick dwarfed by your lordly length.
Two arms for blows or hugging loosely hung
Are mocked by Boa Constrictor's single strength.

How dare men claim their image as my own,
With all those limbs and features sticking out?
You, Snake, with continuity of bone
Need but a spine to coil and cruise about.

Men fear the force of your hypnotic eyes,
Make myths to damn your being wise and deft.
You, Snake, not men, deserve my cosmic prize.
I'm glad you stayed in Eden when they left.

The Profane

Allal

Paul Bowles

He was born in the hotel where his mother worked. The hotel had only three dark rooms, which gave on a courtyard behind the bar. Beyond was another smaller patio with many doors. This was where the servants lived, and where Allal spent his childhood.

The Greek who owned the hotel had sent Allal's mother away. He was indignant because she, a girl of fourteen, had dared to give birth while she was working for him. She would not say who the father was, and it angered him to reflect that he himself had not taken advantage of the situation while he had had the chance. He gave the girl three months' wages and told her to go home to Marrakech. Since the cook and his wife liked the girl and offered to let her live with them for a while, he agreed that she might stay on until the baby was big enough to travel. She remained in the back patio for a few months with the cook and his wife, and then one day she disappeared, leaving the baby behind. No one heard of her again.

As soon as Allal was old enough to carry things, they set him to work. It was not long before he could fetch a pail of water from the well behind the hotel. The cook and his wife were childless, so he played alone.

When he was somewhat older he began to wander over the empty table-land outside. There was nothing else up here but the barracks, and they were enclosed by a high blind wall of red adobe. Everything else was below in the valley: the town, the gardens, and the river winding southward among the thousands of palm trees. He could sit on a point of rock far above and look down at the people walking in the alleys of the town. It was only later that he visited the place and saw what the inhabitants were like. Because he had been left behind by his mother they called him a son of sin, and laughed when they looked at him. It seemed to him that in this way they hoped to make him into a shadow, in order not to have to think of him as real and alive. He awaited with dread the time when he would have to go each morning to the town and work. For the moment he helped in the kitchen and served the officers from the barracks, along with the few motorists who passed through the region. He got small tips in the restaurant, and free food and lodging in a cell of the servants' quarters, but the Greek gave him no wages. Eventually he reached an age when this situation seemed shameful, and he went of his own accord to the town below and began to work, along with older boys of his age, helping to make the mud bricks people used for building their houses.

Living in the town was much as he had imagined it would be. For two years he stayed in a room behind a blacksmith's shop, leading a life without quarrels, and saving whatever money he did not have to spend to keep himself alive. Far from making any friends during this time, he formed a thorough hatred for the people of the town, who never allowed him to forget that he was a son of sin, and therefore not like others, but *meskhot*—damned. Then he found a small house, not much more than a hut, in the palm groves outside the town. The rent was low and no one lived nearby. He went to live there, where the only sound was the wind in the trees, and avoided the people of the town when he could.

One hot summer evening shortly after sunset he was walking under the arcades that faced the town's main square. A few paces ahead of him an old man in a white turban was trying to shift a heavy sack from one shoulder to the other. Suddenly it fell to the ground, and Allal stared as two dark forms flowed out of it and disappeared into the shadows. The old man pounced upon the sack and fastened the top of it, at the same time beginning to shout: Look out for the snakes! Help me find my snakes!

Many people turned quickly around and walked back the way they had come. Others stood at some distance, watching. A few called to the old man: Find your snakes fast and get them out of here! Why are they here? We don't want snakes in this town!

Hopping up and down in his anxiety, the old man turned to Allal. Watch this for me for a moment, my son. He pointed at the sack lying on the earth at his feet, and snatching up a basket he had been carrying, went swiftly around the corner into an alley. Allal stood where he was. No one passed by.

It was not long before the old man returned, panting with triumph. When the onlookers in the square saw him again, they began to call out, this time to Allal: Show that *berrani* the way out of the town! He has no right to carry those things in here. Out! Out!

Allal picked up the big sack and said to the old man: Come on.

They left the square and went through the alleys until they were at the edge of town. The old man looked up then, saw the palm trees black against the fading sky ahead, and turned to the boy beside him.

Come on, said Allal again, and he went to the left along the rough path that led to his house. The old man stood perplexed.

You can stay with me tonight, Allal told him.

And these? He said, pointing first at the sack and then at the basket. They have to be with me.

Allal grinned. They can come.

When they were sitting in the house Allal looked at the sack and the basket. I'm not like the rest of them here, he said.

It made him feel good to hear the words being spoken. He made a contemptuous gesture. Afraid to walk through the square because of a snake. You saw them.

The old man scratched his chin. Snakes are like people, he said. You have to get to know them. Then you can be their friends.

Allal hesitated before he asked: Do you ever let them out?

Always, the old man said with energy. It's bad for them to be inside like this. They've got to be healthy when they get to Taroudant, or the man there won't buy them.

He began a long story about his life as a hunter of snakes, explaining that each year he made a voyage to Taroudant to see a man who bought them for the Aissaoua snake charmers in Marrakech. Allal made tea while he listened, and brought out a bowl of kif paste to eat with the tea. Later, when they were sitting comfortably in the midst of the pipe smoke, the old man chuckled. Allal turned to look at him.

Shall I let them out?

Fine!

But you must sit and keep quiet. Move the lamp nearer.

He untied his sack, shook it a bit, and returned to where he had been sitting. Then in silence Allal watched the long bodies move cautiously out into the light. Among the cobras were others with markings so delicate and perfect that they seemed to have been designed and painted by an artist. One reddish-gold serpent, which coiled itself lazily in the middle of the floor, he found particularly beautiful. As he stared at it, he felt a great desire to own it and have it always with him.

The old man was talking. I've spent my whole life with snakes, he said. I could tell you some things about them. Did you know that if you give them *majoun* you can make them do what you want, and without saying a word? I swear by Allah!

Allal's face assumed a doubtful air. He did not question the truth of the other's statement, but rather the likelihood of his being able to put the knowledge to use. For it was at that moment that the idea of actually taking the snake first came into his head. He was thinking that whatever he was to do must be done quickly, for the old man would be leaving in the morning. Suddenly he felt a great impatience.

Put them away so I can cook dinner, he whispered. Then he sat admiring the ease with which the old man picked up each one by its head and slipped it into the sack. Once again he dropped two of the snakes into the basket, and one of these, Allal noted, was the red one. He imagined he could see the shining of its scales through the lid of the basket.

As he set to work preparing the meal Allal tried to think of other things. Then, since the snake remained in his mind in spite of everything, he began to devise a way of getting it. While he squatted over the fire in a corner, he mixed some kif paste in a bowl of milk and set it aside.

The old man continued to talk. That was good luck, getting the two snakes back like that, in the middle of the town. You can never be sure what people are going to do when they find out you're carrying snakes. Once in El Kelaa they took all of them and killed them, one after the other, in front of me. A year's work. I had to go back home and start all over again.

Even as they ate, Allal saw that his guest was growing sleepy. How will things happen? He wondered. There was no way of knowing beforehand precisely what he was going to do, and the prospect of having to handle the snake worried him. It could kill me, he thought.

Once they had eaten, drunk tea and smoked a few pipes of kif, the old man lay back on the floor and said he was going to sleep. Allal sprang up. In here! he told him, and led him to his own mat in an alcove. The old man lay down and swiftly fell asleep.

Several times during the next half hour Allal went to the alcove and peered in, but neither the body in its burnoose nor the head in its turban had stirred.

First he got out his blanket, and after tying three of its corners together, spread it on the floor with the fourth corner facing the basket. Then he set the bowl of milk and kif paste on the blanket. As he loosened the strap from the cover of the basket the old man coughed. Allal stood immobile, waiting to hear the cracked voice speak. A small breeze had sprung up, making the palm branches rasp one against the other, but there was no further sound from the alcove. He crept to the far side of the room and squatted by the wall, his gaze fixed on the basket.

Several times he thought he saw the cover move slightly, but each time he decided he had been mistaken. Then he caught his breath. The shadow along the base of the basket was moving. One of the creatures had crept out from the far side. It waited for a while before continuing into the light, but when it did, Allal breathed a prayer of thanks. It was the red-and-gold one.

When finally it decided to go to the bowl, it made a complete tour around the edge, looking in from all sides, before lowering its head toward the milk. Allal watched, fearful that the foreign flavor of the kif paste might repel it. The snake remained there without moving.

He waited a half hour or more. The snake stayed where it was, its head in the bowl. From time to time Allal glanced at the basket, to be certain that the second snake was still in it. The breeze went on, rubbing the palm branches together. When he decided it was time, he rose slowly, and keeping an eye on the basket where apparently the other snake still slept, he reached over and gathered together the three tied corners of the blanket. Then he lifted the fourth corner, so that both the snake and the bowl slid to the bottom of the improvised sack. The snake moved slightly, but he did not think it was angry. He knew exactly where he would hide it: between some rocks in the dry riverbed.

Holding the blanket in front of him, he opened the door and stepped out under the stars. It was not far up the road, to a group of high palms, and then to the left down into the oued. There was a space between the boulders where the bundle would be invisible. He pushed it in with care, and hurried back to the house. The old man was asleep.

There was no way of being sure that the other snake was still in the basket, so Allal picked up his burnoose and went outside. He shut the door and lay down on the ground to sleep.

Before the sun was in the sky the old man was awake, lying in the alcove coughing. Allal jumped up, went inside, and began to make a fire in the *mijmah*. A minute later he heard the other exclaim: They're loose again! Out of the basket! Stay where you are and I'll find them.

It was not long before the old man grunted with satisfaction. I have the black one! he cried. Allal did not look up from the corner where he crouched, and the old man came over, waving a cobra. Now I've got to find the other one.

He put the snake away and continued to search. When the fire was blazing, Allal turned and said: Do you want me to help you look for it?

No, no! Stay where you are.

Allal boiled the water and made the tea, and still the old man was crawling on his knees, lifting boxes and pushing sacks. His turban had slipped off and his face ran with sweat.

Come and have tea, Allal told him.

The old man did not seem to have heard him at first. Then he rose and went into the alcove, where he rewound his turban. When he came out he sat down with Allal, and they had breakfast.

Snakes are very clever, the old man said. They can get into places that don't exist. I've moved everything in this house.

After they had finished eating, they went outside and looked for the snake between the close-growing trunks of the palms near the house. When the old man was convinced that it was gone, he went sadly back in.

That was a good snake, he said at last. And now I'm going to Taroudant.

They said good-bye, and the old man took his sack and basket and started up the road toward the highway.

All day long as he worked, Allal thought of the snake, but it was not until sunset that he was able to go to the rocks in the oued and pull out the blanket. He carried it back to the house in a high state of excitement.

Before he untied the blanket, he filled a wide dish with milk and kif paste, and set it on the floor. He ate three spoonfuls of the paste himself

and sat back to watch, drumming on the low wooden tea table with his fingers. Everything happened just as he had hoped. The snake came slowly out
of the blanket, and very soon had found the dish and was drinking the milk.
As long as it drank he kept drumming; when it had finished and raised its
head to look at him, he stopped, and it crawled back inside the blanket.

Later that evening he put down more milk, and drummed again on the
table. After a time the snake's head appeared, and finally all of it, and the
entire pattern of action was repeated.

That night and every night thereafter, Allal sat with the snake, while with
infinite patience he sought to make it his friend. He never attempted to touch
it, but soon he was able to summon it, keep it in front of him for as long as he
pleased, merely by tapping on the table, and dismiss it at will. For the first week
or so he used the kif paste; then he tried the routine without it. In the end the
results were the same. After that he fed it only milk and eggs.

Then one evening as his friend lay gracefully coiled in front of him, he
began to think of the old man, and formed an idea that put all other things
out of his mind. There had not been any kif paste in the house for several
weeks, and he decided to make some. He bought the ingredients the following day, and after work he prepared the paste. When it was done, he mixed a
large amount of it in a bowl with milk and set it down for the snake. Then
he himself ate four spoonfuls, washing them down with tea.

He quickly undressed, and moving the table so he could reach it,
stretched out naked on a mat near the door. This time he continued to tap
on the table, even after the snake had finished drinking the milk. It lay still,
observing him, as if it were in doubt that the familiar drumming came from
the brown body in front of it.

Seeing that even after a long time it remained where it was, staring at him
with its stony yellow eyes, Allal began to say to it over and over: Come here.
He knew it could not hear his voice, but he believed it could feel his mind as
he urged it. You can make them do what you want, without saying a word,
the old man had told him.

Although the snake did not move, he went on repeating his command,
for by now he knew it was going to come. And after another long wait, all at
once it lowered its head and began to move toward him. It reached his hip
and slid along his leg. Then it climbed up his leg and lay for a time across his
chest. Its body was heavy and tepid, its scales wonderfully smooth. After a
time it came to rest, coiled in the space between his head and his shoulder.

By this time the kif paste had completely taken over Allal's mind. He lay in a state of pure delight, feeling the snake's head against his own, without a thought save that he and the snake were together. The patterns forming and melting behind his eyelids seemed to be the same ones that covered the snake's back. Now and then in a huge frenzied movement they all swirled up and shattered into fragments which swiftly became one great yellow eye, split through the middle by the narrow vertical pupil that pulsed with his own heartbeat. Then the eye would recede, through shifting shadow and sunlight, until only the designs of the scales were left, swarming with renewed insistence as they merged and separated. At last the eye returned, so huge this time that it had no edge around it, its pupil dilated to form an aperture almost wide enough for him to enter. As he stared at the blackness within, he understood that he was being slowly propelled toward the open-ing. He put out his hands to touch the polished surface of the eye on each side, and as he did this he felt the pull from within. He slid through the crack and was swallowed by darkness.

On awakening Allal felt that he had returned from somewhere far away. He opened his eyes and saw, very close to him, what looked like the flank of an enormous beast, covered with coarse stiff hair. There was a repeated vibration in the air, like distant thunder curling around the edges of the sky. He sighed, or imagined that he did, for his breath made no sound. Then he shifted his head a bit, to try and see beyond the mass of hair beside him. Next he saw the ear, and he knew he was looking at his own head from the outside. He had not expected this; he had hoped only that his friend would come in and share his mind with him. But it did not strike him as being at all strange; he merely said to himself that now he was seeing through the eyes of the snake, rather than through his own.

Now he understood why the serpent had been so wary of him: from here the boy was a monstrous creature, with all the bristles on his head and his breathing that vibrated inside him like a far-off storm.

He uncoiled himself and glided across the floor to the alcove. There was a break in the mud wall wide enough to let him out. When he had pushed himself through, he lay full length on the ground in the crystalline moon-light, staring at the strangeness of the landscape, where shadows were not shadows.

He crawled around the side of the house and started up the road toward the town, rejoicing in a sense of freedom different from any he had ever imagined. There was no feeling of having a body, for he was perfectly contained in the skin that covered him. It was beautiful to caress the earth with the length of his belly as he moved along the silent road, smelling the sharp veins of wormwood in the wind. When the voice of the muezzin floated out over the countryside from the mosque, he could not hear it, or know that within the hour the night would end.

On catching sight of a man ahead, he left the road and hid behind a rock until the danger had passed. But then as he approached the town there began to be more people, so that he let himself down into the *seguia*, the deep ditch that went along beside the road. Here the stones and clumps of dead plants impeded his progress. He was still struggling along the floor of the *seguia*, pushing himself around the rocks and through the dry tangles of matted stalks left by the water, when dawn began to break.

The coming of daylight made him anxious and unhappy. He clambered up the bank of the *seguia* and raised his head to examine the road. A man walking past saw him, stood quite still, and then turned and ran back. Allal did not wait; he wanted now to get home as fast as possible.

Once he felt the thud of a stone as it struck the ground somewhere behind him. Quickly he threw himself over the edge of the *seguia* and rolled squirming down the bank. He knew the terrain here: where the road crossed the oued, there were two culverts not far apart. A man stood at some distance ahead of him with a shovel, peering down into the *seguia*. Allal kept moving, aware that he would reach the first culvert before the man could get to him.

The floor of the tunnel under the road was ribbed with hard little waves of sand. The smell of the mountains was in the air that moved through. There were places in here where he could have hidden, but he kept moving, and soon reached the other end. Then he continued to the second culvert and went under the road in the other direction, emerging once again into the *seguia*. Behind him several men had gathered at the entrance to the first culvert. One of them was on his knees, his head and shoulders inside the opening.

He now set out for the house in a straight line across the open ground, keeping his eye on the clump of palms beside it. The sun had just come up, and the stones began to cast long bluish shadows. All at once a small boy appeared from behind some nearby palms, saw him, and opened his eyes and mouth wide with fear. He was so close that Allal went straight to him and bit him in the leg. The boy ran wildly toward the group of men in the *seguia*.

Allal hurried on to the house, looking back only as he reached the hole between the mud bricks. Several men were running among the trees toward him. Swiftly he glided through into the alcove. The brown body still lay near the door. But there was no time, and Allal needed time to get back into it, to lie close to its head and say: Come here.

As he stared out into the room at the body, there was a great pounding on the door. The boy was on his feet at the first blow, as if a spring had been released, and Allal saw with despair the expression of total terror on his face, and the eyes with no mind behind them. The boy stood panting, his fists clenched. The door opened and some of the men peered inside. Then with a roar the boy lowered his head and rushed through the doorway. One of the men reached out to seize him, but lost his balance and fell. An instant later all of them turned and began to run through the palm grove after the naked figure.

Even when, from time to time, they lost sight of him, they could hear the screams, and then they would see him, between the palm trunks, still running. Finally he stumbled and fell face downward. It was then that they caught him, bound him, covered his nakedness, and took him away, to be sent one day soon to the hospital at Berrechid.

That afternoon the same group of men came to the house to carry out the search they had meant to make earlier. Allal lay in the alcove, dozing. When he awoke, they were already inside. He turned and crept to the hole. He saw the man waiting out there, a club in his hand.

The rage always had been in his heart; now it burst forth. As if his body were a whip, he sprang out into the room. The men nearest him were on their hands and knees, and Allal had the joy of pushing his fangs into two of them before a third severed his head with an axe.

~

Bad Mouth

Margaret Atwood

There are no leaf-eating snakes.
All are fanged and gorge on blood.
Each one is a hunter's hunter,
nothing more than an endless gullet
pulling itself on over the still-alive prey
like a sock gone ravenous, like an evil glove,
like sheer greed, lithe and devious.

Puff adder buried in hot sand
or poisoning the toes of boots,
for whom killing is easy and careless
as war, as digestion,
why should you be spared?

And you, *Constrictor constrictor*,
sinuous ribbon of true darkness,
one long muscle with eyes and an anus,
looping like thick tar out of the trees

to squeeze the voice from anything edible,
reducing it to scales and belly.

And you, pit viper
with your venomous pallid throat
and teeth like syringes
and your nasty radar
homing in on the deep red shadow
nothing else knows it casts . . .
Shall I concede these deaths?

Between us there is no fellow feeling,
as witness: a snake cannot scream.
Observe the alien
chainmail skin, straight out
of science fiction, pure
shiver, pure Saturn.

Those who can explain them
can explain anything.

Some say they're a snarled puzzle
only gasoline and a match can untangle.

Even their mating is barely sexual,
a romance between two lengths
of cyanide-colored string.
Despite their live births and squirming nests
it's hard to believe in snakes loving.

Alone among the animals
the snake does not sing.
The reason for them is the same
as the reason for stars, and not human.

My Last Cobra

STALKING THE WILD
PREVARICATION

George Plimpton

THE TROUBLE BEGAN on a bird-watching expedition to India and the mountain kingdom of Bhutan a year and a half ago when I developed an aggravated bursitis condition in my left elbow. Fortunately, a doctor was on the expedition, and one evening he lanced my elbow, which looked as though a Ping-Pong ball had been inserted in it. But the relief was only temporary. When we came out of the Black Mountains of Bhutan, my arm had swollen to such proportions that I was forced to loosen my watch strap a couple of holes. At the Adventist Hospital in Bangkok, the elbow, now almost the size of a tennis ball, was lanced again by my doctor friend.

Back in New York the elbow was lanced yet again and my arm set in a cast and a sling. Around town, when asked what was wrong, I replied, "Oh, it's an aggravated bursitis condition. Nothing serious."

Then I made a mistake. It occurred at a cocktail party given by Alexander Chancellor, then the editor of the Talk of the Town department of *The New Yorker*. The usual inquiries were being made about my arm. I thanked those who asked and said it was nothing to worry about—a simple aggravated bursitis condition. Sometimes, if they stayed around, I talked about the cranes we'd seen in India—the rare Siberian, and the Sarus cranes that stand as tall as a man. If the guests stared at my arm in its sling, I talked about the low medical costs in Thailand. (The cost of the facilities given my doctor for the procedure, including nurses, syringes, antibiotics, a sling, and a safety pin to hold it: $40.)

About midway through the party I caught sight of Jason Epstein standing by the door putting on his coat to leave. He is a senior editor at Random House. He called out, "Hey, George, what's wrong with your arm?"

Suddenly, it seemed too boring to give the usual answer. So somewhat to my own astonishment I found myself saying over the chatter of the party: "Well, Jason, the damnedest thing. I was lying in some tall grass at the Bharatpur Reserve, peering at a pair of Sarus cranes through my binoculars, when I sensed some movement to my left. I turned, raised my arm, and was bitten in the elbow by a small cobra!"

Jason's eyes widened. "My God!" he exclaimed. His date, standing beside him, said, "Hey, Jason, we're late!" and before I could admit I was joshing him she had propelled him out the door.

My immediate reaction was one of dismay. Jason is a familiar and popular figure at various social and publishing functions and watering holes around the city. It was inevitable that the cobra story would quickly get about.

Two days later the phone rang, and a man I didn't know came on. "Hey," he said, "I was having lunch with Elizabeth Sifton, the editor at Farrar, Straus & Giroux, today, and she tells me that you've been bitten by a cobra." By the most extraordinary coincidence, it turned out the caller was a doctor of considerable reputation, formerly the head of New York City's Roosevelt Hospital, and an expert on poisons and toxins, including snake venoms. He would be most pleased if I could have lunch with him to discuss what had happened.

This would have been the appropriate time for me to admit that I had been kidding about the cobra. Instead, my heart pounding and my face reddening, I told the doctor that it had been a *small* cobra, really nothing, that my recovery had been swift, without complications, not much to report . . .

"Oh, no!" the doctor said, insisting that anything I could tell him about the incident would be of great value to him. "Please."

I couldn't get out of it. I said that if he really wished, I'd be delighted to have lunch with him in three or four weeks—setting a considerable period of time so that in the interim he might forget that we had a date. We chatted for a while about Gaboon vipers. He sounded as though he could hardly wait for our lunch.

His was the first of a number of calls, enough to make me realize the situation had truly gotten out of hand. I decided to explain matters to my mother, who is ninety-three. She is active in New York social circles—bridge clubs, charity luncheons—and soon enough she would hear that her son had been bitten by a cobra.

So we had lunch. She noticed my arm sling but didn't seem especially curious about it.

"Mother," I said, "You're going to hear about this arm of mine . . . that I've been bitten on the elbow by a small cobra." I waited a beat. I couldn't resist it. "Mother, it's true."

"Stuff and nonsense," she said. "You have an aggravated bursitis condition."

Astonished, I asked, "How do you know?"

"Why, I saw your doctor at a concert two evenings ago," she said. "You might have told me when you got back from India," she went on reproachfully. "It's awkward to hear about such things from others."

The next day my sister called. "Hey!" she said. "I hear you've been bitten by a cobra on the elbow."

"Who told you that?"

"Mother," she said.

It turns out that my mother rather liked the cobra-bite story. I could imagine her sitting down at the bridge table, shuffling the cards, and getting ready to tell her friends, which she does by clearing her throat to get attention.

The cobra story was not only hers to tell. It got into the newspapers. New York's *Daily News* had an item in its gossip column. One paper reported that I was recovering in a hospital in Nairobi, Kenya, from a dangerous cobra bite suffered while on safari in Africa.

What was curious was that as time went on, the cobra experience began to become not only clear in my mind but secure, as if it had actually happened. I could almost smell the marsh grass on which I was lying, the feel of the earth against my belly, the faint movement of something to my left. "Oh, yes," I would say when asked, invariably emphasizing that it had been a *small* cobra. To my shame, I felt no qualms about perpetuating the untruth. After all, I reasoned, it was verified in the nation's press—it had gone out over the wire. The item was now tucked away in countless newspaper files, perhaps to re-emerge at my demise: MAN WHO SURVIVED COBRA BITE DIES.

The only individual I promised myself to come clean with was the doctor from Roosevelt Hospital. He had telephoned a few times since his last call and had not forgotten our luncheon date. Worried about his reaction, I had the inspired thought to have our lunch on April Fools' Day, hoping that he would accept what I had done in the spirit of that occasion. My plan was to lead him on throughout most of the meal . . . until the coffee, say, at which point I would lean forward and, in that sly, unctuous manner of the practical jokester about to break the news, ask the doctor if he realized what day it was.

To prepare for our meeting, I called up the Bronx Zoo to speak to someone in the herpetology department and find out what *does* happen to someone bitten by a cobra.

The scientist was very forthcoming. "There's probably a burning sensation where the cobra bit," he said, "a tingling up the arms, on the lips, as well as evasive saliva. . . ."

"Evasive saliva?"

"Drooling, if you will. There have been reports of euphoria . . . hallucinations, and, of course, local neuropathy, especially around the lung area. That is how people die from a cobra bite—the neural system that works the lungs fails."

"The euphoria does not last for a long time."

"Absolutely not."

"Anything else?"

The scientist paused. "It appears that the vision is affected," he said. "Green leaves in a tree might appear to be red. Vision is likely to be blurred. Of course, all this depends on the severity of the bite. . . ."

The scientist didn't ask me why I wanted the information. I had planned to tell him I was working on a murder thriller in which a cobra is dropped through a trapdoor into a victim's bathtub. Lying was becoming appallingly easy to do.

The doctor and I had lunch at a midtown club. We sat at a window table for two. He was a large man, with a smile so friendly that I winced thinking what was going to happen to it once the news sank in.

Though the doctor had never traveled to Africa or Asia, continents with a plethora of cobras and other poisonous snakes, it turned out that he was the foremost authority in New York City on snakebites. "As a consultant to the City Department of Health, I'm okayed only for snakes," he told me. "It's not kosher for me to handle bites by lionfish, poison frogs, or any other deadly critters. Only snakes."

He had plenty to keep him busy. He said I would be surprised how many amateur collectors would take "difficult" snakes out of their herpetoriums to see how they'd get along on the living-room carpet. He described a baggage handler at JFK airport who, noticing a mild turmoil in a mail sack, had gone over to investigate and had been bitten by a king cobra through the canvas.

"Wow!"

"Astonishing to think you can order snakes through the mail," the doctor said. "You can find advertisements for this in magazines like *Field and Stream*. Here's an interesting case. A woman bought a leather coat that had been made in Okinawa. She developed a severe pain in the arm, and it turned out she had been bitten by a kind of Asian copperhead—a habu, it's called."

"A what?"

"A habu. It apparently was living in the lining of the coat."

"Wow!" I said for the second time. "How long do you think the habu was in there?"

"Quite a while, I would judge." The doctor smiled. "These creatures are very self-sufficient. We had a case of someone who decided to help a cottonmouth shed its skin. They've been doing it successfully for 300 million years. The kid thought the creature needed help and got bitten for his pains. Isn't that a beauty?"

By the time we'd finished the main course, the doctor had described a number of other instances, including an encounter between a biology teacher "who should have known better" and a saw-scaled viper, a Middle Eastern "creature."

"When this viper moves," the doctor explained, "its scales slide one over the other, which makes a quite distinctive sound . . . rather like the sound of Wheaties being crushed between the fingers, though, mind you, that's not a scientific description."

The doctor took a sip of water. He continued: "Anyway, that's why the biology teacher had this creature—an auditory pleasure for him—and when he poked it into motion so he could listen to it, it *got* him. Caused a severe blood disorder. Almost killed him."

"Wow!"

As the dessert arrived, the doctor leaned back in his chair, joined his fingers in a steeple, and asked me to tell him about my cobra. I cleared my throat. "Well, doctor, I was lying in some grass looking through my binoculars at a Sarus crane when I sensed some movement to my left and was bitten in the point of the elbow by this small cobra."

We discussed what kind of cobra it was.

"Small," I said. "Really quite small. You don't suppose it could have been a krait?"

"Oh, no," the doctor said. "Hardly possible. Almost undoubtedly, considering the area, a spectacled cobra."

I thought of the distinctive eye pattern on the back of that particular species' hood and shivered slightly as I reached for a corn muffin.

"And then?" The doctor's eyes glistened behind the glasses.

"I didn't run."

"Capital!" It turned out as our conversation progressed that "capital" (along with "creature" or "critter") was a favorite expression.

I continued: "My friend Peter Matthiessen was a half mile down the spillway, hoping to spot the Siberian crane out there in the marsh. Not much he could have done anyway."

"Of course not."

"So I sat down on a sort of knoll and took off the moleskin shirt I was wearing. I looked at my elbow and I could see that the bite was not so much a puncture as a small tear. There was discomfort, as if acid had been splashed on the wound, but this was counteracted"—I gulped slightly—"by an odd feeling of . . . what? . . . Exaltation? Euphoria? . . ."

"Capital!" the doctor exploded.

"Then I noticed something quite curious. The leaves—"

"Yes, the leaves," the doctor interjected.

"—the leaves on the trees overhead had turned reddish, a kind of autumnal color. Quite odd."

"Oh, this is truly splendid," said the doctor. The reason for his excitement—he went on to explain—was that a long-standing disagreement exists about the working of cobra poison on the human system. The question is whether it works its way up the brain stem and affects the brain itself. Many authorities believe it doesn't, that it simply does its damage below the neck. My description of the discolored leaves supported the doctor's hypothesis that the brain was involved.

"Go on," he said eagerly.

I couldn't bring myself to tell him that sitting there on the knoll I had begun to drool. Besides, the timing was perfect for me to lean forward and let him in on the gag. All I had to do was to remark somewhat roguishly, "Hey, doctor, do you know what day it is?"

I could not bring myself to do it. I have wondered since why I did not fess up. Perhaps it was because I feared that, at what Aristotle referred to as the "moment of recognition," the doctor would rear up out of his chair, aggrieved, with a terrible howl that would turn heads in the august and subdued atmosphere of that midtown men's club.

The other possibility was more upsetting: that I simply could not let it go. I truly liked the fact that my mother was spreading the story at her bridge meetings: "One spade. Have you heard what's happened to my son?"

I can't recall much more about the lunch other than the palpable delight the doctor showed on being told about the chameleonlike leaves.

Almost a year to the day after our April Fools' lunch at the club, I got a letter from the doctor. He said he was writing a long essay or perhaps a short book about his experiences with serious snakebite in an urban setting. Could he use my experience as an anecdote? Presumably he was going to enlist my evidence to support his views on the effect of cobra poison on the brain. I stared at the letter, appalled.

Eventually, a solution came to mind. I would write an account of everything that had happened: the bursitis condition in Bhutan, the arm in the sling, the cocktail party where I'd sprung the cobra-bite story on Jason Epstein, my mother's reaction, the call from the doctor—all this in careful detail, including a harsh look at my own lapses of judgment. When it was all typed up and given a title ("My Last Cobra"), I'd send it off to the doctor, making sure that it got to him at some point on April 1. It occurred to me that it might be wise to send a bouquet of roses along as well.

All that was required was an envelope and some stamps. I had the good doctor's address. And yet there was this curious reluctance to let it go. What greater substantiation of what happened to me in the sedge grass at the

Bharatpur Reserve than to have notice of it in an essay published, say, in a distinguished medical journal! I was tempted to send the doctor a wire: *By all means use what you wish stop delighted to contribute to medical knowledge stop please send copies of article when published*—this last so I could carry clippings from it around in my wallet to bring out at suitable occasions.

I did send the package, of course. In the days following I expected the doctor to write or call—either to express chagrin or, I hoped, to admit he'd been duped but no harm done. A month went by. Then another. An eerie silence. I don't dare call. I have been avoiding the club where we had lunch. If a package arrives in the mail, I shake it slightly to make sure that from within I don't hear a hiss, or a rattle, or, especially, the sound of Wheaties being crushed between the fingers. . . .

~

The Speckled Band

(from: THE ADVENTURES
OF SHERLOCK HOLMS)

Arthur Conan Doyle

ON GLANCING OVER my notes of the seventy odd cases in which I have during the last eight years studied the methods of my friend Sherlock Holmes, I find many tragic, some comic, a large number merely strange, but none commonplace; for, working as he did rather for the love of his art than for the acquirement of wealth, he refused to associate himself with any investigation which did not tend towards the unusual, and even the fantastic. Of all these varied cases, however, I cannot recall any which presented more singular features than that which was associated with the well-known Surrey family of the Roylotts of Stoke Moran. The events in question occurred in the early days of my association with Holmes, when we were sharing rooms as bachelors in Baker Street. It is possible that I might have placed them upon record before, but a promise of secrecy was made at the time, from which I have only been freed during the last month by the untimely death of the lady to whom the pledge was given. It is perhaps as well that the facts should now come to light, for I have reasons to know that there are widespread rumours as to the death of Dr. Grimesby Roylott which tend to make the matter even more terrible than the truth.

It was early in April in the year '83 that I woke one morning to find Sherlock Holmes standing, fully dressed, by the side of my bed. He was a late riser, as a rule, and as the clock on the mantelpiece showed me that it was only a quarter-past seven, I blinked up at him in some surprise, and perhaps just a little resentment, for I was myself regular in my habits.

"Very sorry to knock you up, Watson," said he, "but it's the common lot this morning. Mrs. Hudson has been knocked up, she retorted upon me, and I on you."

"What is it, then—a fire?"

"No; a client. It seems that a young lady has arrived in a considerable state of excitement, who insists upon seeing me. She is waiting now in the sitting-room. Now, when young ladies wander about the metropolis at this hour of the morning, and knock sleepy people up out of their beds, I presume that it is something very pressing which they have to communicate. Should it prove to be an interesting case, you would, I am sure, wish to follow it from the outset. I thought, at any rate, that I should call you and give you the chance."

"My dear fellow, I would not miss it for anything."

I had no keener pleasure than in following Holmes in his professional investigations, and in admiring the rapid deductions, as swift as intuitions, and yet always founded on a logical basis, with which he unravelled the problems which were submitted to him. I rapidly threw on my clothes and was ready in a few minutes to accompany my friend down to the sitting-room. A lady dressed in black and heavily veiled, who had been sitting in the window, rose as we entered.

"Good-morning, madam," said Holmes cheerily. "My name is Sherlock Holmes. This is my intimate friend and associate, Dr. Watson, before whom you can speak as freely as before myself. Ha! I am glad to see that Mrs. Hudson has had the good sense to light the fire. Pray draw up to it, and I shall order you a cup of hot coffee, for I observe that you are shivering."

"It is not cold which makes me shiver," said the woman in a low voice, changing her seat as requested.

"What, then?"

"It is fear, Mr. Holmes. It is terror." She raised her veil as she spoke, and we could see that she was indeed in a pitiable state of agitation, her face all drawn and gray, with restless, frightened eyes, like those of some hunted animal. Her features and figure were those of a woman of thirty, but her hair was shot with premature gray, and her expression was weary and haggard.

Sherlock Holmes ran her over with one of his quick, all-comprehensive glances.

"You must not fear," said he soothingly, bending forward and patting her forearm. "We shall soon set matters right, I have no doubt. You have come in by train this morning, I see."

"You know me, then?"

"No, but I observe the second half of a return ticket in the palm of your left glove. You must have started early, and yet you had a good drive in a dog-cart, along heavy roads, before you reached the station."

The lady gave a violent start and stared in bewilderment at my companion.

"There is no mystery, my dear madam," said he, smiling. "The left arm of your jacket is spattered with mud in no less than seven places. The marks are perfectly fresh. There is no vehicle save a dog-cart which throws up mud in that way, and then only when you sit on the left-hand side of the driver."

"Whatever your reasons may be, you are perfectly correct," said she. "I started from home before six, reached Leatherhead at twenty past, and came in by the first train to Waterloo. Sir, I can stand this strain no longer; I shall go mad if it continues. I have no one to turn to—none, save only one, who cares for me, and he, poor fellow, can be of little aid. I have heard of you, Mr. Holmes; I have heard of you from Mrs. Farintosh, whom you helped in the hour of her sore need. It was from her that I had your address. Oh, sir, do you not think that you could help me, too, and at least throw a little light through the dense darkness which surrounds me? At present it is out of my power to reward you for your services, but in a month or six weeks I shall be married, with the control of my own income, and then at least you shall not find me ungrateful."

Holmes turned to his desk and, unlocking it, drew out a small case-book, which he consulted.

"Farintosh," said he. "Ah yes, I recall the case; it was concerned with an opal tiara. I think it was before your time, Watson. I can only say, madam, that I shall be happy to devote the same care to your case as I did to that of your friend. As to reward, my profession is its own reward; but you are at liberty to defray whatever expenses I may be put to, at the time which suits you best. And now I beg that you will lay before us everything that may help us in forming an opinion upon the matter."

"Alas!" replied our visitor, "the very horror of my situation lies in the fact that my fears are so vague, and my suspicions depend so entirely upon small points, which might seem trivial to another, that even he to whom of all others I have a right to look for help and advice looks upon all that I tell him about it as the fancies of a nervous woman. He does not say so, but I can read it from his soothing answers and averted eyes. But I have heard, Mr. Holmes, that you can see deeply into the manifold wickedness of the human heart. You may advise me how to walk amid the dangers which encompass me."

"I am all attention, madam."

"My name is Helen Stoner, and I am living with my stepfather, who is the last survivor of one of the oldest Saxon families in England, the Roylotts of Stoke Moran, on the western border of Surrey."

Holmes nodded his head. "The name is familiar to me," said he.

"The family was at one time among the richest in England, and the estates extended over the borders into Berkshire in the north, and Hampshire in the west. In the last century, however, four successive heirs were of a dissolute and wasteful disposition, and the family ruin was eventually completed by a gambler in the days of the Regency. Nothing was left save a few acres of ground, and the two-hundred-year-old house, which is itself crushed under a heavy mortgage. The last squire dragged out his existence there, living the horrible life of an aristocratic pauper; but his only son, my stepfather, seeing that he must adapt himself to the new conditions, obtained an advance from a relative, which enabled him to take a medical degree and went out to Calcutta, where, by his professional skill and his force of character, he established a large practice. In a fit of anger, however, caused by some robberies which had been perpetrated in the house, he beat his native butler to death and narrowly escaped a capital sentence. As it was, he suffered a long term of imprisonment and afterwards returned to England a morose and disappointed man.

"When Dr. Roylott was in India he married my mother, Mrs. Stoner, the young widow of Major-General Stoner, of the Bengal Artillery. My sister Julia and I were twins, and we were only two years old at the time of my mother's re-marriage. She had a considerable sum of money—not less than £1000 a year—and this she bequeathed to Dr. Roylott entirely while we resided with him, with a provision that a certain annual sum should be allowed to each of us in the event of our marriage. Shortly after our return to England my mother died—she was killed eight years ago in a railway accident near Crewe. Dr. Roylott then abandoned his attempts to establish himself in practice in London and took us to live with him in the old ancestral house at Stoke Moran. The money which my mother had left was enough for all our wants, and there seemed to be no obstacle to our happiness.

"But a terrible change came over our stepfather about this time. Instead of making friends and exchanging visits with our neighbours, who had at first been overjoyed to see a Roylott of Stoke Moran back in the old family seat, he shut himself up in his house and seldom came out save to indulge in ferocious quarrels with whoever might cross his path. Violence of temper approaching to mania has been hereditary in the men of the family, and in my stepfather's case it had, I believe, been intensified by his long residence in the tropics. A series of disgraceful brawls took place, two of which ended in the police-court, until at last he became the terror of the village, and the folks would fly at his approach, for he is a man of immense strength, and absolutely uncontrollable in his anger.

"Last week he hurled the local blacksmith over a parapet into a stream, and it was only by paying over all the money which I could gather together that I was able to avert another public exposure. He had no friends at all save the wandering gypsies, and he would give these vagabonds leave to encamp upon the few acres of bramble-covered land which represent the family estate, and would accept in return the hospitality of their tents, wandering away with them sometimes for weeks on end. He has a passion also for Indian animals, which are sent over to him by a correspondent, and he has at this moment a cheetah and a baboon, which wander freely over his grounds and are feared by the villagers almost as much as their master.

"You can imagine from what I say that my poor sister Julia and I had no great pleasure in our lives. No servant would stay with us, and for a long time we did all the work of the house. She was but thirty at the time of her death, and yet her hair had already begun to whiten, even as mine has."

"Your sister is dead, then?"

"She died just two years ago, and it is of her death that I wish to speak to you. You can understand that, living the life which I have described, we were little likely to see anyone of our own age and position. We had, however, an aunt, my mother's maiden sister, Miss Honoria Westphail, who lives near Harrow, and we were occasionally allowed to pay short visits at this lady's house. Julia went there at Christmas two years ago, and met there a half-pay major of marines, to whom she became engaged. My stepfather learned of the engagement when my sister returned and offered no objection to the marriage; but within a fortnight of the day which had been fixed for the wedding, the terrible event occurred which has deprived me of my only companion."

Sherlock Holmes had been leaning back in his chair with his eyes closed and his head sunk in a cushion, but he half opened his lids now and glanced across at his visitor.

"Pray be precise as to details," said he.

"It is easy for me to be so, for every event of that dreadful time is seared into my memory. The manor-house is, as I have already said, very old, and only one wing is now inhabited. The bedrooms in this wing are on the ground floor, the sitting-rooms being in the central block of the buildings. Of these bedrooms the first is Dr. Roylott's, the second my sister's, and the third my own. There is no communication between them, but they all open out into the same corridor. Do I make myself plain?"

"Perfectly so."

"The windows of the three rooms open out upon the lawn. That fatal night Dr. Roylott had gone to his room early, though we knew that he had not retired to rest, for my sister was troubled by the smell of the strong Indian cigars which it was his custom to smoke. She left her room, therefore, and came into mine, where she sat for some time, chatting about her approaching wedding. At eleven o'clock she rose to leave me, but she paused at the door and looked back.

" 'Tell me, Helen,' said she, 'have you ever heard anyone whistle in the dead of the night?'

" 'Never,' said I.

" 'I suppose that you could not possibly whistle, yourself, in your sleep?'

" 'Certainly not. But why?'

" 'Because during the last few nights I have always, about three in the morning, heard a low, clear whistle. I am a light sleeper, and it has awakened me. I cannot tell where it came from—perhaps from the next room, perhaps from the lawn. I thought that I would just ask you whether you had heard it.'

" 'No, I have not. It must be those wretched gypsies in the plantation.'

" 'Very likely. And yet if it were on the lawn, I wonder that you did not hear it also.'

" 'Ah, but I sleep more heavily than you.'

" 'Well, it is of no great consequence, at any rate.' She smiled back at me, closed my door, and a few moments later I heard her key turn in the lock."

"Indeed," said Holmes. "Was it your custom always to lock yourselves in at night?"

"Always."

"And why?"

"I think that I mentioned to you that the doctor kept a cheetah and a baboon. We had no feeling of security unless our doors were locked."

"Quite so. Pray proceed with your statement."

"I could not sleep that night. A vague feeling of impending misfortune impressed me. My sister and I, you will recollect, were twins, and you know how subtle are the links which bind two souls which are so closely allied. It was a wild night. The wind was howling outside, and the rain was beating and splashing against the windows. Suddenly, amid all the hubbub of the gale, there burst forth the wild scream of a terrified woman. I knew that it was my sister's voice. I sprang from my bed, wrapped a shawl round me, and rushed into the corridor. As I opened my door I seemed to hear a low whistle, such as my sister described, and a few moments later a clanging sound, as if a mass of metal had fallen. As I ran down the passage, my sister's door was unlocked, and revolved slowly upon its hinges. I stared at it horror-stricken, not knowing what was about to issue from it. By the light of the corridor-lamp I saw my sister appear at the opening, her face blanched with terror, her hands groping for help, her whole figure swaying to and fro like that of a drunkard. I ran to her and threw my arms round her, but at that moment her knees seemed to give way and she fell to the ground. She writhed as one who is in terrible pain, and her limbs were dreadfully convulsed. At first I thought that she had not recognized me, but as I bent over her she suddenly shrieked out in a voice which I shall never forget, 'Oh, my God! Helen! It was the band! The speckled band!' There was something else which she would fain have said, and she stabbed with her finger into the air in the direction of the doctor's room, but a fresh convulsion seized her and choked her words. I rushed out, calling loudly for my stepfather, and I met him hastening from his room in his dressing-gown. When he reached my sister's side she was unconscious, and though he poured brandy down her throat and sent for medical aid from the village, all efforts were in vain, for she slowly sank and died without having recovered her consciousness. Such was the dreadful end of my beloved sister."

"One moment," said Holmes; "are you sure about this whistle and metallic sound? Could you swear to it?"

"That was what the county coroner asked me at the inquiry. It is my strong impression that I heard it, and yet, among the crash of the gale and the creaking of an old house, I may possibly have been deceived."

"Was your sister dressed?"

"No, she was in her night-dress. In her right hand was found the charred stump of a match, and in her left a match-box."

"Showing that she had struck a light and looked about her when the alarm took place. That is important. And what conclusions did the coroner come to?"

"He investigated the case with great care, for Dr. Roylott's conduct had long been notorious in the county, but he was unable to find any satisfactory cause of death. My evidence showed that the door had been fastened upon the inner side, and the windows were blocked by old-fashioned shutters with broad iron bars, which were secured every night. The walls were carefully sounded, and were shown to be quite solid all round, and the flooring was also thoroughly examined, with the same result. The chimney is wide, but is barred up by four large staples. It is certain, therefore, that my sister was quite alone when she met her end. Besides, there were no marks of any violence upon her."

"How about poison?"

"The doctors examined her for it, but without success."

"What do you think that this unfortunate lady died of, then?"

"It is my belief that she died of pure fear and nervous shock, though what it was that frightened her I cannot imagine."

"Were there gypsies in the plantation at the time?"

"Yes, there are nearly always some there."

"Ah, and what did you gather from this allusion to a band—a speckled band?"

"Sometimes I have thought that it was merely the wild talk of delirium, sometimes that it may have referred to some band of people, perhaps to these very gypsies in the plantation. I do not know whether the spotted handkerchiefs which so many of them wear over their heads might have suggested the strange adjective which she used."

Holmes shook his head like a man who is far from being satisfied.

"These are very deep waters," said he; "pray go on with your narrative."

"Two years have passed since then, and my life has been until lately lonelier than ever. A month ago, however, a dear friend, whom I have known for many years, has done me the honour to ask my hand in marriage. His name is Armitage—Percy Armitage—the second son of Mr. Armitage, of Crane Water, near Reading. My stepfather has offered no opposition to the match, and we are to be married in the course of the spring. Two days ago some repairs were started in the west wing of the building, and my bedroom wall has been pierced, so that I have had to move into the chamber in which my sister died, and to sleep in the very bed in which she slept. Imagine, then, my thrill of terror when last night, as I lay awake, thinking over her terrible fate, I suddenly heard in the silence of the night the low whistle which had been the herald of her own death. I sprang up and lit the lamp, but nothing was to be seen in the room. I was too shaken to go to bed again, however, so I dressed, and as soon as it was daylight I slipped down, got a dog-cart at the Crown Inn, which is opposite, and drove to Leatherhead, from whence I have come on this morning with the one object of seeing you and asking your advice."

"You have done wisely," said my friend. "But have you told me all?"

"Yes, all."

"Miss Roylott, you have not. You are screening your stepfather."

"Why, what do you mean?"

For answer Holmes pushed back the frill of black lace which fringed the hand that lay upon our visitor's knee. Five little livid spots, the marks of four fingers and a thumb, were printed upon the white wrist.

"You have been cruelly used," said Holmes.

The lady coloured deeply and covered over her injured wrist. "He is a hard man," she said, "and perhaps he hardly knows his own strength."

There was a long silence, during which Holmes leaned his chin upon his hands and stared into the crackling fire.

"This is a very deep business," he said at last. "There are a thousand details which I should desire to know before I decide upon our course of action. Yet we have not a moment to lose. If we were to come to Stoke Moran to-day, would it be possible for us to see over these rooms without the knowledge of your stepfather?"

"As it happens, he spoke of coming into town to-day upon some most important business. It is probable that he will be away all day, and that there would be nothing to disturb you. We have a housekeeper now, but she is old and foolish, and I could easily get her out of the way."

"Excellent. You are not averse to this trip, Watson?"

"By no means."

"Then we shall both come. What are you going to do yourself?"

"I have one or two things which I would wish to do now that I am in town. But I shall return by the twelve o'clock train, so as to be there in time for your coming."

"And you may expect us early in the afternoon. I have myself some small business matters to attend to. Will you not wait and breakfast?"

"No, I must go. My heart is lightened already since I have confided my trouble to you. I shall look forward to seeing you again this afternoon." She dropped her thick black veil over her face and glided from the room.

"And what do you think of it all, Watson?" asked Sherlock Holmes, leaning back in his chair.

"It seems to me to be a most dark and sinister business."

"Dark enough and sinister enough."

"Yet if the lady is correct in saying that the flooring and walls are sound, and that the door, window, and chimney are impassable, then her sister must have been undoubtedly alone when she met her mysterious end."

"What becomes, then, of these nocturnal whistles, and what of the very peculiar words of the dying woman?"

"I cannot think."

"When you combine the ideas of whistles at night, the presence of a band of gypsies who are on intimate terms with this old doctor, the fact that we have every reason to believe that the doctor has an interest in preventing his stepdaughter's marriage, the dying allusion to a band, and, finally, the fact that Miss Helen Stoner heard a metallic clang, which might have been caused by one of those metal bars that secured the shutters falling back into its place, I think that there is good ground to think that the mystery may be cleared along those lines."

"But what, then, did the gypsies do?"

"I cannot imagine."

"I see many objections to any such theory."

"And so do I. It is precisely for that reason that we are going to Stoke Moran this day. I want to see whether the objections are fatal, or if they may be explained away. But what in the name of the devil!"

The ejaculation had been drawn from my companion by the fact that our door had been suddenly dashed open, and that a huge man had framed himself in the aperture. His costume was a peculiar mixture of the professional and of the agricultural, having a black top-hat, a long frock-coat, and a pair of high gaiters, with a hunting-crop swinging in his hand. So tall was he that his hat actually brushed the cross bar of the doorway, and his breadth seemed to span it across from side to side. A large face, seared with a thousand wrinkles, burned yellow with the sun, and marked with every evil passion, was turned from one to the other of us, while his deep-set, bile-shot eyes, and his high, thin, fleshless nose, gave him somewhat the resemblance to a fierce old bird of prey.

"Which of you is Holmes?" asked this apparition.

"My name, sir; but you have the advantage of me," said my companion quietly.

"I am Dr. Grimesby Roylott, of Stoke Moran."

"Indeed, Doctor," said Holmes blandly. "Pray take a seat."

"I will do nothing of the kind. My stepdaughter has been here. I have traced her. What has she been saying to you?"

"It is a little cold for the time of the year," said Holmes.

"What has she been saying to you?" screamed the old man furiously.

"But I have heard that the crocuses promise well," continued my companion imperturbably.

"Ha! You put me off, do you?" said our new visitor, taking a step forward and shaking his hunting-crop. "I know you, you scoundrel! I have heard of you before. You are Holmes, the meddler."

My friend smiled.

"Holmes, the busybody!"

His smile broadened.

"Holmes, the Scotland Yard Jack-in-office!"

Holmes chuckled heartily. "Your conversation is most entertaining," said he. "When you go out close the door, for there is a decided draught."

"I will go when I have said my say. Don't you dare to meddle with my affairs. I know that Miss Stoner has been here. I traced her! I am a dangerous man to fall foul of! See here." He stepped swiftly forward, seized the poker, and bent it into a curve with his huge brown hands.

"See that you keep yourself out of my grip," he snarled, and hurling the twisted poker into the fireplace he strode out of the room.

"He seems a very amiable person," said Holmes, laughing. "I am not quite so bulky, but if he had remained I might have shown him that my grip was not much more feeble than his own." As he spoke he picked up the steel poker and, with a sudden effort, straightened it out again.

"Fancy his having the insolence to confound me with the official detective force! This incident gives zest to our investigation, however, and I only trust that our little friend will not suffer from her imprudence in allowing this brute to trace her. And now, Watson, we shall order breakfast, and afterwards I shall walk down to Doctors' Commons, where I hope to get some data which may help us in this matter."

It was nearly one o'clock when Sherlock Holmes returned from his excursion. He held in his hand a sheet of blue paper, scrawled over with notes and figures.

"I have seen the will of the deceased wife," said he. "To determine its exact meaning I have been obliged to work out the present prices of the investments with which it is concerned. The total income, which at the time of the wife's death was little short of £1100, is now, through the fall in agricultural prices, not more than £750. Each daughter can claim an income of £250, in case of marriage. It is evident, therefore, that if both girls had married, this beauty would have had a mere pittance, while even one of them would cripple him to a very serious extent. My morning's work has not been wasted, since it has proved that he has the very strongest motives for standing in the way of anything of the sort. And now, Watson, this is too serious for dawdling, especially as the old man is aware that we are interesting ourselves in his affairs; so if you are ready, we shall call a cab and drive to Waterloo. I should be very much obliged if you would slip your revolver into your pocket. An Eley's No. 2 is an excellent argument with gentlemen who can twist steel pokers into knots. That and a tooth-brush are, I think, all that we need."

At Waterloo we were fortunate in catching a train for Leatherhead, where we hired a trap at the station inn and drove for four or five miles through the lovely Surrey lanes. It was a perfect day, with a bright sun and a few fleecy clouds in the heavens. The trees and wayside hedges were just throwing out their first green shoots, and the air was full of the pleasant smell of the moist earth. To me at least there was a strange contrast between the sweet promise of the spring and this sinister quest upon which we were engaged. My companion sat in the front of the trap, his arms folded, his hat pulled down over his eyes, and his chin sunk upon his breast, buried in the deepest thought. Suddenly, however, he started, tapped me on the shoulder, and pointed over the meadows.

"Look there!" said he.

A heavily timbered park stretched up in a gentle slope, thickening into a grove at the highest point. From amid the branches there jutted out the gray gables and high roof-tree of a very old mansion.

"Stoke Moran?" said he.

"Yes, sir, that be the house of Dr. Grimesby Roylott," remarked the driver.

"There is some building going on there," said Holmes; "that is where we are going."

"There's the village," said the driver, pointing to a cluster of roofs some distance to the left; "but if you want to get to the house, you'll find it short-er to get over this stile, and so by the foot-path over the fields. There it is, where the lady is walking."

"And the lady, I fancy, is Miss Stoner," observed Holmes, shading his eyes. "Yes, I think we had better do as you suggest."

We got off, paid our fare, and the trap rattled back on its way to Leatherhead.

"I thought it as well," said Holmes as we climbed the stile, "that this fel-low should think we had come here as architects, or on some definite busi-ness. It may stop his gossip. Good-afternoon, Miss Stoner. You see that we have been as good as our word."

Our client of the morning had hurried forward to meet us with a face which spoke her joy. "I have been waiting so eagerly for you," she cried, shak-ing hands with us warmly. "All has turned out splendidly. Dr. Roylott has gone to town, and it is unlikely that he will be back before evening."

"We have had the pleasure of making the doctor's acquaintance," said Holmes, and in a few words he sketched out what had occurred. Miss Ston-er turned white to the lips as she listened.

"Good heavens!" she cried, "he has followed me, then."

"So it appears."

"He is so cunning that I never know when I am safe from him. What will he say when he returns?"

"He must guard himself, for he may find that there is someone more cun-ning than himself upon his track. You must lock yourself up from him to-night. If he is violent, we shall take you away to your aunt's at Harrow. Now, we must make the best use of our time, so kindly take us at once to the rooms which we are to examine."

The building was of gray, lichen-blotched stone, with a high central por-tion and two curving wings, like the claws of a crab, thrown out on each side.

In one of these wings the windows were broken and blocked with wooden boards, while the roof was partly caved in, a picture of ruin. The central portion was in little better repair, but the right-hand block was comparatively modern, and the blinds in the windows, with the blue smoke curling up from the chimneys, showed that this was where the family resided. Some scaffolding had been erected against the end wall, and the stone-work had been broken into, but there were no signs of any workmen at the moment of our visit. Holmes walked slowly up and down the ill-trimmed lawn and examined with deep attention the outsides of the windows.

"This, I take it, belongs to the room in which you used to sleep, the centre one to your sister's, and the one next to the main building to Dr. Roylott's chamber?"

"Exactly so. But I am now sleeping in the middle one."

"Pending the alterations, as I understand. By the way, there does not seem to be any very pressing need for repairs at that end wall."

"There were none. I believe that it was an excuse to move me from my room."

"Ah! that is suggestive. Now, on the other side of this narrow wing runs the corridor from which these three rooms open. There are windows in it, of course?"

"Yes, but very small ones. Too narrow for anyone to pass through."

"As you both locked your doors at night, your rooms were unapproachable from that side. Now, would you have the kindness to go into your room and bar your shutters?"

Miss Stoner did so, and Holmes, after a careful examination through the open window, endeavoured in every way to force the shutter open, but without success. There was no slit through which a knife could be passed to raise the bar. Then with his lens he tested the hinges, but they were of solid iron, built firmly into the massive masonry. "Hum!" said he, scratching his chin in some perplexity, "my theory certainly presents some difficulties. No one could pass these shutters if they were bolted. Well, we shall see if the inside throws any light upon the matter."

A small side door led into the whitewashed corridor from which the three bedrooms opened. Holmes refused to examine the third chamber, so we passed at once to the second, that in which Miss Stoner was now sleeping, and in which her sister had met with her fate. It was a homely little room, with a low ceiling and a gaping fireplace, after the fashion of old country-houses. A brown chest of drawers stood in one corner, a narrow white-counterpaned bed in another, and a dressing-table on the left-hand side of the window. These articles, with two small wicker-work chairs, made up all the furniture in the room save for a square of Wilton carpet in the centre. The boards round and the panelling of the walls were of brown, worm-eaten oak, so old and discoloured that it may have dated from the original building of the house. Holmes drew one of the chairs into a corner and sat silent, while his eyes travelled round and round and up and down, taking in every detail of the apartment.

"Where does that bell communicate with?" he asked at last, pointing to a thick bell-rope which hung down beside the bed, the tassel actually lying upon the pillow.

"It goes to the housekeeper's room."

"It looks newer than the other things?"

"Yes, it was only put there a couple of years ago."

"Your sister asked for it, I suppose?"

"No, I never heard of her using it. We used always to get what we wanted for ourselves."

"Indeed, it seemed unnecessary to put so nice a bell-pull there. You will excuse me for a few minutes while I satisfy myself as to this floor." He threw himself down upon his face with his lens in his hand and crawled swiftly backward and forward, examining minutely the cracks between the boards. Then he did the same with the wood-work with which the chamber was panelled. Finally he walked over to the bed and spent some time in staring at it and in running his eye up and down the wall. Finally he took the bell-rope in his hand and gave it a brisk tug.

"Why, it's a dummy," said he.

"Won't it ring?"

"No, it is not even attached to a wire. This is very interesting. You can see now that it is fastened to a hook just above where the little opening for the ventilator is."

"How very absurd! I never noticed that before."

"Very strange!" muttered Holmes, pulling at the rope. "There are one or two very singular points about this room. For example, what a fool a builder must be to open a ventilator into another room, when, with the same trouble, he might have communicated with the outside air!"

"That is also quite modern," said the lady.

"Done about the same time as the bell-rope?" remarked Holmes.

"Yes, there were several little changes carried out about that time."

"They seem to have been of a most interesting character—dummy bell-ropes, and ventilators which do not ventilate. With your permission, Miss Stoner, we shall now carry our researches into the inner apartment."

Dr. Grimesby Roylott's chamber was larger than that of his stepdaughter, but was as plainly furnished. A camp-bed, a small wooden shelf full of books, mostly of a technical character, an armchair beside the bed, a plain wooden chair against the wall, a round table, and a large iron safe were the principal things which met the eye. Holmes walked slowly round and examined each and all of them with the keenest interest.

"What's in here?" he asked, tapping the safe.

"My stepfather's business papers."

"Oh! you have seen inside, then?"

"Only once, some years ago. I remember that it was full of papers."

"There isn't a cat in it, for example?"

"No. What a strange idea!"

"Well, look at this!" He took up a small saucer of milk which stood on the top of it.

"No; we don't keep a cat. But there is a cheetah and a baboon."

"Ah, yes, of course! Well, a cheetah is just a big cat, and yet a saucer of milk does not go very far in satisfying its wants, I daresay. There is one point which I should wish to determine." He squatted down in front of the wooden chair and examined the seat of it with the greatest attention.

"Thank you. That is quite settled," said he, rising and putting his lens in his pocket. "Hello! Here is something interesting!"

The object which had caught his eye was a small dog lash hung on one corner of the bed. The lash, however, was curled upon itself and tied so as to make a loop of whipcord.

"What do you make of that, Watson?"

"It's a common enough lash. But I don't know why it should be tied."

"That is not quite so common, is it? Ah, me! it's a wicked world, and when a clever man turns his brains to crime it is the worst of all. I think that I have seen enough now, Miss Stoner, and with your permission we shall walk out upon the lawn."

I had never seen my friend's face so grim or his brow so dark as it was when we turned from the scene of this investigation. We had walked several

times up and down the lawn, neither Miss Stoner nor myself liking to break
in upon his thoughts before he roused himself from his reverie.

"It is very essential, Miss Stoner," said he, "that you should absolutely
follow my advice in every respect."

"I shall most certainly do so."

"The matter is too serious for any hesitation. Your life may depend upon
your compliance."

"I assure you that I am in your hands."

"In the first place, both my friend and I must spend the night in your
room."

Both Miss Stoner and I gazed at him in astonishment.

"Yes, it must be so. Let me explain. I believe that that is the village inn
over there?"

"Yes, that is the Crown."

"Very good. Your windows would be visible from there?"

"Certainly."

"You must confine yourself to your room, on pretence of a headache,
when your stepfather comes back. Then when you hear him retire for the
night, you must open the shutters of your window, undo the hasp, put your
lamp there as a signal to us, and then withdraw quietly with everything
which you are likely to want into the room which you used to occupy. I have
no doubt that, in spite of the repairs, you could manage there for one night."

"Oh, yes, easily."

"The rest you will leave in our hands."

"But what will you do?"

"We shall spend the night in your room, and we shall investigate the
cause of this noise which has disturbed you."

"I believe, Mr. Holmes, that you have already made up your mind," said
Miss Stoner, laying her hand upon my companion's sleeve.

"Perhaps I have."

"Then, for pity's sake, tell me what was the cause of my sister's death."

"I should prefer to have clearer proofs before I speak."

"You can at least tell me whether my own thought is correct, and if she
died from some sudden fright."

"No, I do not think so. I think that there was probably some more tangi-
ble cause. And now, Miss Stoner, we must leave you, for if Dr. Roylott
returned and saw us our journey would be in vain. Good-bye, and be brave,

for if you will do what I have told you you may rest assured that we shall soon drive away the dangers that threaten you."

Sherlock Holmes and I had no difficulty in engaging a bedroom and sitting-room at the Crown Inn. They were on the upper floor, and from our window we could command a view of the avenue gate, and of the inhabited wing of Stoke Moran Manor House. At dusk we saw Dr. Grimesby Roylott drive past, his huge form looming up beside the little figure of the lad who drove him. The boy had some slight difficulty in undoing the heavy iron gates, and we heard the hoarse roar of the doctor's voice and saw the fury with which he shook his clinched fists at him. The trap drove on, and a few minutes later we saw a sudden light spring up among the trees as the lamp was lit in one of the sitting-rooms.

"Do you know, Watson," said Holmes as we sat together in the gathering darkness, "I have really some scruples as to taking you to-night. There is a distinct element of danger."

"Can I be of assistance?"

"Your presence might be invaluable."

"Then I shall certainly come."

"It is very kind of you."

"You speak of danger. You have evidently seen more in these rooms than was visible to me."

"No, but I fancy that I may have deduced a little more. I imagine that you saw all that I did."

"I saw nothing remarkable save the bell-rope, and what purpose that could answer I confess is more than I can imagine."

"You saw the ventilator, too?"

"Yes, but I do not think that it is such a very unusual thing to have a small opening between two rooms. It was so small that a rat could hardly pass through."

"I knew that we should find a ventilator before ever we came to Stoke Moran."

"My dear Holmes!"

"Oh, yes, I did. You remember in her statement she said that her sister could smell Dr. Roylott's cigar. Now, of course that suggested at once that there must be a communication between the two rooms. It could only be a small one, or it would have been remarked upon at the coroner's inquiry. I deduced a ventilator."

"But what harm can there be in that?"

"Well, there is at least a curious coincidence of dates. A ventilator is made, a cord is hung, and a lady who sleeps in the bed dies. Does not that strike you?"

"I cannot as yet see any connection."

"Did you observe anything very peculiar about that bed?"

"No."

"It was clamped to the floor. Did you ever see a bed fastened like that before?"

"I cannot say that I have."

"The lady could not move her bed. It must always be in the same relative position to the ventilator and to the rope—or so we may call it, since it was clearly never meant for a bell-pull."

"Holmes," I cried, "I seem to see dimly what you are hinting at. We are only just in time to prevent some subtle and horrible crime."

"Subtle enough and horrible enough. When a doctor does go wrong he is the first of criminals. He has nerve and he has knowledge. Palmer and Pritchard were among the heads of their profession. This man strikes even deeper, but I think, Watson, that we shall be able to strike deeper still. But we shall have horrors enough before the night is over; for goodness' sake let us have a quiet pipe and turn our minds for a few hours to something more cheerful."

About nine o'clock the light among the trees was extinguished, and all was dark in the direction of the Manor House. Two hours passed slowly away, and then, suddenly, just at the stroke of eleven, a single bright light shone out right in front of us.

"That is our signal," said Holmes, springing to his feet; "it comes from the middle window."

As we passed out he exchanged a few words with the landlord, explaining that we were going on a late visit to an acquaintance, and that it was possible that we might spend the night there. A moment later we were out on the dark road, a chill wind blowing in our faces, and one yellow light twinkling in front of us through the gloom to guide us on our sombre errand.

There was little difficulty in entering the grounds, for unrepaired breach-es gaped in the old park wall. Making our way among the trees, we reached the lawn, crossed it, and were about to enter through the window when out from a clump of laurel bushes there darted what seemed to be a hideous and distorted child, who threw itself upon the grass with writhing limbs and then ran swiftly across the lawn into the darkness.

"My God!" I whispered; "did you see it?"

Holmes was for the moment as startled as I. His hand closed like a vise upon my wrist in his agitation. Then he broke into a low laugh and put his lips to my ear.

"It is a nice household," he murmured. "That is the baboon."

I had forgotten the strange pets which the doctor affected. There was a cheetah, too; perhaps we might find it upon our shoulders at any moment. I confess that I felt easier in my mind when, after following Holmes's example and slipping off my shoes, I found myself inside the bedroom. My companion noiselessly closed the shutters, moved the lamp onto the table, and cast his eyes round the room. All was as we had seen it in the daytime. Then creeping up to me and making a trumpet of his hand, he whispered into my ear again so gently that it was all that I could do to distinguish the words:

"The least sound would be fatal to our plans."

I nodded to show that I had heard.

"We must sit without light. He would see it through the ventilator."

I nodded again.

"Do not go asleep; your very life may depend upon it. Have your pistol ready in case we should need it. I will sit on the side of the bed, and you in that chair."

I took out my revolver and laid it on the corner of the table.

Holmes had brought up a long thin cane, and this he placed upon the bed beside him. By it he laid the box of matches and the stump of a candle. Then he turned down the lamp, and we were left in darkness.

How shall I ever forget that dreadful vigil? I could not hear a sound, not even the drawing of a breath, and yet I knew that my companion sat open-eyed, within a few feet of me, in the same state of nervous tension in which I was myself. The shutters cut off the least ray of light, and we waited in absolute darkness. From outside came the occasional cry of a night-bird, and once at our very window a long-drawn catlike whine, which told us that the cheetah was indeed at liberty. Far away we could hear the deep tones of the parish clock, which boomed out every quarter of an hour. How long they seemed, those quarters! Twelve struck, and one and two and three, and still we sat waiting silently for whatever might befall.

Suddenly there was the momentary gleam of a light up in the direction of the ventilator, which vanished immediately, but was succeeded by a strong smell of burning oil and heated metal. Someone in the next room had lit a dark-lantern. I heard a gentle sound of movement, and then all was silent once more, though the smell grew stronger. For half an hour I sat with straining ears. Then suddenly another sound became audible—a very gentle, soothing sound, like that of a small jet of steam escaping continually from a kettle. The instant that we heard it, Holmes sprang from the bed, struck a match, and lashed furiously with his cane at the bell-pull.

"You see it, Watson?" he yelled. "You see it?"

But I saw nothing. At the moment when Holmes struck the light I heard a low, clear whistle, but the sudden glare flashing into my weary eyes made it impossible for me to tell what it was at which my friend lashed so savagely. I could, however, see that his face was deadly pale and filled with horror and loathing.

He had ceased to strike and was gazing up at the ventilator when suddenly there broke from the silence of the night the most horrible cry to which I have ever listened. It swelled up louder and louder, a hoarse yell of pain and fear and anger all mingled in the one dreadful shriek. They say that away down in the village, and even in the distant parsonage, that cry raised the sleepers from their beds. It struck cold to our hearts, and I stood gazing at Holmes, and he at me, until the last echoes of it had died away into the silence from which it rose.

"What can it mean?" I gasped.

"It means that it is all over," Holmes answered. "And perhaps, after all, it is for the best. Take your pistol, and we will enter Dr. Roylott's room."

With a grave face he lit the lamp and led the way down the corridor. Twice he struck at the chamber door without any reply from within. Then he turned the handle and entered, I at his heels, with the cocked pistol in my hand.

It was a singular sight which met our eyes. On the table stood a dark-lantern with the shutter half open, throwing a brilliant beam of light upon the iron safe, the door of which was ajar. Beside this table, on the wooden chair, sat Dr. Grimesby Roylott, clad in a long gray dressing-gown, his bare ankles protruding beneath, and his feet thrust into red heelless Turkish slippers. Across his lap lay the short stock with the long lash which we had noticed during the day. His chin was cocked upward and his eyes were fixed in a dreadful, rigid stare at the corner of the ceiling. Round his brow he had a peculiar yellow band, with brownish speckles, which seemed to be bound tightly round his head. As we entered he made neither sound nor motion.

"The band! the speckled band!" whispered Holmes.

I took a step forward. In an instant his strange headgear began to move, and there reared itself from among his hair the squat diamond-shaped head and puffed neck of a loathsome serpent.

"It is a swamp adder!" cried Holmes; "the deadliest snake in India. He has died within ten seconds of being bitten. Violence does, in truth, recoil upon the violent, and the schemer falls into the pit which he digs for another. Let us thrust this creature back into its den, and we can then remove Miss Stoner to some place of shelter and let the county police know what has happened."

As he spoke he drew the dog-whip swiftly from the dead man's lap, and throwing the noose round the reptile's neck he drew it from its horrid perch and, carrying it at arm's length, threw it into the iron safe, which he closed upon it.

Such are the true facts of the death of Dr. Grimesby Roylott, of Stoke Moran. It is not necessary that I should prolong a narrative which has already run to too great a length by telling how we broke the sad news to the terrified girl, how we conveyed her by the morning train to the care of her good aunt at Harrow, of how the slow process of official inquiry came to the conclusion that the doctor met his fate while indiscreetly playing with a dangerous pet. The little which I had yet to learn of the case was told me by Sherlock Holmes as we travelled back next day.

"I had," said he, "come to an entirely erroneous conclusion which shows, my dear Watson, how dangerous it always is to reason from insufficient data. The presence of the gypsies, and the use of the word 'band,' which was used by the poor girl, no doubt to explain the appearance which she had caught a hurried glimpse of by the light of her match, were sufficient to put me upon an entirely wrong scent. I can only claim the merit that I instantly reconsidered my position when, however, it became clear to me that whatever danger threatened an occupant of the room could not come either from the window or the door. My attention was speedily drawn, as I have already remarked to you, to this ventilator, and to the bell-rope which hung down to the bed. The discovery that this was a dummy, and that the bed was clamped to the floor, instantly gave rise to the suspicion that the rope was there as a bridge for something passing through the hole and coming to the bed. The idea of a snake instantly occurred to me, and when I coupled it with my knowledge that the doctor was furnished with a supply of creatures from India, I felt that I was probably on the right track. The idea of using a form of poison which could not possibly be discovered by any chemical test was just such a one as would occur to a clever and ruthless man who had had an Eastern training. The rapidity with which such a poison would take effect would also, from his point of view, be an advantage. It would be a sharp-eyed coroner, indeed, who could distinguish the two little dark punctures which would show where the poison fangs had done their work. Then I thought of the whistle. Of course he must recall the snake before the morning light revealed it to the victim. He had trained it, probably by the use of the milk which we saw, to return to him when summoned. He would put it through this ventilator at the hour that he thought best, with the certainty that it would crawl down the rope and land on the bed. It might or might not bite the occupant, perhaps she might escape every night for a week, but sooner or later she must fall a victim.

"I had come to these conclusions before ever I had entered his room. An inspection of his chair showed me that he had been in the habit of standing on it, which of course would be necessary in order that he should reach the ventilator. The sight of the safe, the saucer of milk, and the loop of whipcord were enough to finally dispel any doubts which may have remained. The metallic clang heard by Miss Stoner was obviously caused by her stepfather hastily closing the door of his safe upon its terrible occupant. Having once made up my mind, you know the steps which I took in order to put the matter to the proof. I heard the creature hiss as I have no doubt that you did also, and I instantly lit the light and attacked it."

"With the result of driving it through the ventilator."

"And also with the result of causing it to turn upon its master at the other side. Some of the blows of my cane came home and roused its snakish temper, so that it flew upon the first person it saw. In this way I am no doubt indirectly responsible for Dr. Grimesby Roylott's death, and I cannot say that it is likely to weigh very heavily upon my conscience."

Winter

Peter Sacks

1.

Tonight a portion of the wasting moon rose
red as heresy returning from the world,
as if some other fruit, unseen till now,
hung on the scaffold of the tree—
a north wind gathering the orchard into ice.

And when that spirit blows,
the spirit of the perishable world,
it brings the winter
and the winter is the world.

2.

A life still folded at the crease of exile
flashing back the motherland like sunset on the ice,
frozen palms, flamboyants hung with swords.

Cold effigies, like back into the stone,
it is the season of indifference,
of lovelessness beneath the whistling flute;

a novice conjuring the reptile or the desert wolf,
an adolescent god made old, frigid at heart.

3.

This is our bondage, that we build
the image of undying kings above the tomb,
the basalt boat with its deep lid of stars.

Until we've grown old among our enemies:
leafless, each tree black as charcoal,
the impatient sketch becomes the will of what survives,

of carbon flashing in the light of shorter days,
the diamond and its leaves.
And though such flourishes of hard
unearthly light wait sheathed in repetitions
of each season, I drew back from seeing
past and future fall to the same ash,

who in the quarry laughed
to hear a prince of our own blood,
a killer, stammering, a handler of snakes,

would lead us to the desert—
some said for the week of sacrifice,
while others muttered of a Promised Land.

4.

They said give form to what uncoils—
as if reborn, the body of a snake
still filmed with mucus,
blinking back the light

who knows nothing of us, is older,
will outlive us; though that night
I saw a young snake struck and mangled by a car,

three inches of intestine covering
green-gold diamonds of the skin,
head twisting, mouth-side up, gasping for air,
the jaw unhinged to swallow its own death.

5.

Out of the dust, a whisper,
fanged
but unforgotten

of that
glistening between the leaves,

  (*even the skin is sweet*),

no greater subtlety between the lips,
    the teeth, the tongue
                        (its likeness
stirring in the mouth),

    the flavor entering the mind
as knowledge,

        as imagination
                    fleshed;

    what is our life,
                out of the dust,

what is the mist that rises
    from the earth and then

                            returns

        as rain?

And what is likeness,
            after which
we have been made;

and difference—here within
    the garden, in the midst,

                the tree
    between us,

        wholly beautiful,
forbidden;

tasting which—
    and knowing—

 you will be as gods?

  6.

Now reaching, plucking
  (how it fits the hand—

the branch
  swings back, in flight),

now holding it
  against the mouth,

unbruised.
      Who wouldn't eat

(the shine,
    the fragrance rising

 from the thing itself),

knowing we knew nothing
  but the words

for good,
    for evil,
  and for pain?

And what was sin,
      if not
  the first division

   of our love?

  7.

Oppression stiffening out of magic
into art—the flowing muscle

hardened to a rod, cast down
and slithering again, a living flame,

We live within a season of forbidden prayer,
in which devotion, long suppressed,

has made a ritual of accident
    and of escape

        (I leaned against the stone
of an abandoned house—the word

in mind was *longing*—peering in
as through a childhood dream,

the window filthy, webbed,
a solid mist like skin over the gloom

—and as I straightened up,
the viper, coiling

in a slight depression of the wall
was poised to strike);

until whatever happens or is conjured,
caught between our fear and need

—contracted, hard, opaque—
becomes a mirror for the god.

    8.

Smoke fills the valley air:
beyond the chimney's flame
a longing for the natural world returns—

before moonrise, the ragged lines of geese,
their underwings and bellies flushed with light,
long broken lines in early spring,

still wavering bewildered to the north,
and to the frozen west, caught now, for the first time,
by more than their instinctual flight.

The Dancing Cobra

Richard Wiley

RONALD AND BILL were just out of high school and friends. They had dated Sally and Beverly for almost a year, during which time neither couple was alone very much, though Bill and Beverly talked every day on the phone and had occasional wrestling matches in Beverly's living room when her mother wasn't home. They were young, this quartet, but thus far had remained somewhat circumspect, though desire certainly raged in them all.

One cold evening, when Bill was picking up Beverly (Ronald and Sally were sitting outside in the car) and Beverly kept him waiting, Bill happened to open the linen closet, which was in an upstairs hallway where he wasn't supposed to venture when Beverly's mother wasn't home. He wasn't really looking for anything, just sliding his hands between the pleasing folds of sheets and towels, when he came upon Beverly's mother's new vibrator, which he slowly pulled out.

"Lord have mercy," he said, then just as Beverly was about to open her door, he shoved it in his pants and ran down to sit on the couch where he belonged. He wouldn't have taken it if he'd had time to think, but, of course, time to think changes us all.

Beverly looked lovely, the smell of her powder ballooning before her like an omen. Tonight was going to be the night, maybe. Both Bill, with the vibrator in his pants, and the well-powdered Beverly thought so, though they hadn't talked about it.

At first Bill couldn't wait to share his discovery with Ronald, but by the time they got to the drive-in movie he had decided to keep quiet about it for a while. When the movie started Ronald and Sally scrunched down in the front seat and Bill pulled the vibrator out of his pants and put it inside one of the shoes that he had just taken off. Beverly saw him do it, or rather she saw that his pants had come undone, and said something he had longed to hear her say for weeks by then, and that she had thought about all during the time she'd been powdering herself. She said, "Hey, why not let me do that?" Ronald, in the front seat, heard it, too, and looked at Sally with a firmly set jaw.

Meanwhile, back at Beverly's house, her mother came home. She was single, a hardworking woman, who, as the Fates would have it, had just turned forty that day. The vibrator was a birthday gift she had purchased for herself through the mail and tucked away in the linen closet for a spectacular celebration she was thinking of having that night. When she opened the door she called, "Beverly!" though she knew her daughter wasn't home. Beverly was a wonderful daughter, and would have stayed to celebrate with her mother (in a more traditional way), had her mother not insisted that she go along with Bill. Her mother was an admissions counselor at the local college, the deputy director of admissions, so one can well imagine that to have sent off for the vibrator, and now to actually have it in her house, was an act so contrary to those she performed during the day that she was beside herself. She had not used it yet, that, if she found the courage, was reserved for tonight, but she had unpacked it and loaded it with batteries and turned it on and off a couple of times. It said, *Bzz, bzz.*

In the kitchen, where she put down her bundles, she found a cake that Beverly had made that afternoon, with "Happy Birthday, Mom!" written on it. And the mail was there, too, a card from her sister, a few bills. Forty. She was forty. At school the fathers of prospective students were all pretty close to her age, some of them attractive, but she rarely dated, had locked herself up in work and in Beverly for so long that when men did occasionally ask her out she almost always turned them down, even the ones that, as her own mother used to say, "showed promise." She rarely asked herself why she was so reluctant—she'd been outgoing and friendly when growing up—but there it was, forty, and no one in her life. And then she saw the vibrator ad. And now it was upstairs in the linen closet.

But, of course, it wasn't. Rather it was nestled in Bill's shoe, on the floor of Ronald's father's car at the drive-in movie, where Beverly had her hand down Bill's trousers. She had never done this before with anyone and was tentative, both wanting to please Bill and also hoping to satisfy her own vital urges and curiosity. It was a strange thing to touch, both hard and soft at the same time, like a piece of snipped off garden hose, or, yes, like the pet mouse she'd had once as a girl. Was she really going to let him put it in her? She imagined it laying up against her thigh where she had powdered.

For his part Bill moaned and moved about in spastic pleasure, hoping against hope not to embarrass himself. And Ronald, who *knew* what was happening in the back, had repeatedly taken Sally's hand and put it between his legs. She'd retrieved it firmly each time, but was getting irritated. She didn't mind kissing Ronald, and she liked letting him put his hands beneath her sweater, but she wasn't going farther, not now, not ever with Ronald. So Ronald grew frustrated and suddenly sat up. "Come on, Bill," he ordered, "Let's go down to the concession stand for popcorn and Cokes."

Bill didn't want to go anywhere, but the moment Ronald spoke Beverly pulled her hand out of his pants, and as long as Ronald continued to stare at them, she wasn't putting it back. So he sighed and said, "God, Ronald, your timing's great, but okay." The excitement of what Beverly was doing, and his genuine love for her, had made him forget about the vibrator in his shoe until he bent down to put his shoes back on. And by then Ronald had the door open and the light came on. So Bill could either go buy popcorn in his stocking feet, or shove the vibrator under the seat in front of him. Oh, why had he taken the fool thing? Why hadn't he left it where it was?

He pushed it under the seat and slipped into his shoes, but in his determination to hide it well he had shoved it too far and it hit one of Sally's ankles. He and Ronald were gone, however, by the time she reached down and closed her fist around it, hefting it as if it were a barbell. "That damned Ronald," she said to herself.

Back at home, Beverly's mother was preparing her other secret shame: rare red meat with a baked potato and a nice cold glass of Chablis. And after that a piece of Beverly's birthday cake. And then a hot bath. And then her clandestine meeting with Mr. V. If she dared, if she still had it in her to do such a thing. All during dinner preparations she thought about it. She was mindful about everything, from her role as admissions counselor at the college to cooking for herself and Beverly, but the idea of what sat in her linen closet, the abstract notion of it, disrupted her mindfulness tonight. She forgot to set the timer for her steak (which was eighteen bucks a pound at the butcher shop) and she left the Chablis in the freezer too long. She didn't exactly hurry, her date with Mr. V was for ten o'clock, not sooner, but when the phone rang at eight-thirty, it was jarring, accusatory. And she decided to let the answering machine take the call.

"Hello, Donna?" said a man's voice, "Happy birthday, Donna, if you're there, pick up." It was a voice she knew but didn't recognize, a breathy voice with a cloak of warmth around it that made her take her hand off her wine-glass and put it between her legs. Who was it? Who knew about her birth-day? He waited for the longest time, a half a minute, maybe, before he hung up. And in the following silence she picked up the receiver and then put it down again, so the dial tone wouldn't dislodge the voice from her memory. She would listen for it again, she decided, when she got to work on Monday.

When she remembered that there was a way to discover the number of whomever had called you most recently it was like an electric shock. She had to look in the phone book to learn how to do it, but Beverly had told her it was possible, and it worked, first try. The number was full of sixes and threes, sixes and threes, like a code. She also read how to block her own number from such easy discovery, and had the terrifying thought that she might like to hear that voice again, at around ten o'clock, when (and if) she pulled Mr. V from his grotto. She shuddered, casting the thought aside and then pulling it back and then casting it aside. This was so unlike her! 636-3663.

It was cold outside but warm in the concession stand, and warmer yet in the car, where Ronald had left the engine on while they'd been gone. And the vibrator was warm in Sally's hand while she'd been thinking about Ronald. Was he so insecure, did he have such a fragile confidence in himself that he had brought this along for help? And did he plan on using it on her? She wanted to be outraged, but by the time the car door opened again, she decid-ed to bide her time, and tucked the vibrator out of sight beneath her legs.

"What did we miss?" Ronald asked, but Bill only took his shoes off again and snuggled up next to Beverly. There was a blanket behind them, and he pulled it down and covered them so they might get back to what they were doing before. He had forgotten about the vibrator, for his mind had been entirely taken up with Beverly, about whom he had come to a decision during his long wait in the concession line. This touching was fine, and he wanted more, but he also wanted to tell her that they should go no farther tonight, in the backseat of Ronald's parents' car, but should do it properly, tomorrow or the next day in her bedroom, when her mother was out.

636-3663. It was Beverly's mother's mantra, but the vibrator itself, the still-quiet Mr. V, played just as much havoc on Sally's mind. So while Donna finished her dinner and washed the dishes with as much mindfulness as she could muster (all the while thinking was it Don from Chemistry? Frank from Buildings Maintenance? That new guy, Bob, from her very own office?), Sally was in the throes of unexpected and antithetical emotions, both incensed and intrigued at the same time. At first she kissed Ronald so hard that he almost spilled their Cokes and did upset the popcorn. "Oh, gosh, sorry," he said, as they both got their fingers buttery picking it up.

"Never mind that," said Sally, slipping one of those fingers into his mouth. Her other hand was around the now buttery vibrator, sliding over it like a fireman down a pole. "How dare he bring this here?" she asked herself. Unlike Beverly, Sally wasn't a virgin, though she had not enjoyed the experience (with her previous boyfriend) and had thought of Ronald as a stop-gap, someone to keep her off what her mother liked to call a "slippery slope," for a little while longer. She was about to let her passion get the best of her when suddenly her fingers found the switch that turned the damned thing on. *Bzz*, it said, with such unexpected encroachment that Ronald sat up and started messing with the heater knobs. *Bzz, bzz.* She hid it beneath her legs again and had a small amount of difficulty turning it off.

At home, though it still wasn't ten, Donna went into the basement to dig out, Mr. V's packing box. She hadn't really read the "instructions," she'd been far too nervous unpacking it for that, but she didn't want to hurt herself by misusing her birthday present. What if she got it stuck in there or kept it on too long, or even, God forbid, electrocuted herself? She laughed as she took the box upstairs and sat it on the edge of the tub. "Admissions director dead at forty, vibrated to death." She could see the headlines now.

She put bubbles in her bath and lit candles around the tub, and took off her clothes and slipped down into the churning water with music playing in the background. The music was from a classic rock radio station she liked and the Beatles were just then singing, "I get by with a little help from my friends," and that made her laugh as well. She was still a good-looking woman, only forty for crying out loud. Oh, why had she not been able to put a name to that voice on the phone?

She picked up the box and for the first time saw the cover drawing of a little anthropomorphic, penis-headed snake, with a row of sibilant *S*s coming from its mouth. The vibrator's actual name was "The Dancing Cobra," with the logo, "Find Your Own True HappineSss at Home," written under it in undulating letters, but she already knew it said *bzz*. "Ssss, my ass," she told it, and then the phone rang again, not only downstairs where the answering machine was, but here between the candles, right on the edge of the tub. She didn't usually bring the phone into the bathroom with her, but she had tonight, pulling it from her bedside on a terrifically long cord. "What if it's him?" she asked the snake. She had her refilled wineglass on the tubside, too, and took a sip while she counted the rings. "Three, four . . ." till she heard the answering machine clicking on.

"Yes, hello?" said Donna, grabbing the phone beside her and sitting up in the tub.

"Donna?" said that same man's voice. "You're there, you're home . . ."

"Yes," she said, "Who is this?" She reached over and turned down the radio.

"It's Bob from work," said the voice, "I know this is weird, but I got you a present and wondered if I could bring it over."

"Bob from work?" He had been her third guess, but my God, she'd hardly spoken to him, nothing more than passing chitchat in the halls. How did he know about her birthday? She looked at the photo of "The Dancing Cobra," and dropped the box over the edge of the tub.

"Well, I don't know, Bob," she said. "It is kind of late and Beverly isn't home."

She was immediately ashamed and put a soapy hand to her brow. God, how old was she? Had she really said, "Beverly isn't home"?

"Oh, hell, Bob, what I mean to say is sure. I have no idea why you'd think to get me a present, but of course you can bring it over."

"Great," he said. "What do you think, ten o'clock?"

Ten o'clock, the witching hour. "Sure," she said again. "I'll give you a piece of cake."

When he hung up she dropped the phone onto "The Dancing Cobra" box, then picked up a bar of soap and started to wash. Bob from work. He was her age, or maybe a little bit younger. He'd been hired at the beginning of the spring semester and had been . . . what had he been before? A carpenter? He had a master's degree in counseling but had dropped out of it a decade earlier, and now was deciding to come back. That, in a nutshell, was all she knew about him. And now he was calling her and telling her he'd got her a birthday present and she had said, "Beverly isn't home." My God.

When she stepped from the tub and looked down at "The Dancing Cobra" box, some soap fell from her body and landed on the snake's mouth, making it look even more obscene and leery than it had when it arrived in the mail. How could she have fallen so far and not even known it! Thank God Beverly wasn't home. She hoped, at least, that Beverly would not discover life's miseries for a good long while.

Back at the drive-in movie a woman was sitting in the cabin of a boat with her legs parted and her panties showing, her face both bemused and taunting. "You think you're man enough, Harry, then come and get it," she was saying, as she raised and pointed a pistol. The camera switched to Harry. "What have we here?" he said.

That's what Sally imagined herself telling Ronald, while holding up the buttery vibrator, and when she heard it coming from the man on the screen her anger returned. True, while Ronald had been kissing her and trying to get her clothes off she had just about decided not to say anything, to simply take the vibrator home with her and thus not have to put up with boys like Ronald anymore, but now her hostility came back with a vengeance. What did he think, that he was going to shove the thing up into her and make her think it was him! What a fool he was! How could she have seen anything in him in the first place?

"God, Ronald, get your fat hands off me and take me home," she suddenly said, then she reached into her bag and made the vibrator go *bzz* again for emphasis.

"Huh?" said Ronald. This time he thought the sound was coming from his radio.

"You heard me. Take me home right now, you low-life pervert. Damn you, Ronald, what kind of girl do you think I am?"

"Sally, what the hell?" Ronald said, holding both hands up.

"Just start the engine and drive," she told him. "I've half a mind to tell your father what goes on in his car."

"Why are they fighting?" Bill asked Beverly, when the engine roared to life.

"Search me," said Beverly. "They should learn to get along, like us."

They were under the blanket touching each other again and smiling, their hearts as light as Ronald's was heavy. When the car lurched away from its parking space, however, slamming over the drive-in movie's speed bumps, they sat up.

"Hey, Ron, slow down," said Bill, and Beverly looked at Sally.

"Get your own goddam car if you wanta make out!" bellowed Ronald.

Bill reached up to touch his friend but Ronald was in no mood to be cajoled. "Get your hands off me or I'll stop this car right now and kick you out," he hissed. "And Sally, you can just go fuck yourself."

"Don't mind if I do," she said.

But she was far too pleased with her own cleverness and barked out a couple of harsh laughs. And though Beverly was still dumbfounded, that made Bill say, "Oh, oh." He fell down to search the floor, inside his recently re-removed shoes, and everywhere. He reached so far forward that he brushed Sally's ankle.

"What happened, Bill, did you lose a contact lens?" asked Beverly, and Sally punched Ronald hard in the arm. "Creep!" she cried. "Weasel! Skunk!"

Ronald was furious but he was also baffled, and as they sped along the highway he tried to slow down. All he needed was another ticket and he would lose his driving privileges. "You must be on the rag or something, Sally!" he yelled.

"That's right, hit me," she said, though he still had his hands on the wheel. "Big man Ronald, can't even get it up himself!"

But she had gone too far and she knew it, she couldn't steal the vibrator now without big trouble. So she pulled it back out of her bag. Her first idea was to wave it at Bill and Beverly, so they could see for themselves what a weirdo Ronald was, but if she did that Ronald might really go crazy, running them off the road. And who knew, Bill and Beverly might think it was hers in the first place! So she let out an agonized "OHHHH!" and shoved it back under the seat.

"Found it!" said Bill, pretending the lost contact lens was in his mouth.

"Want my hand mirror, sweetie?" Beverly asked him, but Bill only shook his head and feigned putting the contact back in his eye. And after that they sat there with their shoulders touching, until Ronald pulled up in front of Sally's house, reached across to open her door, and screamed, "Get out!"

Meanwhile, Donna had parted her curtains and was peeking at the street thinking, "Ten o'clock." She wasn't sure why, but she'd brought some of her candles downstairs and she had returned "The Dancing Cobra" box to the basement, tearing it slowly apart. Not only was there cake, but there was sherry, too, and she had gone around the living room fluffing couch pillows and straightening Beverly's various pictures on the walls. It really was over-kill, to have this many photos, there must be four dozen of them, of Beverly at every stage of life, and she vowed to put some of them away tomorrow. Bob would surely think she didn't have a life of her own.

She wanted to part the curtains again when she heard someone pull up outside, but instead went into the kitchen and plugged in the coffeepot. Cof-fee went better with cake than sherry, and gave less of an impression that this was a date. Bob from work. She put the sherry in the cupboard and returned to the living room to open the door.

Beverly and Bill were coming up the walk and behind them Ronald had just zoomed away when another car, an ancient 1950-something Jaguar, pulled into the vacated spot. Beverly and Bill looked bedraggled and so did the Jaguar, which was spotty with lead and primer. Bob from work sat behind the wheel, a large package in the seat beside him. He killed the engine and got out by stepping over the door.

"Sorry, Mom," said Beverly, "But Ronald and Sally were acting all freaked out."

Bob reached back into his car to pick up the box. "Don't you know it's winter?" Donna called, "Doesn't that thing have a top?"

"No more double dating with Ronald and Sally, Mrs. Coolidge," said Bill.

When Donna looked at him her eyes were drawn to the front of his pants. Poor Bill, she thought, and determined to have a talk with Beverly tomorrow.

"Got two tops," said Bob, "A hard one and a soft one both." He had come up behind Beverly and Bill, struggling under the poorly wrapped box.

"Didn't know you were having company, Mom," said Beverly. "Bill and I will go upstairs."

"It's not company, it's Bob from work," said Donna, "And no you won't." She put a hand up to fix her daughter's hair, smiled at poor Bill, and made the introductions. "There's cake, it's my birthday, and I've got this mysterious present. You really shouldn't have, Bob."

"Should have, shouldn't have . . . Back and forth like a seesaw. I've been thinking the same thing all week."

Suddenly Donna remembered that Bob had a son. They'd had a conversa-tion in the cafeteria one day, where both of them put child-rearing between them and lingered over it. His son was coming to live with him and starting school at the college in the fall. "Bob's got a boy only a year older than you guys," she told Beverly and Bill.

Bill helped Bob with the present, which was so poorly wrapped that it began to show itself before they even got it inside. He had another present, too, much smaller and flat like a record, under his arm. They brought the package into the living room and put it on the coffee table. Bob smoothed the paper out and Beverly said she was going to run up and change her clothes and come right back down.

"I'll go with you," said Bill, but Donna gave him a look and he only sat on the couch behind the present. Donna determined right then and there not to leave him alone with Beverly anymore. "Right then and there," had been an expression of her mother's.

"I know it's forward of me coming over here like this," said Bob. "I can hardly even believe I'm doing it." But he couldn't stop smiling as he said it.

"Well you can make up for it by helping me get the coffee and cake," Donna said, smiling back and drawing him into the kitchen.

When he was finally alone Bill dug the vibrator from his pants, looked wildly around for a place to hide it, then shoved it back again when Beverly came bounding down the stairs. She saw the bulge and said, "Wow, Bill, I'm impressed."

"Impressed about what?" called her mother from the kitchen. "And you guys stay there, I'm about to open my present."

"I really have to go to the bathroom," said Bill.

Donna and Bob brought the cake and coffee into the living room on a battered old tea tray, something left to Donna by her mother, and somehow a sort of counterpart to Bob's old Jaguar outside. Bob had a box of candles and while he and Beverly arranged them on the cake, Bill started up the stairs.

"There's a bathroom down here, you know, Bill," Beverly said, but he waved over his head and kept on going. Beverly and Donna looked at each other and smiled, and when Bob lit the candles, Beverly turned off the overhead light. They wavered in the windless room, the people and the candles both, until a much relieved Bill came running back down to join them.

"Now make a wish, Mom," said Beverly, "And blow them out."

"Gosh," said Donna, "This feels like a birthday party all of a sudden." Then she closed her eyes and wished as hard as she could, for her daughter's eternal happiness.

When the candles were smoking toward the ceiling and she finally turned her attention to Bob's gift, it nearly unwrapped itself. It wasn't new, no newer than his car outside, but it delighted her like nothing else she could have imagined. It was an old phonograph, a record player, with a one-inch shaft in its center, made especially for playing 45s. "Well, I'll be damned," she said. It was just like one that had sat in her parents' basement when she was a girl.

"It works," said Bob. "Here, now open this one." He gave her the better-wrapped gift from under his arm.

"You truly shouldn't have, Bob," said Donna.

"I don't know how to be subtle," he told her. "I don't very much know how to ease into things."

While Donna opened the record, Beverly dished up the cake, and Bill helped Bob put the phonograph next to an electrical outlet on the floor.

"Oh, Bob!" said Donna, holding up the odd-looking record.

"What is it, Mom?" asked Beverly, "Bing Crosby singing 'White Christmas'?"

"It's the best two-sided single ever made," Bob said. "From 1958. Your mother wasn't born then, though, so I wasn't sure she'd know it."

"Know it? Ha!" Donna said.

"Well what is it?" Beverly asked again. "Hurry up and put it on."

"Yeah," said Bill. "We can eat the cake and dance."

Donna sat cross-legged by the phonograph, slipped the record over the shaft, and watched as it fell down and started spinning, forty-five revolutions per minute, one for every year of her life, plus five. She laughed again and looked at Bob. The tune was "La Bamba," by Ritchie Valens, killed when he wasn't much older than Beverly, in that plane crash with Buddy Holly and the Big Bopper.

"Para bailar La Bamba
Para bailar La Bamba se necessita una poca de gracia
Una poca de gracia y otra cosita y arriba y arriba
Ay arriba y arriba por ti sere por ti sere por ti sere."

~

Donna and Beverly both knew the words from listening to Donna's radio station and leapt together like Mexican beans, singing like crazy. "Bam-ba Bamba! Bam-ba la Bamba!" Bob sang, too, but did a little "Hand Jive" move-

ment from another song, while Bill took a bite of his cake and made a couple of wishes of his own. He wished his family could be like this, and that
Beverly's mother would leave them alone in the morning.

Though they all loved it, Bob had not bought the record player for "La
Bamba," but for its flip side, a dreamy slow-dance kind of song called,
"Donna." *"I had a girl, and Donna was her name. Since she left me, I've never been the
same. . . ."*

As that side started he took Donna in his arms, and Beverly took Bill's
cake plate from him and the four of them danced. When it ended they
played it again, and then a third time, and then they returned to the cake and
the coffee, eating and smiling at each other.

Though it might not seem like it, this was a life-changing birthday for
Donna. She and Bob were hardly ever apart after that, whether at her house
cooking and listening to music, or at his, working on the Jaguar in his garage.
And the next day Bill got his second wish when Donna did leave them alone,
going out early to poke around with Bob in the auto wrecking yards, while
Beverly took him to her bedroom, the promise of the drive-in movie kept
during the clear light of day.

In the quiet afterwards, and later when Donna and Bob came back, as
well, they each thought they could hear a vague buzzing, distant like a fly in
a jar, or the slightest onslaught of tinnitus. No one thought to mention it,
however, for they each believed it singular to themselves.

All of them, in fact, also began to believe what the side of "The Dancing
Cobra" box had proclaimed; that they had found their own true happineSss
at home.

~

Pro Snake

Virginia Hamilton Adair

Some say the Bible teaches fear of women, snakes,
and God, who killed His Manchild for our sakes
and puts a mark beside our least mistakes,
and beats us all until our spirit breaks.

Must we believe His godly finger shakes
at Eve for every apple pie she bakes?
I'd rather take my chances with the snakes.

~

Growing Up in the Garden of Eden

A Snake in That Garden

Kate Lehrer

TARANTULAS INVADED OUR yard that Texas summer, their holes creating acne scars across our lawn. Scorpions came next. My mother, who had grown up here in Rollins, said she'd never seen anything like this. Summer usually brought nothing more than mosquitoes and chiggers.

Although I was not fond of any insect other than fireflies, the tarantulas and scorpions didn't faze me. My only concession to the plagues was to play "Dance of the Tarantella" on the piano and to wear shoes after dark. My fear and anger I saved for the two growing protuberances contained in the new white cotton brassiere my mother bought and made me wear on the first day of summer vacation. Until that moment, I ignored the changes in my body, and once pointed out, they shocked and aggrieved me. For the first ten summers of my life, I'd been allowed to go topless along with my boy cousins in our own backyards.

When one cousin asked why I'd started wearing sissy blouses all the time, tears hit my eyes as my fist hit his nose. He would tell on me, but avenging held its own sweetness. As my mother had already explained, he would not ever have to wear a brassiere, the word itself a hateful affront. What had been two innocuous brown spots could not be willed back into flatness, into freedom. And so the snake entered my garden.

~

First came a short interlude in Dallas, where I spent a few days with another boy cousin and his mother, my aunt Sally, who made homemade ice cream most summer evenings. I liked Aunt Sally and the ice cream. Johnny had boxes of comic books and height to recommend him. No other boys I played with could reach my eyes, but he was two years older and two inches taller. Though I could no longer wrestle him to the ground, my legs, strong and sure, kept him from wreaking much havoc on me either. As a result, we had a new if unstated regard for each other. His desire to grow up to be an outlaw well suited my new sense of the world.

~

Upon my return from Dallas, I made the happy discovery of summer with girlfriends. Our past summer get-togethers had been sporadic and structured—one of our mothers taking us to the miniature golf course or the amusement park outside Dallas or to the Olympic-size pool in another town thirty miles away. This year we got to roam on our own. We skated, rode bikes or simply walked back and forth all day from one house to another. Though in the same grade school, our houses radiated a mile or more in different directions.

One of our first weeks of freedom found us at Kathy's. Her mother, as did mine, worked and her older sister had left for church camp. Finding we had the house to ourselves, Wanda suggested we play strip poker, this being the most daring game we'd yet discovered. Throughout the winter and spring we had played canasta, poker, blackjack and dominoes. Gambling among our parents, including the Baptist ones, must have been common because all of us came to the games casually. However, we didn't use real money because we didn't have any. From the least to the most affluent, we received neither allowances or pay for tasks performed at home. If we went to a movie, our parents gave us money for that and popcorn. We each bought one comic book a week and traded. None of us questioned this arrangement or asked for much or got much or cared at all.

But with this summer came a restlessness. Our usual games in their usual ways no longer sufficed. We played "dare" on our bikes: how far could we go with no hands? Instead of hanging upside down on the crossbar at school, we walked the second story window ledge of the school building, holding on to the bricks with our fingertips, much as we'd seen done in movies. We hit upon "strip poker" after Laura heard about it from her older brother Mike. We didn't keep each other's clothes. The thrill came in the daring of exposure, as well as the curiosity about what was going on with each body. But my body alone showed the only signs of change, and I wasn't about to let them in on that secret and face their relentless teasing until the same happened to them.

"Strip poker is boring," I said and went in search of cold lavender water inside Kathy's refrigerator. Since Kathy's sister had read in a movie magazine that a lot of California stars doused in cold cologne, we each kept a bottle of this purple substance. Reeking of lavender, I returned with a plan.

"Let's tell the scariest thing that's ever happened to us."

"We did that when we were kids," Laura answered. She shuffled the cards.

"Lots has happened in the meantime. Like last week in Dallas with my cousin Johnny."

"Is he scary?" Wanda wanted to know.

"He saved me." I delivered this line in the solemn tone Aunt Sally uses for Sunday blessing. Dramatic presentations didn't always work on this group. If they thought they could get away with it, they would poke fun at God. But today my ploy worked.

"Saved you from what?" Kathy asked as if she didn't really care, meaning she did. I took my time settling back on the floor and crossing my feet over my knees and trying to figure out where to go from here.

"Last week my cousin Johnny and me rode bikes out miles and miles away from human habitation."

"How can you be miles away from people in Dallas?" Wanda asked. "And how come you had two bikes?" Kathy piped up. She knew Johnny was an only child like me.

"Johnny has two bikes, OK? Ya'll going to let me finish or not?" That hushed them quick enough, but I hesitated another few seconds just to be sure they stayed hushed. "So, Johnny and I rode his bikes—he let me ride his new silver one. The kind that looks like a shiny new silver dollar? He took the old one, a royal blue, just the color of—"

"Get on with it!" Laura interrupted. Kathy, more of an appreciator of fine language, added, "please."

"So, we rode all the way to a meandering brook and found shelter under a tree on the green undulating bank," I continued, ignoring Laura's eyes roll. I hoped the undulating bank wasn't from a book we'd all just read. "We sat down to have our cookies and Dr. Peppers that Johnny carried in his basket.

Johnny stuffed a whole one in his mouth, but I . . ." About to lose my audience, I skipped on. "I saw behind Johnny's back a rattlesnake, all brown with creepy circles and his horny rattler tale, coiled and ready to strike.

"I knew I had to act fast. I jumped on top of Johnny to roll him away. But he thought I'd launched a surprise attack and started scuffling. Then I screamed!" A pause, a lower voice. "Too late. The snake struck my foot and wound itself around my leg. I writhed on the floor, one minute the snake, the next minute me. By now Johnny had taken out his scout pocketknife and, quick as can be, threw it right between that sucker's eyes.

"In death's throes, the snake clutched me tighter, but with my bare hands . . ."

"They don't have rattlers in Dallas. We don't even have them here," Kathy said, her knees hugged to her chest. I wanted to smack that sneer right off her freckled face everybody said was so cute because of her upturned nose, but I looked at her with pity.

"Kathy, I didn't think so either until I got bitten. I didn't think Dallas had turtles either until I saw one."

"What have turtles got to do with anything?" Wanda asked.

I looked at her with pity, too, and gave her a sad smile. "I was just trying to show you how wrong you can be in what you think. It's important to . . ."

"Let's finish the story," Laura scolded all of us. "You were pulling the snake off your leg," she prompted. I stood up.

"And Johnny helped. We had no time to waste. He had to suck out the poison before it hit my bloodstream. He saved my life. Then he pumped me home." Johnny's transformation into this brave, handsome outlaw Robin Hood was as complete in my head as it was in my story. Fending off questions and admiration with equal amounts of modesty and assurance, I was pleased all around although after they left, something kept nagging at me. A guilty conscience, I supposed at first.

~

The snake idea had come to me as happens when thoughts aren't so much formed as felt and envisioned faster than it takes to explain the process. In this case, looking for a way out of strip poker, I had realized that I was about to tell a lie, once more led into temptation as Eve was led into temptation by the snake. I had never understood why the snake and Eve got such a bad rap for what they did and God didn't for what He did, especially since in the Lord's Prayer we still had to plead with God not to lead us into temptation. In bed that night I blamed neither God nor the snake for my latest transgression. I blamed those two things growing out my body. I could only blame myself, though, for what had been nagging me: I had allowed a boy to rescue me.

Before, I'd shared the role of hero with no one.

~

The next day I set out to reclaim my stature as the Lone Ranger, or the Lone Rangerette, as I thought of myself. In Laura's kitchen our group made sandwiches for a bike ride to my uncle Ray's farm. When Laura's older brother walked through, he stopped long enough to look down at my foot, take a bite out of the tuna sandwich I'd just fixed and spoke to me. "Show me that bite." I pointed down. "Gone now," I answered. He gave me a painful frog in my arm while instructing me to watch out for slimy things.

"He said you have a lot more guts than he thought," Laura whispered with excitement, my bravery reflecting well on her as my friend.

~

My resolve to be the Lone Rangerette, the attention of Laura's brother, the new respect I felt from my friends and the getting away with such a brazen lie emboldened me. No doubt also I'd begun to believe my own tale, for after we'd had lunch down by Uncle Ray's creek and run through the usual "dares" the farm provided—walking across a plank over the stream of water, climbing to the very top of the barn's pitched roof—I decided to test us further.

Standing to the widest spot of the creek bed, I dared everyone to jump across.

"Not fair," Laura accused. "Your legs are longer."

"Then find us another spot," I said.

After pacing up and down the bank, we lined up—Laura behind me, then Wanda, then Kathy. I spoke again: "If we fall in, we have to watch out for snakes."

"You've never mentioned snakes here before," Wanda said, her voice rising.

"Aunt Evie said they've seen some this summer. Not rattlers, though."

"Then forget it," Kathy said. The others agreed.

But I now felt compelled to jump. Doing this would establish me for the rest of the summer as the leader. I walked back to the widest spot, close to where the old tractor tire hung. My friends started trying to talk me out of it. My mother would be mad. I shouldn't risk another bite. Kathy began crying.

Nothing deterred me although I had no precedent to believe I could jump this creek. My athletic abilities had a lot more to do with strength than agility, and I knew this. And the more my friend protested and I swaggered, the more I came to believe snakes inhabited that creek. I began to understand why books said people "tasted" fear. I also knew I couldn't back down.

Finally, I walked away from the creek. I sucked in my breath. I ran. I leapt. I made it. I walked the plank back across to where the others waited, the plank seeming nothing now.

~

As we biked back by Uncle Ray's and Aunt Evie's house, my uncle waved from the barn. We usually stopped to talk a minute and drink water from their well, this being the only functioning well we knew. Today we kept biking to the main road. I didn't want any talk of snakes or my leap. If my mother found out what I'd just done, she would never let me come back here again on my own.

~

The next few days I basked in admiration. The very next afternoon Laura's brother grinned and said, "Way to go!" This time he gave me a painful frog in each arm. In bed that night and in the nights to come, I imagined his sucking the poison out of my snakebite. Mornings, instead of jumping up as usual, I lay in bed with my eyes shut, seeing myself run over by a car. Laura's brother would pick up my limp body and carry me inside, holding my hand until the doctor came. He suddenly saw a beauty in me that had escaped him, escaped everyone until now. And so my daydreams continued in one or another version of this basic scenario.

A week or so after my leap and still charged by the fumes of my victory, I let a boy kiss me—my first kiss. We stood behind the changing rooms of the public swimming pool and his closed lips touched my closed lips for a good fifteen seconds. He must have stood on his tiptoes because I didn't stoop down. Now I added this kiss to the repertoire of my new daydreams, but I didn't tell my friends.

We still spent our hot summer days walking or biking from one house to the other. Strip poker came up only once more, but I squelched it. For swimming, I wore a one-piece bathing suit so large that it hung away from my body. I told everyone that it had belonged to a friend of my mother's because my mother couldn't afford to buy me a new one. My friends were too well brought up to tease about that.

Yet the routine of summer couldn't stop my breasts from growing, my romantic daydreams from proliferating or my fear of snakes from haunting. At night, no matter how pleasant the day, I worried about snakes. I began to suspect one lived under my bed, much as I had suspected monsters there when I was small. I must have checked under my dust ruffle twenty times a night. Only by concentrating hard on my romantic fantasies could I finally get to sleep.

One night I had a nightmare. A snake lived inside me and nothing I could do would make it go away. This snake, too, became part of my nightly vigil, a punishment from God, I thought, for telling such a big lie and from kissing a boy. I couldn't do anything about the kiss but every night I resolved to confess the lie. Then I would see my friends and couldn't bear to think of their disregard if I told. I would see Laura's brother and despair of losing those arm-froggings and his look—real or imagined—of approval. Finally I made up my mind to resign myself to a lifetime of snakes rather than take the necessary steps to rid myself of them. Strangely to me, once I made this last decision, the fear, if not the constancy, of the snakes, internal and external let up.

It took me a longer time to stop playing the victim in my daydreams. However much bravado I showed during the day, at night I settled for beautiful and passive. This bothered me, but I wanted to be rescued. I wanted someone to save me. Such a relief, to be saved. For all my self-absorption, I worried about my little family's happiness. The little family made up of my mother and me.

As it happened, I didn't go again to the farm that summer except with my mother and then to sit on the porch with the grown-ups and listen to their stories. I didn't want to risk seeing those snakes I had come to believe in absolutely.

~

Many years later my husband and my children and I spent a month in Tuscany. Because the region suffered a severe drought that summer, by August the snakes—vipers, as the snakebite kit in the refrigerator labeled them—made their way up from the brush to our swimming pool in search of food and water. When our daughter, speaking Italian, told the groundskeeper to get rid of them, he agreed to comply with more than his usual sullenness.

The next time we spot the snake, we run for the gardener and stand there watching as he raises his hoe and sucks in his breath, not from fear but from revulsion for his deed. As the hoe severs the viper's neck from the rest of his body, the body begins wrapping itself around the hoe in its tenacious reflex for life. Tears stream from the man's eyes. "It is a living thing," he says over and over to my daughter. But already I am crying.

~

Snake

Theodore Roethke

I saw a young snake glide
Out of the mottled shade
And hang, limp on a stone:
A thin mouth, and a tongue
Stayed, in the still air.

It turned; it drew away;
Its shadow bent in half;
It quickened, and was gone.

I felt my slow blood warm.
I longed to be that thing,
The pure, sensuous form.

And I may be, some time.

Serpent Tales

THEY WERE LONG, SILENT, AND
SOMETIMES DEADLY . . .

Randall Kenan

"I'LL RACE YA," my cousin said.

At age ten I was fleet of foot, but I never knew, when I raced my cousin, if I beat him with my own swiftness when I beat him, or by his good nature in letting me win. Larry was six years my senior and an athlete who played both football and basketball; tall and muscular at sixteen, with the legs of a gazelle.

I lived on a long dirt road in those days. We were to race to my Aunt Lillian's house, about a quarter of a mile down, and back. As usual, Larry gave me a head start.

I took off, my scrawny legs pumping. Twilight was melting into night and I could barely make out Aunt Lillian's two-story white house set way back from the road. On either side of the dirt road were acres of fields, corn, soybeans, tobacco. And off in the distance were ancient forests of longleaf pine, oak, sassafras, gum, hickory. . . . Behind me I could hear Larry's long strides catching up to me; my own strides lengthened. We were Citation and Secretariat. Soon we were neck and neck.

Three-fourths of the way to Aunt Lillian's house, I spied something in the road. In those days I had superb night vision. A doctor once told me I had hawk-eye vision, 20/10. Not one, but two snakes were in the middle of the road in front of us, and one had raised its head and the front half of its body as snakes do when they investigate or climb or are about to fight.

My reaction came from the base of my brain; it cannot even be called thinking. I pivoted and galloped toward home. I think I might have yelped. My cousin called out my name repeatedly, puzzled, and set out after me. For once, and without a shadow of a doubt in my mind, I'm certain I beat my cousin running.

Copperheads are perhaps the most beautiful of snakes—the North American fer-de-lance.

Their colors are like those of the coleus plant, purples, vivid reds, violent whites, dashes of brown and green; almost iridescent. Rattlesnakes are beautiful in their own way, mesmerizing, not only by the regularity of their diamond designs, but with their creeping legend and unsettling sound. Coral snakes are rarely seen, with bold bands of black, red and yellow, deceptively pretty, almost like a toy. Water moccasins are the ugliest of snakes. Dun black with next to no sheen at all. The cotton of their open mouths always a caution and a grim omen, like pure white poison. The moccasin is also known to be among the most ill-tempered.

Those trouble-bringers are just the venomous snakes. There are milk snakes, garter snakes, green snakes, hognose snakes, black racers, black adders and the seemingly ubiquitous, gluttonous and mischievous chicken snakes—climbers, acrobats, swallowers of whole eggs and rats, dumb yet inquisitive, aggravating in the utmost. This list is by no means a complete catalogue of all the crawling miscreants in the wilds of southeastern North Carolina, but the ones with which I was too well acquainted.

Chinquapin, the small farming community where I grew up, is on the edge of one of the largest swamps in North Carolina, the Angola. Tributaries, creeks, branches, ditches feed the vast marshland from several rivers, and in turn it feeds back a stupendous array of wildlife. In those days farmers talked of seeing black bears in the distance. I saw foxes and wildcats on a number of occasions, though I only witnessed an alligator once. Deer were—and still are—commonplace and the cause of many a motorist's increased insurance rates.

But the bane of my existence, the only reason I regarded summer with dread—aside from field work and humidity—was the reality of snakes, the crawling multitude, the scourge of Eden, the lurking menace, the lot my brother-in-law referred to jokingly as "the boys." From the first snake sight-ing, usually sometime in mid- or late April, till the first frost, when the boys had slunk into hibernation, I was constantly filled with a catlike, free-floating anxiety. It did not matter to me if they were poisonous or harmless, big or small, docile or hateful, I despised snakes with the very fiber of my being, and was sometimes angry with God for having created them in the first place. Most boys, when confronted with real-world danger, hide their fear and try to act like "men." There is understood shame in doing otherwise. However, my fear of snakes was so all-encompassing, so gut-wrenchingly real, that I didn't give a damn if anyone called me a sissy or taunted me. I did not care. I was no fun-loving, straw-chewing nature boy, though I loved to go barefoot. I fear I identified too much with Eva Gabor on *Green Acres* and longed for the benign world of sitcom TV. Opie was never imperiled by venomous vermin. There were no snakes on Gilligan's tropical island.

Summer for me was tobacco farming, cutting grass, vacation Bible school, dogfights, trips to the beach, and snakes. Always snakes.

The old folk would gather on porches in those boyhood days of mine. Their talk would range and I would listen, sometimes intently, sometimes lackadaisically. But one out of four of their conversations would invariably revolve around some experience with a snake. Often chilling, often humorous, but for me always ominous. Of the time a moccasin found its way into somebody's toilet bowl; of the snake that crawled across my uncle's chest while he was napping in the grass, or the snake that fell out of the peach tree onto my father's head; of the snake that killed the old white mule Lightning; of the chicken snake that got into the cupboard. There was the story of the time my elderly cousin Norman saw a snake in the road, drove a mile home, got his shotgun, drove back, found the snake where it had been, and shot it—not realizing that the snake was already dead. And then there was talk of the legendary rattlesnake who lived in the woods around my house, Ole Rattler. He was so long he was said to span the entire width of the dirt road, and to be monstrously thick. Folk recognized him by the marks he bore from past wounds. He was said to be well over sixty years old, if not older.

One day a terrific commotion came from outside. I rushed out to see what the matter was. My cousin Larry, who had been spraying corn with the tractor, had cornered the biggest rattlesnake I had ever seen. It was ten feet if it was an inch. His grandfather told Larry to watch the thing, which was now plenty riled by all the commotion, while he ran to get the shotgun. Everyone said a rattlesnake could jump its own length or more, and you were to always watch out if one began to coil up, for that meant it was about to strike. The warnings of its rattles sent chills through my testicles. It was beginning to coil. Larry's grandfather returned and I was glad to discover he was as good a shot as he sometimes bragged. He dispatched the snake with two shots.

As Larry began to move the snake—after cutting off the head (always a good idea) and removing the rattles (I seem to remember there were twelve)—large, grayish globules began to fall from the expired serpent's body. They were developing snake eggs.

"Well," Larry's grandfather allowed, "that's not that big Ole Rattler then." Rather than being relieved by this snake-murder and serpent-genocide, my dread only intensified. The Emperor of the Boys was still a-slither.

There are a number of floating tall tales about snakes in southeastern North Carolina. Tales that, like urban legends, are always given some authoritative origin, either having been read in the newspaper, or heard on the radio, or told by the brother or cousin or boss of the protagonist. Of all these stories, one is my favorite. The first time I heard it I was completely gulled by it, and repeated it numerous times, saying, "This was in the paper . . ." A story I had not read. Years later I realized the story was a patent lie, but I nonetheless thrilled to hear it again and again, and listened for variations, as with Bach's fugues. The story goes something like this:

A man and a woman, an older couple, are driving in New Bern or Jacksonville. He is a retired Marine or a farmer or both. While driving he feels something move down by his shoe and by his pants leg. He looks down and sees a huge snake (in the better versions, it's a rattlesnake) commencing to crawl up his leg. (In some versions the snake crawls on the outside of his pants, but inside is quintuply horrifying.) With superhuman courage the old man gently pulls the car to the side of the road. (In some versions he keeps on driving.) But he does not agitate the snake in the least, allowing it to complete its terrifying upward journey. The man whispers to his wife to remain quiet and still. The snake travels the length of the man's body (how it got past the man's belt bothered me even then), pauses at the man's face—the moment of death recognized!—and continues to the shoulder and neck. The man slowly puts his arm out the window of the car, and the snake follows his lead, eventually dropping to the ground and leaving the man unharmed.

How did the snake get there? Why didn't it bite? How could either the man or the woman keep this otherworldly composure? In the end, none of that matters. To be sure, snakes find their way into some weird places; to be

sure, there exist individuals with nerves of adamantium. But the truly fascinating thing about this story is the telling and retelling and what that
signifies. On some level it is merely a variation of the spook story: Man
encounters horror and survives. On another level it is man's encounter with
the ineffable, very like the frisson at the center of snake handling. Single-
handedly an individual confronts the symbol of the most unholy—the
devil—and has the faith to withstand its terror, outlast it, to remain.

Poor, put-upon snakes. Does any other world culture demonize this one
animal as mercilessly? ("And the Lord God said unto the serpent, Because
thou hast done this, thou art cursed above all cattle, and above every beast of
the field; upon thy belly shalt thou go, and dust shalt thou eat all the days of
thy life:

"And I will put enmity between thee and the woman, and between thy
seed and her seed; it shall bruise thy head, and thou shalt bruise his heel."
Genesis: 3:14-15.) Thus Yahweh saith at the climax of the Eden story.

My loathing of snakes does not emerge from some fundamentalist,
Protestant bent, but, I suppose, from some hard-wiring in my system that I
cannot overcome; some eons-old genetic code that I cannot erase.

One summer, during my later years in high school, I went to cut my
Great-Great-Aunt Erie's grass. She lived down the road from us, a field apart.
Each week while the grass grew, I'd take her mower from the utility room of
her new brick house and cut her grass, and she'd give me five bucks.

I liked cutting her yard for it was large and regular with only a large
mimosa tree to navigate. Unlike our yard with its many apple trees and wal-
nuts and oaks and sweet gums and plum trees and cedars and magnolias,
rosebushes, holly bushes, azalea bushes and mysterious grape arbor—giving a
snake plenty of places to lurk.

Aunt Erie would often sit on her carport while I pushed and mowed—
she disliked air conditioning. She was in her late eighties and the most plain-
spoken person I have yet to meet.

This day while cutting the grass, I turned the corner of the house and
froze in abject terror. Before me stood this enormous snake. I say stood, for
half the length of its body was raised in the air; stood like the snake I saw
that long-ago twilight night of the race. Regal it was. Swaying slightly. Its
head moving ever so minutely. The snake was looking directly at me. Exam-

ining me. We stood like that for a spell of time to which I cannot attest. By and by I turned and scampered away like the frightened mouse that I was.

"You finished already?" my great-great-aunt asked.

"No, ma'am." My voice trembled with fear. "There's a snake. There's a snake in the yard."

"So?"

I described the monster to her.

To my chagrin she said: "Leave that snake alone. That's that ole king snake lives around here. Snake's older than you. Keeps the bad snakes away. Rats too. Good to have a king snake around. Brings good luck."

I hesitated for a long while.

"Well? What you standing there for? Finish cutting my yard." She could tell I did not want to go.

She gave a loud tsk. "Boy, that snake ain't gone hurt you. Big as you is."

I slowly walked back to the site of my undoing, reaching down into me, trying to grab hold of my dread. At the edge of the house, beyond which the lawn mower noisily burned up gas, I paused. Taking in a gulp, I turned the corner.

~

An Ophidian Affect

Susan Kinsolving

Both spinal and fluid, the movements are
undulating and minacious: sidewinding,
concertina, constriction, coil, and strike.

As a child, I ran home from my favorite
place to play, under willows by a stream,
where suddenly to my horror one came

weaving through the water. The only poison was
its presence, but that proved to be venomous
enough to my sanctuary. So serpents remain

with me: assailants ominous, though unlikely,
but molting in my mind, mythically provoking.
Cobra, boa, rattler, viper, Egyptian asp . . .

~

The Child and the Snake

(*adapted from:*
THE DARK PATH TO THE RIVER)

Joanne Leedom-Ackerman

JENNY CARRIED ERIKA dozing on her shoulder as she scanned the names of stores on Third Avenue. Erika sagged in her arms. At a pizzeria Jenny set her down while she borrowed a phone book.

"I want to go home," Erika whined.

"In a minute." Jenny searched the pages. She'd seen the store she was looking for months ago. She had stood outside for a long while staring into its window.

"I'm tired," Erika argued.

"In a minute," Jenny repeated. "We're almost there. Don't you want a present?"

"What kind of present?" Erika brightened.

"You'll see in a minute." She took her daughter's hand and strode up Third Avenue through the Sunday shoppers, past fruit stalls and cafes. Finally she stopped at an empty shop. Inside, a cardboard sign was taped: SPACE FOR RENT/ Caldonia's Moved to 2153 Third Avenue.

~

Jenny waved for a cab, and Erika dozed on her lap as the taxi sped up the half-empty Sunday streets, through the seventies, the eighties, nineties to 118th Street.

The buildings along the way changed from cafes and galleries and gourmet food shops to boarded-up storefronts, mom-and-pop groceries, garages. Finally the driver stopped in front of a small shop with two cages in the window. Across the street were a discount furniture store, a discount clothing store and an abandoned hardware shop. "Could you wait?" she asked the driver.

"Sorry, lady." And he locked the doors and drove off.

"I want to go home," Erika said.

Jenny drew her over to the window. "See."

Erika blinked in the sunlight. She stared at the cages, then looked up at her mother. "Snakes," she said.

Jenny also peered into the cage where an enormous brown-and-gray snake lay coiled in the sand. In a smaller cage next to it a nest of baby snakes wriggled on top of each other. According to the sign in the window, the snake was a python. As Jenny and Erika stared, the snake suddenly flattened its head and hissed towards the rear of its cage. Erika reached for her mother. "I don't like snakes," she said.

"Neither do I." Jenny took her daughter's hand and entered the shop.

Cages lined the narrow room: brown wooden boxes filled with sand and rocks and bowls of water. Many of the cages looked empty, though on closer inspection, Jenny saw snakes hidden beneath the rocks or in the sand with only their tails or sides protruding. The only other customers were two boys standing in front of the python's cage. When the proprietor wasn't looking, they struck at the snake with a stick, and the snake hissed again.

"You stop that!" the owner called from the back where he was washing sand. A small dark-skinned man came forward shaking his fist. "Get out!" he declared. "You kids, get out!" The boys stepped away from the cage but made no move towards the door. "You come here frighten my snakes. You get out!" They looked at him with indifference when suddenly he opened the cage and hauled out the ten-foot python whose head thrust towards them.

They tripped over each other to the door. Erika grabbed Jenny, who quickly lifted her in her arms and shielded her with her own body. Jenny wondered suddenly if she had made a mistake coming here. She too started for the door, but the snake keeper began to laugh. "Rikki scares away the riff-raff," he said. "I didn't mean to scare your child. Here . . ." He held out the snake, but Jenny stepped back. He stroked the snake who coiled about his arm and shoulders. "He won't hurt you. He wouldn't hurt those boys, but they don't know that."

"Yes . . ." Jenny said, disbelieving.

The man smiled showing his front teeth missing. On this cold day he was dressed in only an undershirt which was ringed with sweat in this warm shop. He again offered the snake to Jenny. "You want to hold him?"

"No," she gasped.

"Rikki, he is very friendly."

Jenny bumped into the cages behind her, then jumped forward for fear the snakes inside might strike. Suddenly she felt breathless. Why had she come here? "No . . . no . . . really. Actually I'm afraid of snakes."

The man frowned. "Why you come to my shop?"

She was having trouble remembering herself. "I don't know. I don't want my daughter to be afraid." She wasn't sure that reason made any sense. She was beginning to suspect that coming here was not a rational act, for she was in fact terrified of snakes. As a child in Texas, she'd been warned of rattlesnakes in the vacant lots around her house. Then one day she'd turned over a rusted oil drum, and in the same moment she saw the coiled brown body, she felt the needles in her leg. She'd screamed. Her mother, alone in the house now, stepped onto the porch. She kept screaming. She was ten years old, and the possibilities overwhelmed her. Her mother ran across the field as the snake cut through the brown grass and disappeared. Even when her mother reached her, she could not quit screaming. Her mother picked her up and quickly carried her into the house where she applied ice, cut the bite and drew out the blood with her own mouth. The snake, it turned out, had not been poisonous, and the cut took longer to heal than the bite. The fear had never entirely healed. But her childhood fear was not why she was here today, though it occurred to her that if she could face down this symbol of her fear, symbol and object in one, that she might master fear itself. She would come home with a snake, meet Kay's brightly colored bird unafraid with her own boa constrictor or python.

"What kind of snake would you recommend for us?" she asked.

"Well . . ." The proprietor slipped the python back into its cage. "You should start smaller . . . a garter snake, perhaps, or small king snake."

He pulled out a green snake and extended it to Jenny, who tentatively touched its scales. "Will it bite?"

"Wanda? No. She's a good snake. Even if she do, she don't hurt." He bent down to show the snake to Erika, who was growing curious. She thrust out her hand to touch it.

"Slow . . . ," the keeper said. "Around snakes you got to move slow." He reached into another cage and brought out a larger brown-and-gray-ringed snake he called Pete.

"How do you know their names?" Erika asked.

"I give them names," he said. "It makes them seem more friendly to people."

He rested the tail of Pete in Erika's chubby hand. She touched the slick, smooth skin. "Snakes won't hurt you," he assured Jenny, "except poison ones, and I don't sell them. But a snake is a snake. It's not a cat or a dog. Mother snake has her babies, leaves them, never looks back. Or sometimes she eats them." At this revelation Erika's eyes opened wide. "She's got no mother feelings like most animals."

He placed Pete back in the cage. "But the worst thing you can do is be afraid of a snake because he knows." He opened another cage. "Take a boa . . ." He pulled out a mottled brown snake. "He feels you get tense, your muscles flex, he's going to clamp down. That's his instinct. He'll squeeze you. The only way to get loose from a boa is to relax. Don't be afraid, then he'll just let go."

Jenny stared at the snake nosing its way around the proprietor's neck. "How do you know which snakes are poisonous?" she asked. "I mean if I came across one."

"I don't guess you would. Unless it was a rattler, and you could hear it."

"Can you take the poison out?" she asked.

The snake keeper frowned. "People gotten poisoned trying to do that."

"I used to think I'd burn them out," she said.

"How's that?"

"Growing up, there were rattlesnakes where I lived. I decided I'd burn them out if I ever found them."

The snake keeper laughed. "You'd've burned down your own home more likely. Snake would have only crawled deeper in his hole and hidden from the fire. Probably wouldn't even have got hurt. You want to get rid of a snake, you got to block up his hole, cut off his air and food. But first you have to find the hole and then make sure he's in it."

Jenny watched the baby snakes in the front window and the giant mother in the next cage. She wondered if the mother really would eat her own babies. Erika was peering into a different cage on the floor. Jenny kneeled beside her. "Which one do you like?" she asked.

"This one," Erika answered. She pointed to a snake about two feet long, an inch wide, with red and black rings around her. The snake appeared to be staring back at Erika with its lidless eyes.

The snake keeper stepped over. "Rosy," he said. "Well, Rosy wouldn't be a bad one for a beginner. She's a little fussy about eating sometimes, but usually she'll eat a mouse every few weeks." He lifted Rosy out of the cage and showed her to Erika. "Rosy's a king snake," he explained. "She's pretty gentle though she will eat other snakes, even rattlesnakes."

"We'll take it," Jenny said.

The man set Rosy back in her cage, and he and Jenny went to the rear of the store. Erika remained on her knees in front of the snake. Jenny paid for the snake, a cage, a water bowl, a light for warmth, a bag of sand, an arched tile where the snake could hide. The snake keeper said he'd give Jenny the snake in the sand bag, and she could assemble the cage at home; but Jenny insisted that he put the box together and install the snake himself.

Finally, after half an hour, Rosy was set into her new quarters, and Jenny and Erika were standing out in the snow on 118th Street with their snake, looking for a cab home.

~

Kay clicked a manicured fingernail against the bird cage. A white bird with yellow tail feathers cocked its head. "He already says, 'Give him the business!' and 'What's cooking, sweetie?' Don't you think Erika will like that?" Kay smiled. She waited for Mark to smile.

Mark sat on the piano bench across from her peering at the bird on the coffee table, but he looked distracted.

Kay kneeled beside the cage nearer Mark. She took a cracker from a box and tried to feed it to the bird, but the bird wasn't interested. Casually she rested her elbow on the stool by Mark's knee. "What's the matter?"

Mark looked at his watch. "I was wondering where Jenny was." He'd hurried home after his meeting this afternoon. He didn't understand what had upset Jenny so at his parents earlier, but he wanted to talk to her now about himself or rather about his concerns over the figures he'd just seen at his meeting and over the cool way the head of the firm had dismissed what he should be concerned about. For the first time he wondered if he were being told the whole truth. He'd come to trust Jenny's intuition though he argued with her. But now she wasn't here. Because she wasn't here and he didn't know where she was, he couldn't work when he sat down at his desk. Finally he'd come in to play the piano, but then Kay had arrived.

"She's probably out shopping," Kay offered.

"Jenny hates shopping. She wanted to write."

Kay leaned towards the bird, increasing the pressure of her hand on Mark's leg. He looked down, noticing the hand for the first time.

"Thank you again for going with me today to see David in the hospital," she said.

Mark watched the bird pecking at its own image in the mirror. "You should buy David a bird. Have you ever bought him a pet?"

Kay glanced at Mark; she couldn't tell if he were criticizing her. "I don't even know if he likes birds."

"You know Erika less well, and you bought her a bird."

"But I knew she loved the bird your cat killed. She told me all about it this morning." Kay's blue eyes shined behind a thin glaze of emotion. "She's a much more open child than David, Mark. You must see that."

"She's only three and a half. I don't know what she'll be like at eleven."

"Probably very much like you." Kay met Mark's eyes with an assertion which made him pause. He stood and let her hand fall.

"In fact, Erika is more like Jenny."

"Oh? I don't see that. Erika seems . . . well, more lively, but then I guess I don't know either of them very well."

At the piano Mark began straightening loose sheets of music. Kay moved over to him. "You've helped me a lot with David. Buying Erika a present seemed a way to thank you." She laughed then. "Certainly the bird is better than that baby rattle I brought her when I first came to visit a few weeks ago. That's the story of my life with David. By the time I think I know what he likes, he's become someone else, grown up, and I'm forever giving him baby rattles."

"Then spend more time with him. For Christ's sakes, Kay, he's your son. Visit him at boarding school. Take him out of boarding school. Don't be so afraid of him."

Kay laughed airily. "You've noticed that. You could always see inside me, Mark. Why did I ever let you go? I'm scared to death of him."

"He's just a boy who needs a mother. I don't know where his father is, but . . ."

"Neither do I."

"So, you're all he's got."

"That scares the breath out of me. I don't know if you can understand—you're so close to Erika—but here's this person, a stranger really, who's part of me, yet doesn't even like me very much. Yet I *am* all he's got, and that makes him dislike me more, I think, because he's so dependent." She took in air. Then in a quiet voice she added, ". . . And yet sometimes I think he might also be my salvation."

She looked up at Mark. Her sincerity touched him, but it lasted only a moment before she grew conscious of herself and what she had said and the effect it might have. Mark saw in her eyes this change and this fundamental flaw. Jenny was mistaken about Kay, he thought. It wasn't manipulation of people or self-interest that was the flaw; it was sincerity she lacked, sincerity which came so naturally to Jenny. And yet his sympathy was stirred because of his own doubts right now and because Kay cared for him. He put his arm on her shoulders. "I hope David can be your salvation," he offered.

The door opened. Erika stepped into the hallway, followed by Jenny carrying a large wooden box. When Jenny saw Mark with his arm about Kay, she stopped. She stared for a moment, then she took Erika's hand and moved towards the back of the apartment. Kay separated from Mark with an exaggerated motion, offering him a guilty look he did not reciprocate.

"Where have you been?" he asked instead, his own defense, instinctively an offense.

"Shopping," Jenny answered.

Erika broke away and ran into the living room. "Daddy, you'll never guess what we got? One clue: her name is Rosy."

Mark dropped to his knees in front of Erika. "Rosy?" he said. "A bird?"

"No!"

"A cat?"

"No!"

"A mous-se?" Mark drew out the question to make Erika laugh. Jenny had paused in the hallway. They both knew he was really playing to her.

"No!" Erika declared in triumph. "A snake!"

"A snake?" Mark looked up at Jenny.

"Her name is Rosy, and I'm going to keep her in my room."

Mark watched his wife. "I thought you were afraid of snakes."

"I'm not afraid," Erika answered. "The man said you got to know them for a while, and I already know Rosy." She took her father's hand and drew him over to the box. "See." Mark stared in at the sand and the tile. Only the tail of the snake was showing. "She's hiding," Erika explained.

Mark glanced up at Jenny. Her eyes were luminous, but her expression was closed off from him. He saw this purchase was not a random act, though he had no idea what it meant. "Why did you buy it?" he asked.

"I don't want Erika to be afraid of snakes."

"I didn't know she was afraid."

"She will be if she doesn't ever see one."

Mark frowned. He was missing some point here. "What about you?"

"I'll be all right," she answered. She looked at the snake instead of Mark. The snake had poked its head out and was peering about. "It's a king snake," she added flatly. "It eats rattlesnakes."

"Oh. Well, that's quite useful in Manhattan." Mark's irony had an edge. Jenny didn't smile. "Jenny, there are no rattlesnakes in New York City."

"You assume that," she answered. The fact didn't mitigate Rosy's value to her. "We don't know where Erika will end up living," she added. She set the box on the floor. "She shouldn't be afraid." She opened the lid, and with evident effort, she reached in her hand, and she drew forth the snake. She held the snake behind its head.

"Oh, my God!" Kay declared. The two-foot Rosy dangled from Jenny's arm flicking her tongue from side to side. "Jenny, it's going to bite you! Put it back."

"She won't hurt me," Jenny recited.

"What if it gets loose. Erika's just a child," Kay insisted.

"She's Erika's snake. She won't hurt Erika."

Kay stared at Jenny as if she were an alien being. She and Jenny had worked together as reporters years ago. She'd been the one who introduced Jenny to Mark. She never had understood Jenny; she wondered that Mark did. She saw now in Mark's face his concern. "Jenny," she tried more patiently, "don't you think Erika is too young for a snake?" She moved to the coffee table by the bird, who had begun making low guttural noises as if it sensed the threat.

"Why don't you ask Erika?" Erika was holding Rosy's tail and stroking her. She hadn't even noticed the bird on the table.

"I hardly think she'd know," Kay answered.

Jenny replaced the snake in the box and closed the lid. "Well . . . that's a difference between you and me." Without elaborating, she proceeded with Erika to her room.

Kay searched Mark's face for a shared reaction, but Mark's expression had turned inwards. "Excuse me," he said and started after Jenny, but before he got to the door, Jenny returned. She was carrying her briefcase.

"I'm going out to work now," she said. "Erika says she's hungry. She hasn't had much of a nap so she should go to bed early."

"Where are you going?" Mark moved towards her.

"Out."

"Where?" He took hold of her arm gently, but she met his eyes with a look which told him not to try to stop her.

"I'm going out to work," she repeated. Glancing into the living room, she added, "If I were you, I'd hang that bird up before the cat eats it." Then she lifted Rosy with her lidless eyes onto the hall table and left her there to watch over her family.

~

In the living room Kay watched Mark, who stood for a moment without moving, then running his hand through his hair, he turned from the door. He yanked his tie from around his neck and threw it on the chair in the hall. Kay looked away. She lifted the birdcage and carried it over to the window where she strained to raise it to the hook on the pole. Mark stepped over to help her.

"I'm sorry," she said. "I guess Jenny's mad at us?"

Mark glanced at her. He started to say, "There is no *us*, Kay," but he didn't bother. He was furious at Jenny. He had come home needing to talk to her. As he'd left his meeting, he'd wanted to be with his wife and listen to her set his world in order, to comfort her too and help ease her pain, whatever it was. But now she had walked out on him for reasons he didn't even understand. The fact that she misinterpreted what she saw with Kay angered him even more. In his mind he justified himself and censured her for not knowing him better. Yet lingering behind his arguments was the possibility that he was at fault, at least he wasn't entirely guiltless. His infidelity was not that he wanted to have an affair with Kay but that Kay fed some vanity of his, some perception of himself as . . . well, noble or good. That was it, wasn't it? And Jenny saw and knew this vanity and had turned her back on it. He didn't answer Kay's question. Instead he asked, "You want to have dinner with us?"

"Yes. I'd like that," she answered. She was arranging the newspaper in the bottom of the bird's cage and picking up stray birdseed and putting it back in the feeder. She didn't look at him.

Mark moved into the kitchen. Kay followed. "What shall we have?" she asked.

Mark opened the cupboard and took down a can of soup. "Whatever you like."

Kay opened the refrigerator. "Would you like grilled cheese sandwiches? I make an outstanding grilled cheese sandwich."

"Fine." Mark emptied soup into a pot as Kay explored the vegetable drawer, pulling out tomatoes and mushrooms. She set a skillet on the stove and dropped in a slab of butter, then began slicing mushrooms into the pan. She was still wearing her white wool dress from the morning and high-heeled gray leather boots. As the mushrooms sizzled, she sat at the table, lift-ed up her leg to the chair and unzipped her boots.

She returned to the stove in her stocking feet. "I don't cook much for myself," she said, "but I think you'll like this." Mark didn't answer. He was staring at the water running in the sink. "Actually I enjoy cooking for some-one else." Already she was imagining herself as the woman in his house. Today had only confirmed what she'd sensed when she'd first visited two weeks ago. With no other reference than her own, she assumed the discontent she saw between Jenny and Mark arose from their discontent with each other; and now quietly, benignly even, with a show of goodwill, she was considering what kind act she might extend to Jenny as compensation for her husband.

Because Mark didn't see the consequence of his own goodwill towards Kay, he didn't imagine the hurt his next words caused. "After dinner could you baby-sit Erika for a while?" he asked.

Kay glanced at him. She wiped her blonde hair from her face with the back of her hand. "Where are you going?"

"I want to find Jenny. We need to talk."

"Oh . . ." She pushed the mushrooms about with a spatula. "Well . . . I've been out all day, Mark . . . what with David and buying that bird. I haven't done any work myself." She hesitated. She searched his face. Perhaps he needed to find Jenny to discuss the breach between them, but his face offered her no encouragement. She didn't know what she did see, but she saw no clear opening for herself. She answered, "I've got quite a lot to do before tomorrow. Ordinarily I'd be glad to help, but . . ."

Mark just nodded. He poured the water into the saucepan.

Mark and Kay and Erika ate chicken noodle soup and cheese and mush-room and tomato sandwiches in silence at the kitchen table. Erika was so tired that she almost fell asleep twice with her head beside her plate. After dinner Mark revived her long enough for Kay to present the bird, but by then she was too sleepy to focus on it. Mark carried her into her room where he put her to bed in her clothes.

In the living room Kay had gathered up her briefcase and was waiting at the table for Mark. She'd put back on her boots and her white coat with the white fox collar. "I imagine I'll be quite late," she said, standing when he entered. "You still keep your key over the door? I'll just take a couch . . . in your study or in the living room, whatever's available."

Mark walked her to the door. "I'm sorry I can't help you out, Mark." She forced a smile. "Maybe Jenny will be home soon." She leaned over and kissed him on the cheek; then she walked away with the awkward, flat-footed gait of a child.

It was 6:30. The apartment was quiet. In the living room the new bird was clicking its tongue against its beak as if trying to decide what words to offer in its new home. Mark walked about the silent rooms. He was wide awake, unable to work. Downstairs the neighbors were arguing with each other. Mark stood in the middle of the living room listening, then he went to the phone and dialed their apartment. The argument stopped for a moment as Mrs. Rousseau answered: "Now? . . . Well, well, yes. All right. Fifteen minutes," she said.

Mark went to the bedroom, where he took off the sweater and shirt he'd been wearing all day. In his undershirt he stood at the sink and washed his face. He lathered his cheeks and shaved off the day's shadow, then he brushed his teeth and returned to the bedroom. He put on a fresh blue shirt and blue crewneck sweater.

Returning to the kitchen, he began to wash the dishes while he waited for Mrs. Rousseau. Whenever Jenny was upset with him for reasons he didn't understand, he washed dishes. The ritual dated back to one of their earliest arguments about household chores, and the act had an unspoken meaning between them. It was an admission of his own helplessness in the face of feelings he didn't comprehend. When Mrs. Rousseau arrived, he told her he didn't know how long he would be. He went in and kissed Erika again and covered her up. At Erika's request he moved the snake, sleeping now coiled in the sand, into her room, settling it onto a shelf with her toys so that Rosy would be there to greet her when she woke up; then he went to find his wife.

~

The Woods, Fishing, and a Skunk . . . and a Snake

(from: MY DOG SKIP*)*

Willie Morris

THESE WOODS WERE so much a part of our lives, my father's and Skip's and mine, only a half-hour's drive or so from town that I grew up taking them for granted. Only later did I realize that they were the last and largest of the great Delta forests, that it was only at the bottom of that lower triangle of the Delta, where we were, that the remnants of the primordial wilderness had been left untouched by the incursions of man. It was to this spectral country, but closer to the Mississippi River, as I would read many years later in "Delta Autumn," that William Faulkner's character Uncle Ike McCaslin came on his last hunt, having to drive "two hundred miles from Jefferson when once it had been thirty." Little wonder that as I grew older I always in my memory associated these woods with boyhood and Old Skip.

My father and I were in one of these places on December 7, 1941, when I was seven, sometime before I got Skip; I can remember the day by the news that greeted us when we went home. And we had been there many times before then. At first I used a .22, though Daddy once let me shoot his 12-gauge, out of nothing but maliciousness, because after I squeezed the trigger that gun knocked me for a twisting nosedive into the mud. On my twelfth birthday I got a shiny new 16-gauge smelling richly of oil, and the next time we went into the woods I wasted a whole box of shells out of sheer exuberance, and Skip thought I had gone insane.

One afternoon we were walking through a stretch of swamp-bottom with Owen McGinty, one of the town firemen. All of a sudden Owen shouted "Jump!" just as my foot hit something soft and wet, and I jumped with all the enthusiasm I could muster. "Look at *that*," Owen said, rolling out the "*that*," and my father went "*Wheew*." There was a rattlesnake that must have been eight feet long, right in my path. Even Skip, intrepid in all things, but young at the time, was intimidated by the sight of this menacing serpent, and backed off a few feet and merely stared at it. "Let the boy shoot him," Owen said, and I aimed my new shotgun and killed him through the head. Owen pulled out his knife and cut off his rattlers and handed them to me. The next day I took the rattlers to school, and my classmates gathered around and said, "He was a *big* 'un." But Miss Abbott, my teacher, found out about it and made me take my trophy home. If the dust from the insides got in your eyes, she said, you would be blinded for life. My father said Miss Abbott got that from an *old wives' tale*.

Several times in the woods around Panther Creek we ran across a man my father knew—a hanger-on, he called him. The man lived right in the middle of the woods, in a little crooked shanty he had made for himself. He had a scraggly black beard and wore beat-up khakis and a slouch hat; in back of his shack was a vegetable garden. The game wardens ignored him, and he lived off the animals he could kill, and made money now and then guiding deer hunters. My father later told me that the man would eat anything just so it wasn't alive, and even then he might eat it if the gravy was good. Skip took to this man right away, perhaps because the old fellow gave him fried squirrel and allowed him to tease his numerous squawking chickens. "I'll give you five dollars for that dog," he said to me one day. I refused, replying that although Skip had a lot of the woods in him, he was mainly a town dog.

Later, when I lived in England, I saw places that the English called woods, but compared with the Delta swamp-bottoms of that boyhood time they could have been grown in the shop of a florist. Similarly, the lakes where my father, Skip, and I went to fish, compared with the man-made lakes I would see later in Central Texas, were real lakes, of a piece with the stark heavy earth that enveloped them. Their waters were murky and oppressive, and the worst death I ever heard about took place at one of them, when a water-skier got tangled in a school of water moccasins.

Sweet is the Swamp

Emily Dickinson

Sweet is the swamp with its secrets,
Until we meet a snake;
'Tis then we sigh for houses,
And our departure take

At that enthralling gallup
That only childhood knows.
A snake is summer's treason,
And guile is where it goes.

~

From: *The Little Prince*

Antoine De Saint-Exupéry

ONCE WHEN I WAS six I saw a magnificent picture in a book about the jungle, called *True Stories*. It was a boa constrictor swallowing a wild beast. Here is a copy of the picture:

In the book it said: "Boa constrictors swallow their prey whole, without chewing. Afterward they are no longer able to move, and they sleep during the six months of their digestion."

In those days I thought a lot about jungle adventures, and eventually managed to make my first drawing, using a colored pencil. My drawing Number One looked like this:

I showed the grown-ups my masterpiece, and I asked them if my drawing scared them.

They answered, "Why be scared of a hat?"

My drawing was not a picture of a hat. It was a picture of a boa constrictor digesting an elephant. Then I drew the inside of the boa constrictor, so the grown-ups could understand. They always need explanations. My drawing Number Two looked like this:

The grown-ups advised me to put away my drawings of boa constrictors, outside or inside, and apply myself instead to geography, history, arithmetic, and grammar. That is why I abandoned, at the age of six, a magnificent career as an artist. I had been discouraged by the failure of my drawing Number One and of my drawing Number Two. Grown-ups never understand anything by themselves, and it is exhausting for children to have to provide explanations over and over again.

So then I had to choose another career, and I learned to pilot airplanes. I have flown almost everywhere in the world. And, as a matter of fact, geography has been a big help to me. I could tell China from Arizona at first glance, which is very useful if you get lost during the night.

So I have had, in the course of my life, lots of encounters with lots of serious people. I have spent lots of time with grown-ups. I have seen them at close range . . . which hasn't much improved my opinion of them.

Whenever I encountered a grown-up who seemed to me at all enlightened, I would experiment on him with my drawing Number One, which I have always kept. I wanted to see if he really understood anything. But he would always answer, "That's a hat." Then I wouldn't talk about boa constrictors or jungles or stars. I would put myself on his level and talk about bridge and golf and politics and neckties. And my grown-up was glad to know such a reasonable person.

~

The Python

Ogden Nash

The python has, and I fib no fibs,
318 pairs of ribs.
In stating this I place reliance
On a séance with one who died for science.
This figure is sworn to and attested;
He counted them while being digested.

Tending the Garden

Snake

J. D. McClatchy

Close by the creepered wall,
On the cinquefoil's shaggy border,
He takes the sun, and the unwary fly.
The snake is named Disorder.

This garter's all reversed,
Elastic frayed, the yellow stripe
Of species a dirty, bulging seam—
Precision's antitype.

He's a pile of himself!
Too old, too devil-may-care. And yet . . .
That staring eye and wrap-around grin
Unearth a buried debt.

To what? You back away,
Then turn to cultivate some quarter
Of the garden, sulking rows that say
The snake is named Disorder.

My Snakes

Gail Godwin

"There is nothing so simple or so commonplace as a serpent, and yet by virtue of this very simplicity nothing which shocks the spirit more."
—*The Penguin Dictionary of Symbols*,
Jean Chevalier and Alain Gheerbrant,
translated by John Buchanan-Brown

WE LIVED IN the middle of a town and the snakes of my childhood came out of books or out of other people's stories.

Mother read to me from a children's book her mother had read to her. It was about a family of garter snakes. My favorite picture was the one of the mother snake entertaining her friends at tea, all of them wearing bonnets and sitting upright in their garden chairs, their tails drooping decorously beneath them.

And then, a few years later, I found *The Jungle Books*:

That afternoon Mowgli was sitting in the circle of Kaa's great coils, fingering the flaked and broken old skin that lay all looped and twisted among the rocks just as Kaa had left it. Kaa had very courteously packed himself under Mowgli's broad, bare shoulders so that the boy was really resting in a living arm chair.

—"The King's Ankus," *The Second Jungle Book*

Rudyard Kipling had just turned thirty when he wrote this wonderful tale about Mowgli's friendship with Kaa, the old python. Newly married, living on his American wife's Brattleboro, Vermont, estate, already rich and famous for his work, Kipling had nevertheless left his heart—some say for the remainder of his life—back in the jungles of his beloved India. His home-sickness magically combined with his evocative powers to create a jungle which a nine-year-old girl living on a suburban street in Asheville, North Carolina, could escape into. I lay on top of the family car, hidden by the overarching branches of a maple tree, my back supported by a triangular reading pillow with arm supports that my grandmother's generation called a "husband." The car top was my rock, the leafy tree my jungle, and the "hus-band" so comfortably upholding my shoulders was none other than the "liv-ing arm chair" of the courteous old python, who has just shed his skin, "which always makes a snake moody and depressed till the new skin begins to shine and look beautiful."

"Even to the scales of the eyes it is perfect," said Mowgli, under his breath, playing with the old skin. "Strange to see the covering of one's own head at one's own feet."

"Ay, but I lack feet," said Kaa; "and since this is the custom of all my people, I do not find it strange. Does thy skin never feel old and harsh?"

"Then go I and wash, Flathead; but, it is true, in the great heats I have wished I could slough off my skin without pain and run skinless."

~

And then there were the very different snakes of our local folk narratives:

"Allus look afore you put yer foot down in a boat, little girl. Ole *Mon*-roe, he's jist steppin into his rowboat he keeps over thar on Beaver Lake when this six foot devil of a water moccasin been sunnin hisself under the struts lash-es out and strikes him on the ankle. Luckily he's wearin his brogan shoes and he stomps that nasty sumbitch to a pulp. I seen the blood and intestines all over the sole. *Mon*-roe was right put out, though, because they was his brand new brogans."

"Lord, honey, I was never so scared in my whole life. Here Randy and I were fixing to have a nice quiet evening, Randy'd brought the logs in from the woodpile and was laying the fire, when out pours this gigantic rattler and commences to slither across my new carpet, heading for the front door. Randy grabs his thirty-eight and I'm saying, 'Please, please! Not on my new carpet!' So Randy waits til he's *off* the carpet and shoots him square between the eyes just as he's flipping himself over the threshold out into the dark."

"But . . ."

"But *what*, hon?"

"Well, I mean, if it was already out the door, you could have let it go on and live."

"Gail, are you crazy? A rattlesnake'll kill you soon as look at you. Whose side are you on, anyway?"

Literature had already done its dirty work: I was on the snakes' side.

Sunbathing in a delicious slice of golden warmth, rough boards scratching my long tummy—perhaps I would shed my skin in this nice enclosure—when suddenly a clumsy brown shiny thing threatens my peace. I lash out, my fang strikes the evil-smelling monster to no avail, then every nerve in my body shrieks and all goes dark.

Curled up with my family amongst the logs when a shuddering upheaval isolates me from my kin and I am borne through chill space, though mysteriously still wrapped in logs. Then another upheaval, and I'm nearly smashed by a falling log but manage to re-orient myself and wriggle past two jerky upright four limbed creatures and flip over in, I must say, an impressive somersault and am pouring myself out into the evening to rejoin my people when my head shatters and all goes dark.

~

It was my thirty-sixth summer, the summer Robert and I moved to a rented farmhouse in the Catskills, before I got to meet a real snake.

One June afternoon I was reading outside on our stone terrace overlooking the fields when a little boy suddenly materialized:

"Can I still play here?"

I wasn't exactly overjoyed to have my deep country reverie disrupted by who knew what kind of juvenile antics, but he looked so serious and *alone*, one of those children people like to refer to as "old souls," that I said, "Well, okay, if you won't make noise or run around too much."

"We'll be awful quiet, I promise."

We? His imaginary friend, no doubt.

That said, he jumped down off the terrace, being careful to skim the rhubarb patch, and, after lifting and replacing several of the flagstones along the edge of the terrace, he squatted in the grass with his back to me and made rapid movements with his hands, like someone practicing magician's passes. I went back to my book, but soon found I was only using it as a foil so I could spy on him.

The rapid passes continued, broken by the occasional dive forward into the grass, where he would grope about, engage with something on the move, then, muting his squeal of triumph for my benefit, capture whatever it was and resume the squatting posture with his back to me, executing his passes.

The suspense was killing me. I closed the book. " What have you got there?" I called.

He turned and held up a hand with something extra about it. I am very near-sighted.

"Bring it up here."

He hopped up on the terrace and proffered the little brownish-pink snake curled around his finger.

"He's not poisonous. Want to touch him?"

"Well, I just might." For the first time in my life I made contact with this junior member of an ancient, myth-laden race. To my surprise, he was warm and dry, rather crispy, in fact. His red forked tongue flickered along my finger then set out for my knuckles.

"That's the way he smells you," the boy said.

"How do you know it's a he?"

"You scratch the tail under here. If two little ding-dongs pop out he's a male. I'd do it for you but my auntie says it's rude."

~

Years have gone by and I'm still living in the Catskills, in the house Robert and I built fifteen years ago. I've been seduced by the deep country and no longer sleep well when I'm out of it. My sanity is shored up each day by the grazing deer, the wild turkeys parading across the lawn, the coyotes' a capella concert at dusk, a buzzard taking a dirt bath, skittish brother fox keeping to the edge of the woods, mother bear flipping over the capstones on the bluestone wall so she and her cubs can gobble up the ants and wasps underneath. A family of garter snakes took up residence in this wall the summer it was laid, and this morning, June fifth, the big garter snake was back in her customary spot at the far end of the wall, where there is sun all day long. Wearing my distance glasses, I've been checking the corner every day for several weeks, and when I spotted my thirty-inch black-and-yellow friend, who can trace her ancestors back 130 million years, looped over herself in the vinca this morning, I rejoiced that summer had officially begun.

No. Let's tell it as it was: after I had screamed and clutched my heart, I welcomed her back. That's the mysterious part. No matter how often I go looking for my snakes, I always scream and clutch my heart when we first make contact. The thrill of a snake's sheer *otherness* never seems to wear off.

I choose to believe she's a matriarch, though I wouldn't dream of scratching the under side of her tail, nor would she lie still to let me. From my reading I've learned that female snakes are generally larger than the males. One more thing you may not know: I didn't until I read *The Snake Scientist,* by Sy Montgomery, a young adult book, with lavish photographs by Nic Bishop, about Bob Mason's groundbreaking research at a garter snake preserve in Manitoba: When a male snake crawls on top of another snake in hopes of mating, he may find himself rejected, either because he's climbed aboard another male, or the female he's rubbing against would rather not mate with him. Before anything can happen, the female snake's pheromones, her body perfume, has to be scented by the male snake's tongue. Even then the female still has the last word. She can flip him off at the last minute if she doesn't like the feel of him. Research has learned she prefers the heft of a larger-sized male covering her, but research doesn't know why yet.

~

My landscape designer has lent me his best gardener for the day. The young man speaks no English, so I have this message ready for him on a notecard:

HAY UNA CULABRITA
QUI VIVE EN EL JARDIN
PERO SI LA VES
POR FAVOR
NO LA MATES

Culebra being the Spanish for "harmless snake"—plus the diminutive, *-ita,* to convey added affection. Posionous snakes are *víboras,* vipers.

My *culebrita* lives in the garden, but if you see her please don't kill her. This can happen. A friend who raises cornsnakes (an increasingly popular domestic species, whose colors can attain breathtaking shades of pink and orange through selective breeding) came home one afternoon to be told by a proud new gardener's assistant: "There was this big old pink snake laying right on your porch, but don't worry, I killed it."

And it was a sad day, a few summers ago, when I found a large garter snake choked in a mesh fence I had put up to keep the deer out of the perennial garden. It was too late, but as I cut it out of the mesh I kept say-

ing, "I'm sorry, I'm so sorry." I carried the lifeless body by the tail and left it
down in the field for the crows and the turkey buzzards. I dismantled the
ugly fence, let the deer eat what they liked down to the ground, and then
filled in the spaces with the things they didn't like.

~

> Wondering what it's like to be a serpent
> takes me to the edge of the explainable . . .
> —Harry W. Greene
> *Snakes, the Evolution of Mystery in Nature*

One morning as the cat and I were making our rounds, we spied the Matriarch snake, as I think of her, draped languidly across a rock beneath the
blooming sage bush. She was so still; her usually bright yellow eye was dull.

When we returned to the sage bush in the afternoon, I thought she had
died because there she was, in the exact same position. I was preparing for
another sad good-bye, followed by the ecological disposal down in the field,
until I looked closer and saw it was her skin draped over the rock. I picked it
up, delicate and brittle as filo pastry, and carried it inside to show Robert in his
studio. Carefully we laid it out across the shiny black lid of his Yamaha grand.

"Look," he said, "there's even the molding of the eyes. There's her fang!
How do they manage to crawl out of themselves without rupturing the
shape of the mouth?"

We fetched a tape measure.

"Three and a half feet," I said. "If she makes it to her next shedding, the
next one will be longer."

"Just imagine if we could do that," said Robert. "Drape ourselves over a
rock whenever we felt damaged and worn, and feel the tired old stuff loosen
and fall away . . ."

"And then we'd say, 'That's over, that's not me anymore,' and crawl out of
our discarded sheath and slither onward and upward."

"Thank you, my love, for bringing it in," he said. "I feel honored."

I took the skin outside. It floated and danced like a ghost snake on my
upturned wrists. I placed it under a laurel near a favorite bird nest site, and
the next morning it was gone.

~

Black Snake This Time

Mary Oliver

lay
under the oak trees
in the early morning
in a half knot,

in a curl,
and, like anyone
catching the runner at rest,
I stared

at that thick black length
whose neck, all summer
was a river,
whose body was the same river—

whose whole life was a flowing—
whose tail could lash—
who, footless, could spin
like a black tendril and hang

upside down in the branches
gazing at everything
out of seed-shaped red eyes
as it swung to and fro,

the tail making its quick sizzle,
the head lifted
like a black spout.
Was it alive?

Of course it was alive.
This was the quick wrist of early summer,
when everything was alive.
Then I knelt down, I saw

that the snake was gone—
that the face, like a black bud,
had pushed out of the broken petals
of the old year, and it had emerged

on the hundred hoops of its belly,
the tongue sputtering its thread of smoke,
the work of the pearl-colored lung
never pausing, as it pushed

from the chin,
from the crown of the head,
leaving only an empty skin
for the mice to nibble and the breeze to blow

as over the oak leaves and across the creek
and up the far hill it had gone,
damp and shining in the starlight
like a rollicking finger of snow.

Coincidental Copperhead Saga

Marie Ridder

"A COPPERHEAD JUST bit me."

Emergency room doctors at big Washington hospitals see a lot of things, but middle-aged women with snake venom inching towards their hearts are not a big part of their daily practice. I knew therefore that my declaration would brand me as a bit of an odd duck—medically speaking. I understood all of that, even though at that particular moment my sense of ironic detachment had been distinctly muted by an awareness that my obit in *The Washington Post* the next morning might strike most readers as a bit bizarre.

And so I was somewhat anxious that the distinguished looking doctor speaking on the telephone in front of me terminate his conversation. His reassuringly mature gray hair suggested clinical gravitas. That was good. But why was he looking at me in such amazement, even as he hung up the phone? Was I his first snakebite victim?

Actually, I was his second.

"I have had two potentially fatal snakebites in my entire practice," said Dr. Pasmodi, dispensing with normal doctor-patient pleasantries. "And, my dear, they have both been you."

It was true. Nine years earlier, a similar encounter with a copperhead had

also triggered a mad dash to the emergency room, although the trauma of
the occasion had blurred my visual memory of the doctor whose first-ever
treatment had saved my life.

Actually, local lore should have warned my husband and me forty-one
years earlier when we moved to our spectacularly situated house on a high
Virginia bluff overlooking the Potomac. We were moving into a region pop-
ularly known as "Copperhead Hills." Somehow, someone forgot to tell us. It
was only as I was lying in the critical care unit at Washington's Sibley Hospital recovering from my second copperhead bite that I learned that reptiles
had a prior claim on our property.

At the same time, there had been enough incidents to put me on notice:
my youngest daughter was twelve when she discovered a copperhead curled
lazily on her bedroom pillow. My son nearly sat on another such critter during breakfast one sunny morning. Not even our guests have been spared. A
distinguished French foreign correspondent, Count Ziggy de Sejanzac, was
unceremoniously ushered from our dining room when a copper-colored reptile slithering across the parquet rudely greeted him.

My neighbors have had their share of near misses: snakes found coiled
around the laundry tub, hidden in attic beams, stretched across driveways,
napping in the swimming pool machinery. Some weeks after my second bite,
a kindly woman from the National Poison Control Center called to tell me
that my record is unique.

"We would very much like to know if you get bitten a third time," she said.

"Why?" I asked.

"Well, either you have by now developed your own antivenom . . ."

She paused before continuing.

"Or it could be . . . well, it'll kill you."

Even without that helpful and concerned warning, I'm not likely to forget my encounters with my slithering neighbors. As I write, my left foot tingles. The pain has disappeared, but a large swelling of my knee remains as a
reminder of a moonlit September night when my husband, Walter, and I set
out for dinner and, later, an evening of waltzing. Preparing to get in the car,
I stepped in some leaves. My foot, fashionably exposed by an open evening
slipper, rustled pleasantly through the leaves, until . . .

"Ouch," I exclaimed. "What a sharp prick."

"Bees," I added, ignorantly.

"Probably a copperhead," Walter suggested jokingly after having inspected the unthreatening leaves at my feet.

At dinner, however, my foot swelled alarmingly. I showed it to my dinner partner, a prominent orthopedist.

"Best you keep moving," he declared with great authority as if diagnosing a sprained ankle.

So, I hobbled to the dance floor, where agony awaited. But I endured. After all, I was following medical advice, which could not have been more inappropriate. Every hobbling waltz-time movement caused the venom to spread.

Abed that night, I tried to ignore the stiffening, swelling limb that I had once thought of as my left leg. By morning it was purple.

Still operating on the assumption that I had really irritated some bees, I called my doctor, Tom Connally.

"Some bee," Tom said skeptically when I described my symptoms. "I'll meet you at the emergency room at Sibley."

One glance turned his skepticism into urgency.

"That's no bee sting. That's a copperhead. She could lose her leg," he barked as he hustled the emergency-room staff into high gear.

Tests quickly established that I was violently allergic to the antivenom. So instead I was given lots of fluids and released after several days with a very swollen, very painful, but happily intact, leg. It was weeks before I could walk on it and years to make peace with my need for a bigger left shoe and with the unsightly swelling of my knee.

Nine years later, Claire Dwoskin, a neighbor, and I were inspecting the rabbit damage to our gardens. Plucking a weed from a battered bed, I felt a stinging sensation.

"I've been stung by a damn bee," I declared.

By now older and wiser, I looked more closely at my hand. Sure enough, there were the fang marks. Cautiously parting a day lily, I spotted an enormous coiled snake. It lay there, indolently, in the sun of the June morning, its head up and copper markings plain.

I announced my discovery to Claire who challenged me.

"Are you sure?" asked Claire who, unwisely, leaned in for a close look.

"Jesus, you're right," she said, as she jumped away, shocked.

Second time around, I knew time was of the essence.

With Claire insisting on doing the driving, I was hooked up to intravenous fluids seventeen minutes later.

I wasn't any too soon.

This time, the snake had struck a much more dangerous place. The swelling was galloping up my arm towards my lung and heart. Among the risks: paralysis in my right hand.

"Poison control says we must give you the antivenom," Dr. Pasmodi said. "I know from our records you are very allergic to it, but we have no choice."

Everything was done to mitigate the effects of what is primarily horse serum. I was given intravenous Benadryl. Oxygen was brought into the room. Nurses and doctors surrounded me. The allergic reaction materialized in no time flat. I couldn't breath. I had pains in my back and chest. I vomited. But in front of my eyes the swelling started to recede. Pasmodi's gamble worked. The first few weeks after the emergency I had fever, hives, the shakes and difficulty breathing. But at least I survived with an unscathed hand.

Over the years I have heard many copperhead stories. Several neighbors of my farm in the Blue Ridge country have stiff hands or walk with a limp. One old friend, given too much antivenom, now suffers with terrible heart problems. Another lost a niece of eleven, who stumbled into a nest and died from multiple bites. Most victims survive, using simple country remedies such as a tourniquet, ice water baths and lots of fluids. There is a complicated remedy that I don't understand that involves hitching yourself to a car battery and giving yourself a good jolt of electricity; the shock is supposed to arrest the venom's advance—assuming you don't electrocute yourself in the bargain.

I remarked once to a real country expert—a woodcutter—that I had not met many people who had died of copperhead bites. He judiciously drawled his reply: "If he's daid, he's not likely to be talking to you about it."

My own multiple experiences with copperhead bites makes me grateful to modern medicine. But does it make me wary? No. Those suckers can disguise themselves against a pipe, a stone wall, the woodpile or even the stone border of a swimming pool. They can slink invisibly through the grass, along a road, in a dimly lit room.

Doctors and nurses are eminently sensible about all of this. "Move to a condo." "Give up your garden." "Wear high boots and gloves."

As this torrent of advice threatens to drown me, I hear the clear voice of my oldest daughter, Cary.

"I know you all mean well, but she isn't ready for a condo. And she won't give up her beautiful garden."

And I'm thinking to myself, "Two bites in a long life and the pleasures of a riverbank and an enchanting rural pond? Hey, there's always that car battery."

~

A Narrow Fellow in the Grass

Emily Dickinson

A narrow fellow in the grass
Occasionally rides;
You may have met him,—did you not,
His notice sudden is.
The grass divides as with a comb,
A spotted shaft is seen;
And then it closes at your feet
And opens further on.
He likes a boggy acre,
A floor too cool for corn.
Yet when a child, and barefoot,
I more than once, at morn,
Have passed, I thought, a whip-lash
Unbraiding in the sun,—
When, stooping to secure it,
It wrinkled, and was gone.
Several of nature's people
I know, and they know me;
I feel for them a transport
Of cordiality;
But never met this fellow,
Attended or alone,
Without a tighter breathing,
And zero at the bone.

Snake Stories (A True One)

Susan Eisenhower

ONE MONTH AFTER we moved to the country a snake fell on my head. I was standing under a large tree when a heavy plop landed on top of me. Turning around I saw a black snake writhing and slithering, just next to my feet.

Cardiac arrest!

When we moved out of the city we knew there would be wildlife, but I had Thumper and Bambi in mind, not six-foot snakes that slink up trees and coil there in wait. Childhood experiences provided no positive preparation for the shock either. When I was growing up my brother David was given a snake egg at a local animal farm, which he kept in a shoebox, waiting for it to hatch. It wasn't until the box began to smell that it was clear the egg would never produce anything more than a stink.

My cousin Fletcher, however, actually had a pet snake. He kept it in an aquarium—sans the water. The thing stayed curled up all day long. When the snake was hungry (how can you tell?) Fletcher would pop a frozen mouse into a microwave, and then throw it into the glass container. If you wanted to, you could spend all day watching the snake digest its fast-food snack.

Though repelled by these memories, worst-case wildlife, I thought naively, were raccoons under the porch, ground hogs in the garden, or *maybe* bats in the barn. But snakes? No way. We were grateful refugees from city life, after all, consumed by the romance of country living—where the only things "disturbing the peace" were the sounds of armies of geese flying off to the south, squawking in formation like young recruits at boot camp.

My reveries were interrupted only once while touring a potential property. In a dusty recess of the garage, I saw the container of a product advertised as snake repellant. (Apparently this and snake oil fall into the same category.) I asked our real estate agent about it. Glancing at the bottle, she replied, her nose beginning to grow: "I've lived around here for most of my life and I haven't seen a snake in maybe twenty years." I believed her and put it out of my mind.

After much looking we settled on an old house—a nineteenth-century "diamond in the rough." Everything in the house needed to be done—the roof, the plumbing, the siding and the wiring had to be replaced, and plaster was falling off walls. But none of this worried me: I was in control.

But we were there only one week when I got the first hint of trouble. Breathlessly my daughter ran into the kitchen shouting that she'd just found a snakeskin within feet of our house. Several days later, wide-eyed, she reported that she'd seen more skins in the attic. "The attic?" I wailed to my husband. "It's not possible."

Then, less than a month later, the mother of all snakes literally landed on my head.

From that moment onwards, "the problem" took on new urgency. There wasn't a person I didn't press for a solution: friends, neighbors, contractors, gardening experts, even total strangers. All had stories, some of which were even worse than my own.

One man told me of removing the sheeting on a porch ceiling, only to find thirty or more snakes roiling together as they fell to the floor. Another told me of a close encounter he'd had in removing an old cistern. Families of snakes had made it their home for years. "You should be delighted you have only black snakes," he said with authority. With hideous but memorable detail he outlined the differences between the big benign black ones and the snakes that could do you in.

I also heard about an old house with a basement dubbed "the dungeon" by workmen on the property. Once when they went down to repair the heating system they hit their heads on several black snakes dangling from the hot water pipes in the cozy recesses of the furnace room. The snakes stayed—but they didn't.

"But what about solutions?" I asked plaintively. "Get yourself a gun" was a typical response, or a meat cleaver. Or a rottweiler.

The idealists among them, however, had less confrontational proposals.

"We had our house fumigated before we bought it," reported a woman who'd moved to the country the same time we did. "I have to tell you when they finished, there were more than sixty dead snakes in the downstairs alone. They had literally come out of the woodwork."

This was not what I wanted to hear. Even if we could tent our three-story house—turret and all—there was no guarantee that they wouldn't come back again.

"What you need are cats," another friend told me as she waved her hand toward a flock of overfed cats, splayed out on the sunny side of her porch. She called them her "secret weapons," brought into her household for the sole purpose of keeping the snakes out. She told me that she had not seen one snake in her house since she'd taken these measures. She was proud that once her feline force ganged up on a long black snake that had wandered into the area, perhaps to find a cool dark place to escape the blistering summer sun. Hissing, six or seven cats, like barroom bouncers, escorted the unwelcome visitor down a long slope and out of view.

If my friend had found a solution to the snake problem, it did not come without a cost. She was only a weekend resident—that meant that twice a week she had to drive out from the city to feed her cats, otherwise, they would wander off the property.

There had to be an easier way.

"Well, there is," Graham, a Southern friend of mine, said with a drawl. "Yew got two full-proof options. Move or get used to 'em." At his mountain retreat, he told me, he sees snakes all the time, and not just black snakes. He regularly deals with copperheads. "You do?" I asked with admiration. "In the house?"

Graham brushes even the poisonous ones into dustpans or garbage cans with a broom and takes them outside. "Honna, ah learned to *live* with 'em," he said.

Then uttering the greatest cliché of the great outdoors, he added, "They're more frightened of yew than yew are of theam. Let's put it this way, they don't see *yew* as their next meal."

That simple thought was the beginning of recovery. But living Graham's advice was another matter.

During the next two years our contractor took a few big ones away (preferably to another state, I suggested), we saw several on our property and found a few inside the house. Once, I nearly tripped over (ironically) a milk snake on my way to the kitchen—before my first bowl of oatmeal. Coiled up, poised to strike. I backed up repeating, "I am not his next meal." My husband came rushing to my aid, after hearing my screams, and using the recommended broom and dustpan method he scooped it up and took it outside.

Living with snakes has been part of a hard-earned maturing process. But sometimes the thought of seeing a snake still makes my palms sweat. Though it hasn't happened yet, I know that one day I will be called upon to face a confrontation alone, when my husband is not home and my contractor can't be summoned. I'm not sure how I'll react, but I will prevail, or at least survive, most probably by locking up the thing in a room until my husband does arrive.

Nevertheless coming to terms with snakes has been a small trade-off for the open spaces, the fresh breezes and the long vistas that glimmer gold as the evening sun offers its last rays. Indeed, this pursuit of peaceful coexistence is a small sacrifice for living where one can still be awed by the sharp clarity of the nighttime sky, the silence after a snowfall, and the loamy smell of spring earth. Glorious nature is everywhere! It is there for the taking!

But you can be sure that I will never stand under a tree again.

~

The Snakes of September

Stanley Kunitz

All summer I heard them
rustling in the shrubbery,
outracing me from tier
to tier in my garden,
a whisper among the viburnums,
a signal flashed from the hedgerow,
a shadow pulsing
in the barberry thicket.
Now that the nights are chill
and the annuals spent,
I should have thought them gone,
in a torpor of blood
slipped to the nether world
before the sickle frost.
Not so. In the deceptive balm
of noon, as if defiant of the curse
that spoiled another garden,
these two appear on show
through a narrow slit
in the dense green brocade

of a north-country spruce,
dangling head-down, entwined
in a brazen love-knot.
I put out my hand and stroke
the fine, dry grit of their skins.
After all,
we are partners in this land,
co-signers of a covenant.
At my touch the wild
braid of creation
trembles.

~

Snake Lady

Mary Lynn Kotz

YOU'D NEVER KNOW that my mother shot snakes—killed them dead with a .50 caliber pistol or her rare and keen pistol-barrel shotgun, with its neat little .410 shells. Sometimes she whacked off their heads with a sharp hoe, pinned them down with a steel rake while she hollered for somebody to bring the axe, or even found a metal pipe or sturdy limb to beat them to death. "Whoooh, it's a *bad* snake," she'd say, taking aim. And they were: deadly moccasins, copperheads and cottonmouths, and something they called "rattlesnake pilots," creeping along the gullies and creek banks, cotton fields and vegetable gardens in Choctaw County, Mississippi.

Usually Ms. Booth (the new and entirely apropos way to spell "Miz"—a married woman's title in the Deep South) was as ladyfied as she could be, playing the organ at church, or the piano at every secular event in the hill country, on the radio stations with "Ms. Booth's Hymn Time," and at the many schools in the north central part of the state and in the vast, flat Delta, where she taught music for sixty years. She entertained at teas, Sunday dinners, and green punch receptions in Southern finishing-school style; she behaved with equal and educated gentility as a frequent guest in other folks' homes or at a club meeting or the Women's Missionary Union. She'd think nothing at all of driving 150 miles to Memphis to the opera, or 120 to Jackson for the symphony, her children squirming in the backseat of the green '39 Ford.

Every "lyceum" at Wood College, her alma mater, every concert or play at nearby Mississippi State, she'd install us as close to the front row as possible. With Mrs. Burdine, her best friend and 1926 classmate, she'd take in movies at least three times a week (my father didn't enjoy "pictures," preferring to stay home and study, or weave baskets while listening to the radio). Her below-the-waist strawberry-blond hair swept up in a chignon or in braided circles around her head, wearing a lace dress (with jacket, of course) and heels, a splash of pink *Tangee* lipstick and matching nails, she cut an imposing, occasionally elegant, modestly plump figure of womanhood.

But her passion, her thrilling warm-weather pastime, was fishing. Cane-pole, worms or crickets, even cockroaches—fishing from the banks of the Big Black River, which began as a trickle near our house in Mathiston, or the By-Wy canal, deep in the county, and on any lake or pond where she could get permission to fish. In the early days, before my father had a pond dug for her in our pasture to keep her at home, she'd saddle up Minnie Lee, her fast Tennessee Walker, and dash off to someone's farm down in the country, where she had stashed poles and hooks. With the hoe, which she'd borrow and sometimes sharpen, she would dig worms and arm herself. Against the snakes.

When we were old enough, she would take us in the car with poles, bucket, hooks, bobbers, and a tin-can full of earthworms from her own worm beds (a composty stash in an abandoned deep-freeze). In her element—sunlight shimmering on the murky water, frogs gulping beside the bank, worm threaded on the hook—she was ready for the mess of crappie, sun perch, bluegills, goggle-eyes, the rare trout, and of course the slimy, whiskered, bottom-feeding catfish, to fill the bucket or the string floating in the water. Beside her, the .410.

The gun was nothing short of beautiful. It was delicate, a pistol with a single, narrow, steel barrel, about a foot long, of a deep, almost iridescent blue. The shells, too, were small, red-paper cylinders the size of Tootsie rolls, with a copper bottom tinier than a penny. The gun was always unloaded until she spotted the enemy. "Shhhh," she'd warn. "Get back. Stay back." I'd watch fearfully as she cracked open the barrel with the quiet, pleasing metal thud like a car door closing, popped in the shell, and sat down on the ground, against a tree. "It'll kick," she'd whisper every time, meaning the gun, not the snake. "Cover up your ears," she'd say, raising the gun to take aim. And there she'd sit, waiting patiently until the snake's head came squarely into her sight.

I hated the next part. The enormous explosion, so close to my hand-covered ears, always scared me to death. My head rang, my heart pounded. The noise was worse than the snake, I thought, hoping fervently that she'd hit her target. She almost always did, on the first shot. The moccasin's dark body would hump up out of the murky water in three sections (or more if it were really long), showing its creamy white underbelly. A circle of bright red then quickly spread out from where its head had been. I would stare hypnotized by the body writhing on long after its head had been blown off, writhing even while it sank below the surface, soon to be turtle supper. "Keep a good lookout for another one," she instructed, reaching into the coffee can for a squirming worm.

My mother made out like going fishing with her was a rare privilege, only to be earned. She taught me to bait my own hook when I was five. She couldn't concentrate on her own fishing if she had to work for me, too, she said. She taught me how to tell a perch from a catfish from the tug on the line. The perch were nibblers ("Watch out, they're going to steal your bait"). You had to play along with them until they dived really deep, and stayed low. Like bass, catfish were one-bite fellows. One big bite and down to the bottom they'd go. She taught me how to pull the caught fish high out of the water, and swing the pole around to flop them down on the grassy bank. If you didn't, they'd figure out a way to flop themselves right back into the pond. And then I had to learn to wiggle the hooks out of their mouths without hurting them. (I hated it when the fish swallowed the hook, and I'd have to pull and tug until blood and guts came out with the worm. More turtle fodder.) When I was eight, she taught me to clean the fish, dressing them for the frying pan. "If you're going to go fishing with me, you'll have to clean your own catch," she announced. And hers, too, I learned. My mother never cleaned her own fish after that, and I was proud of using a sharp knife to chop off their heads and scraping backwards, remove their scales and their insides, making a little incision in the belly, then operating from there. I absolutely refused to skin a catfish, though. They were ugly, menacing creatures with spears that hurt, and cause infections. Besides, I didn't like the oily, muddy taste of catfish. They required immersion in a pot of boiling water, which once spilled over and had killed a little child of my acquaintance. My fish cleaned and offered up to my mother, I'd scrub my hands with soap and rinse with lemon juice, go inside to practice piano while sniffing fresh fish rolled in cornmeal, sizzling in the skillet.

She never let me touch the gun. Or even know where, in our big old house, it was hidden away. It was as forbidden as touch-dancing, mixed-bathing (swimming with boys) or spotted-cards, which were used for bridge, poker, or old maid. No, the gun was Ms. Booth's, used only rarely by my father to shoot a stray suspected "mad dog" or an incurably lame horse.

My father didn't care much for fishing. He sang, made speeches, taught Bible, and fixed everything himself. Sometimes, when mother would take Mrs. Burdine and me to see the latest Irene Dunne or Greer Garson picture, Daddy and Mr. Burdine would get together and plan their latest horticulture project. Mr. Burdine was a naturalist, knew all kinds of woods lore, and loved to experiment with growing things exotic to the Mississippi hill country. He had a flock of peacocks, a banana tree, guinea hens; collected strange rocks that fell from the skies, or ones that had great fossils in them. He and my father grafted limbs from Texas' large paper-shell pecan trees onto our native hard-as-rock-shell trees (over time, the hard shells won out). They planted bamboo groves, and kept them thinned out to see if their trunks could grow wider than just skinny fishing poles, which they did. One rare day, they decided to go fishing, in a boat, in the Big Black, which they'd heard was yielding some good-sized bass. They drove off in our hump-backed green 1939 Ford, rods and reels, buckets, minnows, and Mr. Burdine's seine stuffed in the trunk.

They came back, way after dark, and Daddy drove into our backyard. Mama ran out to see their catch, and I heard her angry voice. "Whooo! Why in the *world* didn't you kill that thing?" Then, "No sir! No sirree! Not in my backyard. Not anywhere near my pond. I've got children here." At which point I ran out to investigate. "You get back inside that house," my mother ordered.

"It's a monster snake," Mr. Burdine explained. "Big around as my thigh," said my father, a good-sized man. "About as long as I am," said Mr. Burdine, a rather tall, lean fellow. "We're going to take it down to Jackson to the zoo, tomorrow morning early," my father said, as if seeking my approval. "What kind of snake is it?" I asked, having seen Tarzan wrestle off a boa constrictor or anaconda in one of my favorite pictures. "A cotton-mouth moccasin," Mr. Burdine said. "He went after our minnows and we pulled him in, in the seine." Mr. Booth as Lord of the Jungle, I imagined proudly, wrestling a giant reptile into a rowboat.

"Can I see him?" I ventured. "No, ma'am!" My mother grabbed my arm. "You all get that thing away from here before it gets out and bites somebody to death." Which was not an uncommon occurrence in those days in our swamps and backwoods. Not everybody was armed in those days. Except for my mother, the pistol-packing organist whose sworn enemy was the same as Eve's. "You better take the gun," Mama warned Daddy, but they drove off without it.

"What in the world did you all do with that snake?" she wanted to know, when my father came home, a few hours later into the night. "Fixed a holding pen for it in Burdine's yard," he said. "We wrapped the snake in a tarpaulin and tied it up good. Put it under a big iron washtub, big heavy rocks on top and all around. We're going to take it to Jackson first thing in the morning."

"And what did Celia Burdine say about that snake in her yard?"

"Not a word. You know she's not talking to Pearl." Daddy laughed.

"Hmmph," Mama acknowledged. "You better take the gun."

Next morning early before bright, my father drove over to the Burdines' in the Ford, armed with the sizeable Colt pistol, another tarp, and a snake-head holder he'd fashioned from a fire poker and some croquet hoops. Mr. Burdine had a real one, being a naturalist and Boy Scout leader, but they'd allowed it wasn't big enough for this monster. "The snake's as big around as that plum tree," Daddy explained.

He came back before suppertime, though, sooner than we'd expected. Jackson was about three, four hours away back then, before the Natchez Trace was completed. He shook his head, still frowning. "It got away during the night," he said quietly. "We covered every inch of the Burdine place, over and over again. Cannot understand how it got out, but it did. The people in Jackson are still waiting."

"Mrs. Burdine must be terrified," Mama commented.

"Don't know. She didn't say."

"You all are crazy as coots," said my mother.

I was dying to tell somebody, but my father and Mr. Burdine both made us swear not to tell. They didn't want to be known as responsible for bringing such a dangerous creature into the town. Mr. Burdine especially didn't want the Ellises next door to hear about it, as they'd been feuding over a strip of land between their properties. (I seem to remember that Mrs. Ellis didn't like peacock noises, either.)

About a week later, my father was back on his mail route—he called himself the gossip peddler when he wasn't teaching Bible—where the social aspect of the job was the best part. Everybody would come out to the mailbox to find out what was going on, to share vegetables from their gardens, to buy stamps—or to ask to be taken to the doctor. Mr. Burdine came out, as he did every day, shaking his head, silent. Gone. My father shook his head, raised his eyebrows like he always did when he couldn't solve a puzzle. Gone where?

At the next mailbox, Mrs. Ellis came running out, hoe in hand, panting. "Mr. Booth, Mr. Booth, you've got to come see this. I found the biggest snake I ever saw in my life, right here in my little cotton patch. I like to never killed that thing." She was hysterical. My father got out of the Ford, and walked to the killing field, dreading and hoping at the same time. There, headless and still twitching, lay a cottonmouth, big around as his own thigh or our plum tree, six feet and one inch long if you counted the head. She'd measured it.

He recognized his prize catch, old as the hills and clever enough to have survived many, many years in the Big Black bottom and one night swaddled in burlap sacks, a tied up tarp, under a black wash-pot weighted down with small boulders. "My goodness. That surely is a big snake," allowed my father, keeping a very straight face. "I wish I had my camera."

When he reported the remarkable news at home, my mother said, "Serves you right. You all should have known better than to fool with a moccasin."

She took no measure from moccasins. Once, a few years later after she'd stopped horseback riding and had a car of her own, we drove to Uncle Jimmy's to fish in his pond. She was dressed for the occasion, from ground up: high-top overshoes over her oxfords, brown cotton stockings under my father's paja-ma bottoms, a slender cotton dress under the pajamas to her silky hair piled underneath a broad-brim straw hat. She carried the hoe and the poles, I had bait and tackle box, tagging along behind, walking through high pasture grass when—"Whoo! Stay back, Mary. Stay back. It's a *bad* one. Stay back." "Whoo!" she hollered with each whack of the hoe. "Whoo! Stay back." I couldn't see, nor did I want to move. What if there was more than one? A nest?

"I got him," she said finally. "This hoe was dull. He's huge." And he was. Quite the biggest snake I'd ever seen. A copper-belly copperhead—a con-quest so important we went back to the house so we could call people down to marvel at the size of the thing. "It was a *bad* snake," my mother said, awe in her voice. "I should have had my gun." Thereafter, the pistol lived under-neath the driver's seat, shells in the glove compartment, under every fishing trip "off campus"—in subsequent Fords, Chevys, Jeeps, Studebaker—and finally, a carefully tended boat of an LTD.

The beautiful blue-barreled .410, old to begin with, became too cumbersome, its barrel poking out at her ankles. My brother took it away; it was subsequently stolen. The pistol, however, a heavy old six-shooter, lay beside her as she slept alone after my father went to the nursing home, and later throughout her widowhood. One morning, when she was ninety-three, with one artificial hip and two steel knees, with macular degeneration in her eyes, she looked out onto her back patio and saw . . . another copperhead, sunning itself on the concrete. "Whoo!" she said to Gerlean, her helper, "it's a *bad* snake." Clumping along in her walker, she made her way back to her bedroom, opened the bedside table drawers, fetched the pistol, made her way back to the sliding-glass doors to the patio, and took aim. "Miz Booth," Gerlean cried in horror, "you're going to shoot your foot off." My mother stood just inside the open door, and blew the head off the unwelcome visitor.

Soon after, she stepped down as organist at the church, and reluctantly gave up the wheel of her car. Her eyesight and her mobility had worsened. My son stealthily unloaded her gun—and removed all the bullets from the house. For the next three years, snakes stayed away.

On the day of her wake, at ninety-six, everyone who came to the house was in full Mississippi steam: "Did you see the size of that snake, down at Dobbs Road and 15?" "Whoo! That was a big monster!" Some car had done in the reptile; someone had flung the carcass off the highway so it could inspire snake stories all week. "Mr. Bollis killed one like that with a hoe—got up on his porch." "Biggest snake I ever saw was out at Amos and Andy pond—right where the Leggett boys were grappling catfish." And so on.

"My mother shot snakes like that," I ventured. "You don't mean it!" said one of the deacons who had only known her in her lace dresses or stylish suits, playing Chopin on the piano or "Amazing Grace" on the organ, dignity itself.

The next day, as the funeral procession snaked along highway 15 to turn into LaGrange Road toward the cemetery, everybody craned necks at Dobbs Road, to see if the large, dead body was still there.

It was, lying as if in salute.

The Snake

Michael Collier

A cross of oak twigs marks the place
among the ferns and ivy where the children
dug the grave and coiled the baby python
in the dirt. Why feel regret and sadness
for a thing I would not touch?
Why be anything other than annoyed about the hundred bucks
it cost, on sale! And the accessories—
glass terrarium, heating pad, thermometer,
the driftwood pedestal, the strip of Astro Turf
that lined its floor, and the sun lamp—
that cost as much. Why lament a creature
who stared down the good but nervous meal of mouse
and starved itself? Why write except to notice
how love captures love or how my wife and children
could reach inside the artificial world
and lift the serpent with their hands
and hold it like a pliable divining rod
so they could drape it over their shoulders
and laugh a creepy kind of laugh I've never laughed
as the snake constricts around their necks,
its skin a loose diamond basket weave, its shape
a necklace or a noose.

The Snake and the Reporter

Jim Lehrer

MY SNAKE STORY really began as a names story. It occurred in the news-room of a Dallas newspaper in the late 1960s.

First, the managing editor passed on an ultimatum to me and all other reporters and editors. *Names!* he proclaimed. *The publisher wants more names in this newspaper! Give me names. Names, names and more names. We don't have enough names. Give me names.*

Within minutes a piece of news copy mysteriously—and anonymously—appeared on the newsroom bulletin board. In correct newspaper style there was typed, as if legitimate, the following story:

"Seventy-five thousand six hundred and thirty-two people watched the Texas Longhorns whomp the Oklahoma Sooners 23-3 in their traditional football clash at the Cotton Bowl in Dallas Saturday.

"They were:

"Benjamin B. Adams, John Astin, James F. Bowie, Martha C. Brooks, Josef Caldwell, Mark Carliner, Emanuel F. Chambers, David Wilson Crockett, T. Rex Dickens, Stanley M. Grantland, Harry T. Hines, Billy Bob Inwood, S. Sue Jackson, Joe Kenton, L. Lane, Felix R. McKnight, Henry Morgan, James C. Marquette, Nelson Nathan, Thomas Ogden, Mary Peters, Louise Phinney, Frank Quincy, Houston Samyels, Pamela Tiffin, William Barrett Travis, Jonathan Wayne, Richard Widmark . . ."

You want names. Here were names.

Then a short time later there came from On High an opposite kind of word about snakes.

"From this day forward, this newspaper will no longer publish photo-graphs or stories about snakes," said our editors. "Our ownership and man-agement believe any references to and images of snakes unduly scare our readers, some of whom are women and children."

None of us could recall any recent photo or story in our paper about snakes. What happened? What prompted this antisnake outburst?

"The publisher hates snakes, that's all," we were told. In other words, it was a preemptive strike.

It didn't take long for the newsroom bulletin board to be full of would-be stories that fit the new policy.

"President _____ chose _____ to be his Secretary of State today . . .

"Dallas mayor _____ and city manager _____ agreed today on a new approach to public transportation . . .

"Former Texas governor _____ died today of a _____ bite at his farm in South Texas . . ."

"Congressman _____ today accused Congressman _____ of being a 'real _____-in-the-grass' for his attempts to undermine new funding for a post office in Denton . . ."

"Mr. _____ was a _____-oil salesman in his early years in business before joining General Motors . . ."

The most prominently displayed story was about the publisher of our newspaper.

"Prominent Texas publisher _____ was murdered today in his downtown Dallas office by _____, the paper's society editor. A police spokesman said a poisonous _____ was the murder weapon. The accused, reportedly angered over a sweeping new anti-_____ policy that would eliminate 90 percent of the paper's stories and photos of Dallas high society people, allegedly enticed the _____ to bite the victim on that part of his body on which he was sitting while composing a new direc-tive to his dedicated staff.

"There was no immediate word on the subject of the new directive."

Beneath the story was a piece of layout paper with a blank three-column square box where clearly there was to be no photograph of the deceased.

Mortal Combat

*"Think him as a serpent's egg
which, hatch'd, would, as his kind, grow mischievous,
And kill him in the shell."*
—William Shakespeare,
Julius Caesar, ACT 2, SC. 1

From: *Inez*

Carlos Fuentes

YOU WILL STOP and look at the sea. You will not know how you got here. You will not know what you are supposed to do. You will run your hands over your body and it will feel sticky, smeared from head to toes with the same viscous substance that will coat your face. You will not be able to clean yourself with your hands because they too will be covered. Your hair will be a tangled, filthy nest and a thick paste will dribble down into your eyes, blinding you.

When you wake you will be perched among the branches of a tree with your face cradled against your knees and your hands covering your ears to block out the screeches of the capuchin monkey that will club to death the serpent that will never reach the leafy branches where you will be hiding. The capuchin will be doing what you would like to do yourself. Kill the serpent. Now the serpent will not prevent you from climbing down from the tree. But the strength the monkey will reveal as it kills the serpent will frighten you as much as the threat of the snake, or maybe more.

You will not know how long you will have been here, fem, living alone beneath the jungle canopy. There will be moments when you will not be able to think clearly. You will put a hand to your forehead every time you try to weigh the difference between the threat of the serpent and the violence with which the capuchin will kill it but not kill your fear. You will make a great effort to think that first the serpent will threaten you, and that that will happen *before, before,* and the capuchin monkey will club it and kill it, but that will happen *after, after.*

Now the monkey will lope away with an air of indifference, dragging the heavy stick and making noises with its mouth, moving its tongue the color of salmon. The salmon will swim upriver, against the current: that memory will illuminate you, you will feel happy because for a few instants you will have remembered something—although the next instant you will believe that you have only dreamed, imagined, foreseen it. The salmon will swim against the current to give and to win life, to leave their eggs, to await their hatch. . . . But the capuchin will kill the serpent, that will be certain, as it will also be certain that the monkey will make noises with its mouth as it completes its work, and the serpent will be able to do no more than hiss something with its forked tongue, and it will also be certain that now the animal with spiky bristles will approach the motionless serpent and begin to strip away its jungle-colored skin and devour its moon-colored flesh. It will be time to climb down from the tree. There will be no danger now. The forest will protect you forever. You will always be able to return here and hide in the thicket where there is no sun. . . .

~

Rikki-Tikki-Tavi

Rudyard Kipling

At the hole where he went in
Red-Eye called to Wrinkle-Skin.
Hear what little Red-Eye saith:
"Nag, come up and dance with death!"
Eye to eye and head to head,
(Keep the measure, Nag.)
This shall end when one is dead;
(At thy pleasure, Nag.)
Turn for turn and twist for twist—
(Run and hide thee, Nag.)
Hah! The hooded Death has missed!
(Woe betide thee, Nag!)

This is the story of the great war that Rikki-tikki-tavi fought single-handed, through the bath-rooms of the big bungalow in Segowlee cantonment. Darzee, the tailor-bird, helped him, and Chuchundra, the musk-rat, who never comes out into the middle of the floor, but always creeps round by the wall, gave him advice; but Rikki-tikki did the real fighting.

He was a mongoose, rather like a little cat in his fur and his tail, but quite like a weasel in his head and his habits. His eyes and the end of his restless nose were pink; he could scratch himself anywhere he pleased, with any leg,

front or back, that he chose to use; he could fluff up his tail till it looked like
a bottle-brush, and his war-cry, as he scuttled through the long grass, was:
"*Rikk-tikk-tikki-tikki-tchk!*"

One day, a high summer flood washed him out of the burrow where he
lived with his father and mother, and carried him, kicking and clucking,
down a roadside ditch. He found a little wisp of grass floating there, and
clung to it till he lost his senses. When he revived, he was lying in the hot sun
on the middle of a garden path, very draggled indeed, and a small boy was
saying: "Here's a dead mongoose. Let's have a funeral."

"No," said his mother; "let's take him in and dry him. Perhaps he isn't
really dead."

They took him into the house, and a big man picked him up between his
finger and thumb, and said he was not dead but half choked; so they wrapped
him in cotton-wool, and warmed him, and he opened his eyes and sneezed.

"Now," said the big man (he was an Englishman who had just moved into
the bungalow); "don't frighten him, and we'll see what he'll do."

It is the hardest thing in the world to frighten a mongoose, because he is
eaten up from nose to tail with curiosity. The motto of all the mongoose
family is "Run and find out"; and Rikki-tikki was a true mongoose. He
looked at the cotton-wool, decided that it was not good to eat, ran all
around the table, sat up and put his fur in order, scratched himself, and
jumped on the small boy's shoulder.

"Don't be frightened, Teddy," said his father. "That's his way of making
friends."

"Ouch! He's tickling under my chin," said Teddy.

Rikki-tikki looked down between the boy's collar and neck, snuffed at his
ear, and climbed down to the floor, where he sat rubbing his nose.

"Good gracious," said Teddy's mother, "and that's a wild creature! I suppose he's so tame because we've been kind to him."

"All mongooses are like that," said her husband. "If Teddy doesn't pick
him up by the tail, or try to put him in a cage, he'll run in and out of the
house all day long. Let's give him something to eat."

They gave him a little piece of raw meat. Rikki-tikki liked it immensely,
and when it was finished he went out into the verandah and sat in the sunshine and fluffed up his fur to make it dry to the roots. Then he felt better.

"There are more things to find out about in this house," he said to himself, "than all my family could find out in all their lives. I shall certainly stay
and find out."

He spent all that day roaming over the house. He nearly drowned himself in the bath-tubs, put his nose into the ink on a writing table, and burnt it on the end of the big man's cigar, for he climbed up in the big man's lap to see how writing was done. At nightfall he ran into Teddy's nursery to watch how kerosene-lamps were lighted, and when Teddy went to bed Rikki-tikki climbed up too; but he was a restless companion, because he had to get up and attend to every noise all through the night, and find out what made it. Teddy's mother and father came in, the last thing, to look at their boy, and Rikki-tikki was awake on the pillow. "I don't like that," said Teddy's mother; "he may bite the child." "He'll do no such thing," said the father. "Teddy's safer with that little beast than if he had a bloodhound to watch him. If a snake came into the nursery now—"

But Teddy's mother wouldn't think of anything so awful.

Early in the morning Rikki-tikki came to early breakfast in the verandah riding on Teddy's shoulder, and they gave him banana and some boiled egg; and he sat on all their laps one after the other, because every well-brought-up mongoose always hopes to be a house-mongoose some day and have rooms to run about in, and Rikki-tikki's mother (she used to live in the General's house at Segowlee) had carefully told Rikki what to do if ever he came across white men.

Then Rikki-tikki went out into the garden to see what was to be seen. It was a large garden, only half cultivated, with bushes as big as summer-houses of Marshal Niel roses, lime and orange trees, clumps of bamboos, and thickets of high grass. Rikki-tikki licked his lips. "This is a splendid hunting-ground," he said, and his tail grew bottle-brushy at the thought of it, and he scuttled up and down the garden, snuffing here and there till he heard very sorrowful voices in a thorn-bush.

It was Darzee, the tailor-bird, and his wife. They had made a beautiful nest by pulling two big leaves together and stitching them up the edges with fibres, and had filled the hollow with cotton and downy fluff. The nest swayed to and fro, as they sat on the rim and cried.

"What is the matter?" asked Rikki-tikki.

"We are very miserable," said Darzee. "One of our babies fell out of the nest yesterday, and Nag ate him."

"H'm!" said Rikki-tikki, "that is very sad—but I am a stranger here. Who is Nag?"

Darzee and his wife only cowered down in the nest without answering, for from the thick grass at the foot of the bush there came a low hiss—a horrid cold sound that made Rikki-tikki jump back two clear feet. Then inch by inch out of the grass rose up the head and spread hood of Nag, the big black cobra, and he was five feet long from tongue to tail. When he had lifted one-third of himself clear of the ground, he stayed balancing to and fro exactly as a dandelion-tuft balances in the wind, and he looked at Rikki-tikki with the wicked snake's eyes that never change their expression, whatever the snake may be thinking of.

"Who is Nag?" said he. "*I* am Nag. The great god Brahm put his mark upon all our people when the first cobra spread his hood to keep the sun off Brahm as he slept. Look, and be afraid!"

He spread out his hood more than ever, and Rikki-tikki saw the spectacle-mark on the back of it that looks exactly like the eye part of a hook-and-eye fastening. He was afraid for the minute; but it is impossible for a mongoose to stay frightened for any length of time, and though Rikki-tikki had never met a live cobra before, his mother had fed him on dead ones, and he knew that all a grown mongoose's business in life was to fight and eat snakes. Nag knew that too, and at the bottom of his cold heart he was afraid.

"Well," said Rikki-tikki, and his tail began to fluff up again, "marks or no marks, do you think it is right for you to eat fledglings out of a nest?"

Nag was thinking to himself, and watching the least little movement in the grass behind Rikki-tikki. He knew that mongooses in the garden meant death sooner or later for him and his family, but he wanted to get Rikki-tikki off his guard. So he dropped his head a little, and put it on one side.

"Let us talk," he said. "You eat eggs. Why should not I eat birds?"

"Behind you! Look behind you!" sang Darzee.

Rikki-tikki knew better than to waste time in staring. He jumped up in the air as high as he could go, and just under him whizzed by the head of Nagaina, Nag's wicked wife. She had crept up behind him as he was talking, to make an end of him; and he heard her savage hiss as the stroke missed. He came down almost across her back, and if he had been an old mongoose he would have known that then was the time to break her back with one bite; but he was afraid of the terrible lashing return-stroke of the cobra. He bit, indeed, but did not bite long enough, and he jumped clear of the whisking tail, leaving Nagaina torn and angry.

"Wicked, wicked Darzee!" said Nag, lashing up as high as he could reach toward the nest in the thornbush; but Darzee had built it out of reach of snakes, and it only swayed to and fro.

Rikki-tikki felt his eyes growing red and hot (when a mongoose's eyes grow red, he is angry), and he sat back on his tail and hind legs like a little kangaroo, and looked all round him, and chattered with rage. But Nag and Nagaina had disappeared into the grass. When a snake misses its stroke, it never says anything or gives any sign of what it means to do next. Rikki-tikki did not care to follow them, for he did not feel sure that he could manage two snakes at once. So he trotted off to the gravel path near the house, and sat down to think. It was a serious matter for him.

If you read the old books of natural history, you will find they say that when the mongoose fights the snake and happens to get bitten, he runs off and eats some herb that cures him. That is not true. The victory is only a matter of quickness of eye and quickness of foot,—snake's blow against mongoose's jump,—and as no eye can follow the motion of a snake's head when it strikes, that makes things much more wonderful than any magic herb. Rikki-tikki knew he was a young mongoose, and it made him all the more pleased to think that he had managed to escape a blow from behind. It gave him confidence in himself, and when Teddy came running down the path, Rikki-tikki was ready to be petted.

But just as Teddy was stooping, something flinched a little in the dust, and a tiny voice said: "Be careful. I am death!" It was Karait, the dusty brown snakeling that lies for choice on the dusty earth; and his bite is as dangerous as the cobra's. But he is so small that nobody thinks of him, and so he does the more harm to people.

Rikki-tikki's eyes grew red again, and he danced up to Karait with the peculiar rocking, swaying motion that he had inherited from his family. It looks very funny, but it is so perfectly balanced a gait that you can fly off from it at any angle you please; and in dealing with snakes this is an advantage. If Rikki-tikki had only known, he was doing a much more dangerous thing than fighting Nag, for Karait is so small, and can turn so quickly, that unless Rikki bit him close to the back of the head, he would get the return-stroke in his eye or lip. But Rikki did not know: his eyes were all red, and he rocked back and forth, looking for a good place to hold. Karait struck out. Rikki jumped sideways and tried to run in, but the wicked little dusty gray head lashed within a fraction of his shoulder, and he had to jump over the body, and the head followed his heels close.

Teddy shouted to the house: "Oh, look here! Our mongoose is killing a snake"; and Rikki-tikki heard a scream from Teddy's mother. His father ran out with a stick, but by the time he came up, Karait had lunged out once too far, and Rikki-tikki had sprung, jumped on the snake's back, dropped his head far between his fore-legs, bitten as high up the back as he could get hold, and rolled away. That bite paralysed Karait, and Rikki-tikki was just going to eat him up from the tail, after the custom of his family at dinner, when he remembered that a full meal makes a slow mongoose, and if he wanted all his strength and quickness ready, he must keep himself thin.

He went away for a dust-bath under the castor-oil bushes, while Teddy's father beat the dead Karait. "What is the use of that?" thought Rikki-tikki. "I have settled it all"; and then Teddy's mother picked him up from the dust and hugged him, crying that he had saved Teddy from death, and Teddy's father said that he was a providence, and Teddy looked on with big scared eyes. Rikki-tikki was rather amused at all the fuss, which, of course, he did not understand. Teddy's mother might just as well have petted Teddy for playing in the dust. Rikki was thoroughly enjoying himself.

That night, at dinner, walking to and fro among the wine-glasses on the table, he could have stuffed himself three times over with nice things; but he remembered Nag and Nagaina, and though it was very pleasant to be patted and petted by Teddy's mother, and to sit on Teddy's shoulder, his eyes would get red from time to time, and he would go off into his long war-cry of "Rikk-tikk-tikki-tikki-tchk!"

Teddy carried him off to bed, and insisted on Rikki-tikki sleeping under his chin. Rikki-tikki was too well bred to bite or scratch, but as soon as Teddy was asleep he went off for his nightly walk round the house, and in the dark he ran up against Chuchundra, the musk-rat, creeping round by the wall. Chuchundra is a broken-hearted little beast. He whimpers and cheeps all the night, trying to make up his mind to run into the middle of the room, but he never gets there.

"Don't kill me," said Chuchundra, almost weeping. "Rikki-tikki, don't kill me."

"Do you think a snake-killer kills musk-rats?" said Rikki-tikki scornfully.

"Those who kill snakes get killed by snakes," said Chuchundra, more sorrowfully than ever. "And how am I to be sure that Nag won't mistake me for you some dark night?"

"There's not the least danger," said Rikki-tikki; "but Nag is in the garden, and I know you don't go there."

"My cousin Chua, the rat, told me——" said Chuchundra, and then he stopped.

"Told you what?"

"H'sh! Nag is everywhere, Rikki-tikki. You should have talked to Chua in the garden."

"I didn't—so you must tell me. Quick Chuchundra, or I'll bite you!"

Chuchundra sat down and cried till the tears rolled off his whiskers. "I am a very poor man," he sobbed. "I never had spirit enough to run out into the middle of the room. H'sh! I mustn't tell you anything. Can't you *hear*, Rikki-tikki?"

Rikki-tikki listened. The house was as still as still, but he thought he could just catch the faintest *scratch-scratch* in the world,—a noise as faint as that of a wasp walking on a window-pane—the dry scratch of a snake's scales on brick-work.

"That's Nag or Nagaina," he said to himself; "and he is crawling into the bath-room sluice. You're right Chuchundra; I should have talked to Chua."

He stole off to Teddy's bath-room, but there was nothing there, and then to Teddy's mother's bathroom. At the bottom of the smooth plaster wall there was a brick pulled out to make a sluice for the bath-water, and as Rikki-tikki stole in by the masonry curb where the bath is put, he heard Nag and Nagaina whispering together outside in the moonlight.

"When the house is emptied of people," said Nagaina to her husband, "*he* will have to go away, and then the garden will be our own again. Go in quietly, and remember that the big man who killed Karait is the first one to bite. Then come out and tell me, and we will hunt for Rikki-tikki together."

"But are you sure that there is anything to be gained by killing the people?" said Nag.

"Everything. When there were no people in the bungalow, did we have any mongoose in the garden? So long as the bungalow is empty, we are king and queen of the garden; and remember that as soon as our eggs in the melon-bed hatch (as they may to-morrow), our children will need room and quiet."

'I had not thought of that," said Nag. "I will go, but there is no need that we should hunt for Rikki-tikki afterward. I will kill the big man and his wife, and the child if I can, and come away quietly. Then the bungalow will be empty, and Rikki-tikki will go."

Rikki-tikki tingled all over with rage and hatred at this, and then Nag's head came through the sluice, and his five feet of cold body followed it. Angry as he was, Rikki-tikki was very frightened as he saw the size of the big cobra. Nag coiled himself up, raised his head, and looked into the bath-room in the dark, and Rikki could see his eyes glitter.

"Now, if I kill him here, Nagaina will know; and if I fight him on the open floor, the odds are in his favour. What am I to do?" said Rikki-tikki-tavi.

Nag waved to and fro, and then Rikki-tikki heard him drinking from the biggest water-jar that was used to fill the bath. "That is good," said the snake. "Now, when Karait was killed, the big man had a stick. He may have that stick still, but when he comes in to bathe in the morning he will not have a stick. I shall wait here till he comes. Nagaina—do you hear me?—I shall wait here in the cool till daytime."

There was no answer from outside, so Rikki-tikki knew Nagaina had gone away. Nag coiled himself down, coil by coil, round the bulge at the bottom of the water-jar, and Rikki-tikki stayed still as death. After an hour he began to move, muscle by muscle, toward the jar. Nag was asleep, and Rikki-tikki looked at his big back, wondering which would be the best place for a good hold. "If I don't break his back at the first jump," said Rikki, "he can still fight; and if he fights—O Rikki!" He looked at the thickness of the neck below the hood, but that was too much for him; and a bite near the tail would only make Nag savage.

"It must be the head," he said at last; "the head above the hood; and when I am once there, I must not let go."

Then he jumped. The head was lying a little clear of the water-jar, under the curve of it; and, as his teeth met, Rikki braced his back against the bulge of the red earthenware to hold down the head. This gave him just one second's purchase, and he made the most of it. Then he was battered to and fro as a rat is shaken by a dog—to and fro on the floor, up and down, and round in great circles; but his eyes were red, and he held on as the body cart-whipped over the floor, upsetting the tin dipper and the soap-dish and the flesh-brush, and banged against the tin side of the bath. As he held he closed his jaws tighter and tighter, for he made sure he would be banged to death, and, for the honour of his family, he preferred to be found with his teeth locked. He was dizzy, aching, and felt shaken to pieces when something went off like a thunderclap just behind him; a hot wind knocked him sense-less, and red fire singed his fur. The big man had been wakened by the noise, and had fired both barrels of a shot-gun into Nag just behind the hood.

Rikki-tikki held on with his eyes shut, for now he was quite sure he was dead; but the head did not move, and the big man picked him up and said: "It's the mongoose again, Alice; the little chap has saved *our* lives now." Then Teddy's mother came in with a very white face, and saw what was left of Nag, and Rikki-tikki dragged himself to Teddy's bedroom and spent half the rest of the night shaking himself tenderly to find out whether he was really broken into forty pieces, as he fancied.

When morning came he was very stiff, but well pleased with his doings. "Now I have Nagaina to settle with, and she will be worse than five Nags, and there's no knowing when the eggs she spoke of will hatch. Goodness! I must go and see Darzee," he said.

Without waiting for breakfast, Rikki-tikki ran to the thorn-bush where Darzee was singing a song of triumph at the top of his voice. The news of Nag's death was all over the garden, for the sweeper had thrown the body on the rubbish-heap.

"Oh, you stupid tuft of feathers!" said Rikki-tikki angrily. "Is this the time to sing?"

"Nag is dead—is dead—is dead!" sang Darzee. "The valiant Rikki-tikki caught him by the head and held fast. The big man brought the bang-stick, and Nag fell in two pieces! He will never eat my babies again."

"All that's true enough; but where's Nagaina?" said Rikki-tikki, looking carefully round him.

"Nagaina came to the bath-room sluice and called for Nag," Darzee went on; "and Nag came out on the end of a stick—the sweeper picked him up on the end of a stick and threw him upon the rubbish-heap. Let us sing about the great, the red-eyed Rikki-tikki!" and Darzee filled his throat and sang.

"If I could get up to your nest, I'd roll all your babies out!" said Rikki-tikki. "You don't know when to do the right thing at the right time. You're safe enough in your nest there, but it's war for me down here. Stop singing a minute, Darzee."

"For the great, the beautiful Rikki-tikki's sake I will stop," said Darzee. "What is it, O Killer of the terrible Nag?"

"Where is Nagaina, for the third time?"

"On the rubbish-heap by the stables, mourning for Nag. Great is Rikki-tikki with the white teeth."

"Bother my white teeth! Have you ever heard where she keeps her eggs?"

"In the melon-bed, on the end nearest the wall, where the sun strikes nearly all day. She hid them there weeks ago."

"And you never thought it worth while to tell me? The end nearest the wall, you said?"

"Rikki-tikki, you are not going to eat her eggs?"

"Not eat exactly; no. Darzee, if you have a grain of sense you will fly off to the stables and pretend that your wing is broken, and let Nagaina chase you away to this bush. I must get to the melon-bed, and if I went there now she'd see me."

Darzee was a feather-brained little fellow who could never hold more than one idea at a time in his head; and just because he knew that Nagaina's children were born in eggs like his own, he didn't think at first that it was fair to kill them. But his wife was a sensible bird, and she knew that cobra's eggs meant young cobras later on; so she flew off from the nest, and left Darzee to keep the babies warm, and continue his song about the death of Nag. Darzee was very like a man in some ways.

She fluttered in front of Nagaina by the rubbish heap, and cried out, "Oh, my wing is broken! The boy in the house threw a stone at me and broke it." Then she fluttered more desperately than ever.

Nagaina lifted up her head and hissed, "You warned Rikki-tikki when I would have killed him. Indeed and truly, you've chosed a bad place to be lame in." And she moved toward Darzee's wife, slipping along over the dust.

"The boy broke it with a stone!" shrieked Darzee's wife.

"Well! It may be some consolation to you when you're dead to know that I shall settle accounts with the boy. My husband lies on the rubbish-heap this morning, but before the night the boy in the house will lie very still. What is the use of running away? I am sure to catch you. Little fool, look at me!"

Darzee's wife knew better than to do *that*, for a bird who looks at a snake's eyes gets so frightened that she cannot move. Darzee's wife fluttered on, piping sorrowfully, and never leaving the ground, and Nagaina quickened her pace.

Rikki-tikki heard them going up the path from the stables, and he raced for the end of the melon-patch near the wall. There, in the warm litter about the melons, very cunningly hidden, he found twenty-five eggs, about the size of a bantam's eggs, but with whitish skin instead of shell.

"I was not a day too soon," he said; for he could see the baby cobras curled up inside the skin, and he knew that the minute they were hatched they could each kill a man or a mongoose. He bit off the tops of the eggs as fast as he could, taking care to crush the young cobras, and turned over the litter from time to time to see whether he had missed any. At last there were only three eggs left, and Rikki-tikki began to chuckle to himself, when he heard Darzee's wife screaming:

"Rikki-tikki, I led Nagaina toward the house, and she has gone into the verandah, and—oh, come quickly—she means killing!"

Rikki-tikki smashed two eggs, and tumbled backward down the melon-bed with the third egg in his mouth, and scuttled to the verandah as hard as he could put foot to the ground. Teddy and his mother and father were there at early breakfast; but Rikki-tikki saw that they were not eating anything.

They sat stone-still, and their faces were white. Nagaina was coiled up on the matting by Teddy's chair, within easy striking-distance of Teddy's bare leg, and she was swaying to and fro singing a song of triumph.

"Son of the big man that killed Nag," she hissed, "stay still. I am not ready yet. Wait a little. Keep very still, all you three. If you move I strike, and if you do not move I strike. Oh, foolish people, who killed my Nag!"

Teddy's eyes were fixed on his father, and all his father could do was to whisper, "Sit still, Teddy. You mustn't move. Teddy, keep still."

Then Rikki-tikki came up and cried: "Turn round Nagaina; turn and fight!"

"All in good time," said she, without moving her eyes. "I will settle my account with *you* presently. Look at your friends, Rikki-tikki. They are still and white; they are afraid. They dare not move, and if you come a step nearer I strike."

"Look at your eggs," said Rikki-tikki, "in the melon-bed near the wall. Go and look, Nagaina."

The big snake turned half round, and saw the egg on the verandah. "Ah-h! Give it to me," she said.

Rikki-tikki put his paws one on each side of the egg, and his eyes were blood-red. "What price for a snake's egg? For a young cobra? For a young king-cobra? For the last—the very last of the brood? The ants are eating all the others down by the melon-bed."

Nagaina spun clear round, forgetting everything for the sake of the one egg; and Rikki-tikki saw Teddy's father shoot out a big hand, catch Teddy by the shoulder, and drag him across the little table with the teacups, safe and out of reach of Nagaina.

"Tricked! Tricked! Tricked! *Rikk-tchk-tchk!*" chuckled Rikki-tikki. "The boy is safe, and it was I—I—I that caught Nag by the hood last night in the bathroom." Then he began to jump up and down, all four feet together, his head close to the floor. "He threw me to and fro, but he could not shake me off. He was dead before the big man blew him in two. I did it. *Rikki-tikki-tchk-tchk!* Come then, Nagaina, Come and fight with me. You shall not be a widow long."

Nagaina saw that she had lost her chance of killing Teddy, and the egg lay between Rikki-tikki's paws. "Give me the egg, Rikki-tikki. Give me the last of my eggs, and I will go away and never come back," she said, lowering her hood.

"Yes, you will go away, and you will never come back; for you will go to the rubbish-heap with Nag. Fight, widow! The big man has gone for his gun! Fight!"

Rikki-tikki was bounding all round Nagaina, keeping just out of reach of her stroke, his little eyes like hot coals. Nagaina gathered herself together, and flung out at him. Rikki-tikki jumped up and backward. Again and again and again she struck, and each time her head came with a whack on the matting of the verandah, and she gathered herself together like a watch-spring. Then Rikki-tikki danced in a circle to get behind her, and Nagaina spun round to keep her head to his head, so that the rustle of her tail on the matting sounded like dry leaves blown along by the wind.

He had forgotten the egg. It still lay on the verandah, and Nagaina came nearer and nearer to it, till at last, while Rikki-tikki was drawing breath, she caught it in her mouth, turned to the verandah steps, and flew like an arrow down the path, with Rikki-tikki behind her. When the cobra runs for her life, she goes like a whip-lash flicked across a horse's neck.

Rikki-tikki knew that he must catch her, or all the trouble would begin again. She headed straight for the long grass by the thorn-bush, and as he was running Rikki-tikki heard Darzee still singing his foolish little song of triumph. But Darzee's wife was wiser. She flew off her nest as Nagaina came along, and flapped her wings about Nagaina's head. If Darzee had helped they might have turned her; but Nagaina only lowered her hood and went on. Still, the instant's delay brought Rikki-tikki up to her, and as she plunged into the rat-hole where she and Nag used to live, his little white teeth were clenched on her tail, and he went down with her—and very few mongooses, however wise and old they may be, care to follow a cobra into its hole. It was dark in the hole; and Rikki-tikki never knew when it might open out and give Nagaina room to turn and strike at him. He held on savagely, and struck out his feet to act as brakes on the dark slope of the hot, moist earth.

Then the grass by the mouth of the hole stopped waving, and Darzee said: "It is all over with Rikki-tikki! We must sing his death song. Valiant Rikki-tikki is dead! For Nagaina will surely kill him underground."

So he sang a very mournful song that he made up on the spur of the minute, and just as he got to the most touching part the grass quivered again, and Rikki-tikki, covered with dirt, dragged himself out of the hole leg by leg, licking his whiskers. Darzee stopped with a little shout. Rikki-tikki shook some of the dust out of his fur and sneezed. "It is all over," he said. "The widow will never come out again." And the red ants that live between the grass stems heard him, and began to troop down one after another to see if he had spoken the truth.

Rikki-tikki curled himself up in the grass and slept where he was—slept and slept till it was late in the afternoon, for he had done a hard day's work.

"Now," he said, when he awoke, "I will go back to the house. Tell the Coppersmith, Darzee, and he will tell the garden that Nagaina is dead."

The Coppersmith is a bird who makes a noise exactly like the beating of a little hammer on a copper pot; and the reason he is always making it is because he is the town-crier to every Indian garden, and tells all the news to everybody who cares to listen. As Rikki-tikki went up the path, he heard his "attention" notes like a tiny dinner-gong; and then the steady *"Ding-dong-tock! Nag is dead—dong! Nagaina is dead! Ding-dong-tock!"* That set all the birds in the garden singing, and frogs croaking; for Nag and Nagaina used to eat frogs as well as little birds.

When Rikki got to the house, Teddy and Teddy's mother (she still looked very white, for she had been fainting) and Teddy's father came out and almost cried over him; and that night he ate all that was given him till he could eat no more, and went to bed on Teddy's shoulder, where Teddy's mother saw him when she came to look late at night.

"He saved our lives and Teddy's life," she said to her husband. "Just think, he saved all our lives!"

Rikki-tikki woke up with a jump, for all the mongooses are light sleepers.

"Oh, it's you," said he. "What are you bothering for? All the cobras are dead; and if they weren't, I'm here."

Rikki-tikki had a right to be proud of himself; but he did not grow too proud, and he kept that garden as a mongoose should keep it, with tooth and jump and spring and bit, till never a cobra dared show its head inside the walls.

~

Darzee's Chaunt

(SUNG IN HONOUR OF
RIKKI-TIKKI-TAVI)

Singer and tailor am I—
Doubled the joys that I know—
Proud of my lilt through the sky,
Proud of the house that I sew—
Over and under, so weave I my music—so weave I the
house that I sew.
Sing to your fledglings again,
Mother, oh lift up your head!
Evil that plagued us is slain,
Death in the garden lies dead.
Terror that hid in the roses is impotent—flung on the
dung-hill and dead!
Who hath delivered us, who?
Tell me his nest and his name.
Rikki, the valiant, the true,
Tikki, with eyeballs of flame,
Rik-tikki-tikki, the ivory-fanged, the hunter with eye-
balls of flame.
Give him the Thanks of the birds,
Bowing with tail-feathers spread!
Praise him with nightingale-words—
Nay, I will praise him instead.
Hear! I will sing you the praise of the bottle-tailed
Rikki, with eyeballs of red!
(Here Rikki-tikki interrupted, and the rest of the song is lost.)

~

Imitating the Anaconda

Susan Kinsolving

Open wide. Wider. Unhinge your jaws. Wider.
Now swallow that piglet. Gulp again. Go a-
head. There it goes! Down to its tiny twisted
tail. Your gastric juices will dissolve skin, bone
teeth, hair. (Feathers too!) Size can't stop you: feels great
to engorge and ingurgitate. There's nothing
quite like being fed an idea bigger
than your head, a thought that takes days to digest
will duly internalize to manifest.

~

The Green Mamba

(*from*: GOING SOLO)

Roald Dahl

OH, THOSE SNAKES! How I hated them! They were the only fearful thing about Tanganyika, and a newcomer very quickly learnt to identify most of them and to know which were deadly and which were simply poisonous. The killers, apart from the black mambas, were the green mambas, the cobras and the tiny little puff adders that looked very much like small sticks lying motionless in the middle of a dusty path, and so easy to step on.

One Sunday evening I was invited to go and have a sundowner at the house of an Englishman called Fuller who worked in the Customs office in Dar es Salaam. He lived with his wife and two small children in a plain white wooden house that stood alone some way back from the road in a rough grassy piece of ground with coconut trees scattered about. I was walking across the grass towards the house and was about twenty yards away when I saw a large green snake go gliding straight up the veranda steps of Fuller's house and in through the open front door. The brilliant yellowy-green skin and its great size made me certain it was a green mamba, a creature almost as deadly as the black mamba, and for a few seconds I was so startled and dumbfounded and horrified that I froze to the spot. Then I pulled myself together and ran round to the back of the house shouting, "Mr. Fuller! Mr. Fuller!"

Mrs. Fuller popped her head out of an upstairs window. "What on earth's the matter?" she said.

"You've got a large green mamba in your front room!" I shouted. "I saw it go up the veranda steps and right in through the door!"

"Fred!" Mrs. Fuller shouted, turning round. "Fred! Come here!"

Freddy Fuller's round red face appeared at the window beside his wife. "What's up?" he asked.

"There's a green mamba in your living-room!" I shouted.

Without hesitation and without wasting time with more questions, he said to me, "Stay there. I'm going to lower the children down to you one at a time." He was completely cool and unruffled. He didn't even raise his voice.

A small girl was lowered down to me by her wrists and I was able to catch her easily by the legs. Then came a small boy. Then Freddy Fuller lowered his wife and I caught her by the waist and put her on the ground. Then came Fuller himself. He hung by his hands from the window-sill and when he let go he landed neatly on his two feet.

We stood in a little group on the grass at the back of the house and I told Fuller exactly what I had seen.

The mother was holding the two children by the hand, one on each side of her. They didn't seem to be particularly alarmed.

"What happens now?" I asked.

"Go down to the road, all of you," Fuller said. "I'm off to fetch the snake-man." He trotted away and got into his small ancient black car and drove off. Mrs. Fuller and the two small children and I went down to the road and sat in the shade of a large mango tree.

"Who is this snake-man?" I asked Mrs. Fuller.

"He is an old Englishman who has been out here for years," Mrs. Fuller said. "He actually *likes* snakes. He understands them and never kills them. He catches them and sells them to zoos and laboratories all over the world. Every native for miles around knows about him and whenever one of them sees a snake, he marks its hiding place and runs, often for great distances, to tell the snake-man. Then the snake-man comes along and captures it. The snake-man's strict rule is that he will never buy a captured snake from the natives."

"Why not?" I asked.

"To discourage them from trying to catch snakes themselves," Mrs. Fuller said. "In his early days he used to buy caught snakes, but so many natives got bitten trying to catch them, and so many died, that he decided to put a stop to it. Now any native who brings in a caught snake, no matter how rare, gets turned away."

"That's good," I said.

"What is the snake-man's name?" I asked.

"Donald Macfarlane," she said. "I believe he's Scottish."

"Is the snake in the house, Mummy?" the small girl asked.

"Yes, darling. But the snake-man is going to get it out."

"He'll bite Jack," the girl said.

"Oh, my God!" Mrs. Fuller cried, jumping to her feet. "I forgot about Jack!" She began calling out, "Jack! Come here, Jack! Jack! . . . Jack! . . . Jack!"

The children jumped up as well and all of them started calling to the dog. But no dog came out of the open front door.

"He's bitten Jack!" the small girl cried out. "He must have bitten him!" She began to cry and so did her brother who was a year or so younger than she was. Mrs. Fuller looked grim.

"Jack's probably hiding upstairs," she said. "You know how clever he is."

Mrs. Fuller and I seated ourselves again on the grass, but the children remained standing. In between their tears they went on calling to the dog.

"Would you like me to take you down to the Maddens' house?" their mother asked.

"No!" they cried. "No, no, no! We want Jack!"

"Here's Daddy!" Mrs. Fuller cried, pointing at the tiny black car coming up the road in a swirl of dust. I noticed a long wooden pole sticking out through one of the car windows.

The children ran to meet the car. "Jack's inside the house and he's been bitten by the snake!" they wailed. "We know he's been bitten! He doesn't come when we call him!"

Mr. Fuller and the snake-man got out of the car. The snake-man was small and very old, probably over seventy. He wore leather boots made of thick cowhide and he had long gauntlet-type gloves on his hands made of the same stuff. The gloves reached above his elbows. In his right hand he carried an extraordinary implement, an eight-foot-long wooden pole with a forked end. The two prongs of the fork were made, so it seemed, of black rubber, about an inch thick and quite flexible, and it was clear that if the fork was pressed against the ground the two prongs would bend outwards, allowing the neck of the fork to go down as close to the ground as necessary. In his left hand he carried an ordinary brown sack.

Donald Macfarlane, the snake-man, may have been old and small but he was an impressive-looking character. His eyes were pale blue, deep-set in a face round and dark and wrinkled as a walnut. Above the blue eyes, the eyebrows were thick and startlingly white but the hair on his head was almost black. In spite of the thick leather boots, he moved like a leopard, with soft slow cat-like strides, and he came straight up to me and said, "Who are you?"

"He's with Shell," Fuller said. "He hasn't been here long."

"You want to watch?" the snake-man said to me.

"Watch?" I said, wavering. "Watch? How do you mean watch? I mean where from? Not in the house?"

"You can stand out on the veranda and look through the window," the snake-man said.

"Come on," Fuller said. "We'll both watch."

"Now don't do anything silly," Mrs. Fuller said.

The two children stood there forlorn and miserable, with tears all over their cheeks.

The snake-man and Fuller and I walked over the grass towards the house, and as we approached the veranda steps the snake-man whispered, "Tread softly on the wooden boards or he'll pick up the vibration. Wait until I've gone in, then walk up quietly and stand by the window."

The snake-man went up the steps first and he made absolutely no sound at all with his feet. He moved soft and cat-like onto the veranda and straight through the front door and then he quickly but very quietly closed the door behind him.

I felt better with the door closed. What I mean is I felt better for myself. I certainly didn't feel better for the snake-man. I figured he was committing suicide. I followed Fuller onto the veranda and we both crept over to the window. The window was open, but it had a fine mesh mosquito-netting all over it. That made me feel better still. We peered through the netting.

The living-room was simple and ordinary, coconut matting on the floor, a red sofa, a coffee-table and a couple of armchairs. The dog was sprawled on the matting under the coffee-table, a large Airedale with curly brown and black hair. He was stone dead.

The snake-man was standing absolutely still just inside the door of the living-room. The brown sack was now slung over his left shoulder and he was grasping the long pole with both hands, holding it out in front of him, parallel to the ground. I couldn't see the snake. I didn't think the snake-man had seen it yet either.

A minute went by . . . two minutes . . . three . . . four . . . five. Nobody moved. There was death in that room. The air was heavy with death and the snake-man stood as motionless as a pillar of stone, with the long rod held out in front of him.

And still he waited. Another minute . . . and another . . . and another.

And now I saw the snake-man beginning to bend his knees. Very slowly he bent his knees until he was almost squatting on the floor, and from that position he tried to peer under the sofa and the armchairs.

And still it didn't look as though he was seeing anything.

Slowly he straightened his legs again, and then his head began to swivel around the room. Over to the right, in the far corner, a staircase led up to the floor above. The snake-man looked at the stairs, and I knew very well what was going through his head. Quite abruptly, he took one step forward and stopped.

Nothing happened.

A moment later I caught sight of the snake. It was lying full-length along the skirting of the right-hand wall, but hidden from the snake-man's view by the back of the sofa. It lay there like a long, beautiful, deadly shaft of green glass, quite motionless, perhaps asleep. It was facing away from us who were at the window, with its small triangular head resting on the matting near the foot of the stairs.

I nudged Fuller and whispered, "It's over there against the wall." I pointed and Fuller saw the snake. At once, he started waving both hands, palms outward, back and forth across the window hoping to get the snake-man's attention. The snake-man didn't see him. Very softly, Fuller said, "Pssst!" and the snake-man looked up sharply. Fuller pointed. The snake-man understood and gave a nod.

Now the snake-man began working his way very, very slowly to the back wall of the room so as to get a view of the snake behind the sofa. He never walked on his toes as you or I would have done. His feet remained flat on the ground all the time. The cowhide boots were like moccasins, with neither soles nor heels. Gradually, he worked his way over to the back wall, and from there he was able to see at least the head and two or three feet of the snake itself.

But the snake also saw him. With a movement so fast it was invisible, the snake's head came up about two feet off the floor and the front of the body arched backwards, ready to strike. Almost simultaneously, it bunched its whole body into a series of curves, ready to flash forward.

The snake-man was just a bit too far away from the snake to reach it with the end of his pole. He waited, staring at the snake and the snake stared back at him with two small malevolent black eyes.

Then the snake-man started speaking to the snake. "Come along, my pretty," he whispered in a soft wheedling voice. "There's a good boy. Nobody's going to hurt you. Nobody's going to harm you, my pretty little thing. Just lie still and relax. . . ." He took a step forward towards the snake, holding the pole out in front of him.

What the snake did next was so fast that the whole movement couldn't have taken more than a hundredth of a second, like the flick of a camera shutter. There was a green flash as the snake darted forward at least ten feet and struck at the snake-man's leg. Nobody could have got out of the way of that one. I heard the snake's head strike against the thick cowhide boot with a sharp little *crack*, and then at once the head was back in the same deadly back-ward-curving position, ready to strike again.

"There's a good boy," the snake-man said softly. "There's a clever boy. There's a lovely fellow. You mustn't get excited. Keep calm and everything's going to be all right." As he was speaking, he was slowly lowering the end of the pole until the forked prongs were about twelve inches above the middle of the snake's body. "There's a lovely fellow," he whispered. "There's a good kind little chap. Keep still now, my beauty. Keep still, my pretty. Keep quite still. Daddy's not going to hurt you."

I could see a thin dark trickle of venom running down the snake-man's right boot where the snake had struck.

The snake, head raised and arcing backwards, was as tense as a tight-wound spring and ready to strike again. "Keep still, my lovely," the snake man whispered. "Don't move now. Keep still. No one's going to hurt you."

Then *wham*, the rubber prongs came down right across the snake's body, about midway along its length, and pinned it to the floor. All I could see was a green blur as the snake thrashed around furiously in an effort to free itself. But the snake-man kept up the pressure on the prongs and the snake was trapped.

What happens next? I wondered. There was no way he could catch hold of that madly twisting flailing length of green muscle with his hands, and even if he could have done so, the head would surely have flashed around and bitten him in the face.

Holding the very end of the eight-foot pole, the snake man began to work his way around the room until he was at the tail end of the snake. Then, in spite of the flailing and the thrashing, he started pushing the prongs forward along the snake's body towards the head. Very, very slowly he did it, pushing the rubber prongs forward over the snake's flailing body, keeping the snake pinned down all the time and pushing, pushing, pushing the long wooden rod forward millimeter by millimeter. It was a fascinating and frightening thing to watch, the little man with white eyebrows and black hair carefully manipulating his long implement and sliding the fork ever so slowly along the length of the twisting snake towards the head. The snake's body was thumping against the coconut matting with such a noise that if you had been upstairs you might have thought two big men were wrestling on the floor.

Then at last the prongs were right behind the head itself, pinning it down, and at that point the snake-man reached forward with one gloved hand and grasped the snake very firmly by the neck. He threw away the pole. He took the sack off his shoulder with his free hand. He lifted the great still twisting length of the deadly green snake and pushed the head into the sack. Then he let go the head and bundled the rest of the creature in and closed the sack. The sack started jumping about as though there were fifty angry rats inside it, but the snake-man was now totally relaxed and he held the sack casually in one hand as if it contained no more than a few pounds of pota-toes. He stooped and picked up his pole from the floor, then he turned and looked towards the window where we were peering in.

"Pity about the dog," he said. "You'd better get it out of the way before the children see it."

From: *I Dreamed of Africa*

CHAPTER THIRTY:
The Snake of Good Luck

Kuki Gallmann

WE HAD A wonderful time at Easter, with all the Douglas-Hamiltons stay-ing. We went for early-morning walks with Oria and Iain and Luka, rhino-tracking, and we watched elephants drinking at the treetop tank and at Paolo's Dam at Kuti.

The treetop was a simple look-out which I had built on the top of a large gerardia, in a favourite site for elephant. One could climb the tree and hide high among the branches like a bird in a nest, looking out unseen from the concealing leaves at the animals coming to drink at the water tank just below. So close were the elephants that one could smell them, and the sucking of their trunks in the silted water and the low stomach rumbles were the only noise in the high silence of noon.

Emanuele took off on his motorbike one morning to visit Ferina, who was staying with her family for a few days down at Baringo, and on his way back in the evening he ran out of petrol just inside the ranch. He called us on the hand-set radio, and I went to look for him with Saba, bringing a full jerrycan of fuel. We found the bike in the middle of a path, but no sign of Ema. I could not even find his tracks in the dust, as if he had vanished into the air. It was by now evening, and there were signs of elephant everywhere, and leopard spoor. We searched for him, calling, and just as I was beginning to get worried, a stifled giggle attracted our attention. Emanuele was perched on the very top of a large *Acacia gerardia* drinking a beer, laughing down at us. Saba jumped on the back of the bike and I drove behind them.

In the car lights, eyes of secret creatures shone phosphorescent. Hair windblown, talking and laughing to each other in the majestic African night with its shapes and shadows, they were a picture of youth, privilege and freedom which I shall not forget.

For lunch the next day I made a gigantic Easter egg for Sveva, and chocolate bunnies for everybody. Oria took photographs of Emanuele sitting at the head of the table in the place which had been Paolo's, Sveva on his lap and Saba and Dudu each holding an assorted handful of harmless green grass snakes and sand snakes, each girl with a snake or two coiled around her neck.

We went for a barbecue picnic down the river at Mukutan Spring. On our way we saw many vultures gathering at a spot just close to the road, where we found a young eland just killed by a lion. Emanuele and Luka carved the fillet out for us and we left the rest to the lion. Emanuele had come with his blue-and-yellow Yamaha, and Oria took photographs of him overtaking the car. In the evening, I noticed the youngsters plotting something, and Kipiego and Rachel came in grinning and served me a round chocolate flan on a silver platter, which turned out to be a large elephant turd covered in cocoa and coloured sugar, and decorated with flowers.

The evening had ended with Emanuele and the girls, who looked beautiful in tight leopard- and tiger-patterned leotards, dancing on the cedar beams of the sitting-room roof to the music of "Cat's People," and of Emma's favourite tape of the time, "Heat of the Moment." Iain, Oria and I, the older generation at floor level, dressed in ample caftans, laughed and took photographs of the sleek young ones dancing above. Moments of happiness forever frozen in memory.

The news came as a shock at breakfast on Easter Monday, passed on through the Laikipia Security network. Jack Block had died while trout-fishing in a river in Chile, where Jeremy now lived. The body had not been found and it was not clear whether he had drowned, or whether he had had a stroke. Jack's brother Tubby and his wife Aino had been up in Laikipia only a few days before for Paolo's anniversary. Involved in wildlife conservation and in tourism, Jack was a popular figure in the country, respected and admired by African and European alike. Lively and interesting, compassionate and loyal, it was hard to believe he had met such an odd, dramatic death in a far-away country.

The news shocked us all and cast a shadow on our day. It made me reflect once again on the thin thread which separates us from disappearing into nothingness. I became pensive, and for the rest of the day we were all quiet. I decided to drive down next day to Nairobi to offer Tubby my condolences.

In the afternoon, Emanuele asked me to go fishing with him and he drove me to the Big Dam. The mood still hung on me, and I ended up sitting on the shore looking at him casting and swiftly getting one black bass after another.

Sitting there on the rocky red earth, I talked to him about the temporariness of our passage on earth, and about the importance of living in the here and now. I spoke of Paolo and of his feelings for this place, our commitment to keep the balance between the wild and the tame. Again I told him about my last Will in case anything happened to me. He listened in silence, apparently absorbed in his fishing, and so quiet was he that I almost thought he had not paid attention. When I finished, he folded the rod, put it neatly aside, and came towards me. He sat on his haunches just in front of me, looked straight into my eyes and said seriously: "Fine, Pep. I got all that. Now I would like to tell you what I would like you to do if I die first."

The sun was setting behind the dam wall, and in the evening shadows I could not see his eyes. A flock of pelicans landed in the water feet first, balanced on wide white wings, with hardly a ripple.

"You cannot die. You are seventeen." Even to me, the feeble denial sounded lame.

He did not note my interruption. "I would like to be buried close to Paolo. I would like a yellow fever tree on my grave too. For the music, *Bolero*, by Ravel. That cushion you made for me, with NO, PEP embroidered on it, under my head. Champagne, for my anniversary. And, as you just said to me, I also would like you to go on with life and to take care of Sveva."

In the fear which gripped my mind, I could only realize that he had thought about this before. On the mirror-like surface of the lake a fish jumped. A loud chattering of birds heralded the approaching silence of the night. My voice was hollow and out came only a whisper. "Whatever could you die of, at your age?"

A sudden smile transformed his face for a second, and in that moment I knew what he was going to say. He squeezed my hand, as if to reassure me. His voice was quiet, patient, with just a touch of irony, as if explaining the obvious to a child. He chose Swahili, as if the exotic language was more appropriate to an exotic death: *"Nyoka tu"* ("Just a snake").

He stood up. I stared at his long bare legs, covered almost to the knee in the motorbike boots. I had not yet noticed how tall he had grown in recent months. In the stillness before night fell, darkness gathered fast, painting greys and blacks on what seconds before had been molten gold and vivid warmth. It was as if only he and I remained in all the world. I shivered. "Please don't. If you died, it would be my end also."

He collected the rod and the fish, and started walking towards the car. I could sense he was smiling, "No, Pep. You are a survivor. You will make it. Let's go and clean this fish."

A reply died on my lips. We drove home in silence.

~

After the intense weekend everyone seemed tired. Emanuele wrote his diary as usual, the slim muscular legs in tight jeans outstretched in front of him. The white shirt with a round open collar, and a blue waistcoat, set off his young, strong neck. Oria took a few more photographs at the table, catching his serious eyes in the flickering candlelight, and the dark halo of his hair.

The Douglas-Hamiltons left early next morning for the coast. Emanuele drove them to the airstrip, and they flew back to Kuti for the customary goodbye, flying low over Paolo's grave and down towards me. Having anticipated Iain's trick of making me go down flat on my stomach I stood with my back to the tallest petria for protection, waving and sending kisses to their four smiling faces.

I drove straight to Nairobi to see Tubby. Jack's body had been finally found and it was discovered that he had died of a heart attack after all. Perhaps, to his fisherman's heart, the largest trout he had ever caught had brought too much joy. There would be a memorial service later in the month at Longonot Farm in Naivasha. I promised I would come down for it, and I drove back to Laikipia the same day. I was uneasy, with a sense of foreboding, and I wanted to be with my children.

All seemed fine there, but Emanuele told me next morning that his female cobra had escaped. He was worried because she had been sick with a sort of mouth rot, and he was determined to find her. I was playing with Sveva, a round fair little angel, when he approached us across the lawn, and I could see from the look on his face that something had happened to upset him. A snake was slung across his shoulder, looking limp and dead. It was larger and thicker than I had imagined, and it was the cobra.

"I killed her," Emanuele announced in his matter-of-fact voice, but with a tinge of regret. "Mapengo and I smoked her out of the hole where she was hiding. We miscalculated the amount of smoke and she suffocated. Her heart has stopped. She's quite dead. It is my fault."

It often happened that I could foresee what Emanuele was about to say. Now, I saw a thought dart through his mind, and I knew he was thinking of an episode which occurred a few days earlier, when Colin had revived a young calf by blowing down its lungs through a pipe. We had been very impressed, and Emanuele had asked many questions. Now he stood suddenly, a determined expression in his eyes, and started walking towards the house, the snake swinging around his neck like a thick wet towel, saying over his shoulder, "I am getting one of those silver straws of yours from the bar. The ones you use for Pimm's. I'll try to revive her."

I closed my eyes wearily. There seemed to be no end to this. Yet Emanuele had a way of making even something as absurd as trying to revive a spitting cobra through mouth-to-mouth resuscitation seem a perfectly normal exercise. Sensing my dismay, he stopped for a moment and came back a few paces to reassure me. "She has no spit left anyway. She has just spat from the hole, at my goggles." He pointed to the goggles hanging round his neck, smudged with grey, sticky saliva. I shuddered.

When he came back a little later, I could see he had succeeded. His face was slight, transformed as only his face could be. He explained to me how the heart had started beating again, and the elation he had felt at being able to resuscitate her. That night he described the story in his diary in great detail and ended: ". . . and if she lives, I shall call her Bahati, 'the Snake of Good Luck," because she came back from the dead."

It had worked for the snake.

~

CHAPTER THIRTY-ONE:
The End of the World

"... Who is Mungu?" I asked.
"Mungu lives up there," they answered, "and if he wants you to live,
you live and if he wants you to die, you die."

Llewelyn Powys, *Confessions of Two Brothers*

IT BEGAN LIKE any other day with the tea brought after a knock at the door
of my bedroom in Laikipia. Simon's smiling *"Jambo Memsaab,"* and all the
dogs coming in to greet me, cold noses against my cheek and tails wagging.
Simon's tall frame was silhouetted against the windows as he pulled the curtains to let in a fierce sun. It was already hot. The rains were late. It was 12
April 1983, during the Easter holidays. Soon after Sveva came in, hugging her
favourite African doll. She was two-and-a-half years old, a blonde cherub
with deep blue eyes and beautiful easily tanned peach-bronze skin, like Paolo.

I was drinking my tea when Emanuele knocked and walked in, followed
by his dog Angus, a large yellow Alsatian, the best-looking of Gordon's sons,
and stopped at the foot of my bed. I observed how tall he had become, how
broad were his shoulders, and how his shaven jaw was no longer a child's. He
wore khaki shorts and a khaki shirt, sleeves rolled at the elbows. From the
belt hung a knife, and the inevitable snake-tongs. He was seventeen. A handsome young man with quiet ways, a brilliant mind and an intriguing personality, which made him extremely attractive to girls.

"Buongiorno, Pep," he said with his new husky man-voice, "can I have a
rubber band?"

I knew what he wanted the rubber band for. He used them regularly, to tighten a piece of plastic round the neck of a sterilized jar. He would push the glass against the fangs of a deadly puff-adder viper. The gland was squeezed against the rim of the glass, and the venom spurted out in a spray. Emanuele then crystallized it, using a chemical procedure. We found the band.

"I am going to milk the snakes."

"I hate you doing that," I could not help saying.

He looked at me in his peculiar way, straight in the eye, with just a glint of amusement. "You always worry. I have done it dozens of times." I knew he was right.

His face was suddenly transformed by one of his unexpected smiles, he touched Sveva's cheek affectionately, and he was gone, his dog following.

I stood looking at him from the door.

Off he went in the light of the early morning, with the shadow of the house on the lawn, as the sun rose behind it. His shadow was long on the grass and the sun on his back streaked his hair with a golden halo. He was young and strong and handsome . . . and no longer mine. He walked in long easy strides through the glory of the bushes in bloom, under the shade of the yellow fever trees, the snake-tongs swinging at his waist, past the swimming-pool, towards the snake pit.

He went away, and he never turned back.

I watched him with a strange feeling about me, like a cloud of premonition which closed round my stomach like a painful fist. When I could see him no longer the lawn looked suddenly empty. I sighed, and went to have my shower. Sveva followed me, with her doll. I was toweling my hair dry when I realized someone was knocking.

The urgency made the glass of the door rattle and my saliva dry out. I stopped drying my hair and shouted in answer: *"Kitu gani?"* ("What happens?").

"Mama." Only Mapengo, Emanuele's snake man, called me then "Mama," the familiar respectful African way of addressing a married woman. His voice sent a chill down my spine. It was low and altered, unnaturally hesitant and unrecognizable. In the hollow stillness of doom, the only sound was the echo of my terror.

"Mama, *iko taabu kidogo.* . . ." ("There is a small problem. . . .").

"Emanuele? *Nyoka?"* ("A snake?")

"Ndiyo." ("Yes.")

"Terepupa?" ("A puff-adder?")

"Ndiyo."

"Wapi?" ("Where?")

"Gikoni." ("In the kitchen.")

I did not stop to think for a second. With a conscious effort which took everything out of me, I refused to indulge in useless despair. Not just yet. I knew I could not afford hysterics, and I knew I could not lose time. I was alone, far from help, twenty minutes' drive from our airstrip and eight kilometers from Colin's house. I was the only one who could drive, and the only one who could help. I also knew that if I lost my head nothing could be done to save him. . . . Save him? I knew instinctively it was already too late, but that I had to try in every way I could.

That day and the night and the day which followed, I shed layers of my being as a snake sheds its skin. I kept coming in and out of myself, watching myself acting as from a great distance, and suddenly re-entering my body and the agony of my tormented soul.

Now I watched one part of me splitting from the other, and taking over.

The new Kuki grabbed yesterday's clothes from the laundry basket. Like an efficient, emotionless robot, she took the glasses without which she knew she could not see, and the hand-set radio. Before reaching the door in two strides she was already screaming into the set, trying to keep her voice steady and clear. "Emanuele has been bitten by a puff-adder. A puff-adder. Very seriously. Call the flying doctors. Now. Immediately. I am driving him down." She repeated the message twice, in English and Swahili, while running towards the kitchen, ignoring Sveva's bewildered screams, and once she was sure the message had been received, threw the radio aside. The stones of the passage were cold under her running bare feet. She was there.

The kitchen walls were green and the silence hung like a shroud. They stood silent as only Africans can, and the eyes moved to her in unison, expressionless, then returned to the shape on the floor.

Emanuele sat rigid, legs spread out on the green cement, facing the window. With a feeling of overwhelming unreality, she crouched in front of him. From his open mouth, green saliva dribbled in ugly bubbles. The skin was grey, the eyes staring and glassy. She waved a hand in front of them and he did not flinch. With a pang of anguish, she realized he was blind.

At that moment, I again became his mother.

With his right hand, he cradled his left: in the first joint of the index finger was a tiny black mark, unswollen, which he had already cut with his knife. No blood: the snakebite.

I looked at the fingers with the very short nails and the brass bracelet around his wrist, the gift of a girl he would kiss no more. I took his hand gently in mine and I sucked the small wound from which the life I had given him was seeping away. I sucked and I spat and nothing came out.

Where was the adrenalin? Where did he say he kept it? Was there time to look for it? The serum. In the fridge. Now. In the urgency, I tore the fridge door from the hinges: the uncanny strength of despair and impotence.

"Emanuele. Emanuele *ascoltami. Ti taglio la mano?* Do I cut your hand? Do I cut your arm?" Useless questions dictated by hopelessness and desperation. Emanuele was dying and I knew there was nothing I could do. Bitten in the snake pit with a lethal dose, he had climbed out, walked all the way to the kitchen and collapsed there. Through the exertion, the poison had reached his heart. His blood was coagulating.

"Emanuele." My desperation to make contact a last time, to hear again his voice, to bring him back to consciousness. Was he deaf too? This could not really be happening to me.

The eyes flickered weakly, focused on mine for an instant with immense fatigue, and there was a faint glimmer of recognition. The strangled voice was no longer his voice. There was no fear and no expression in it.

The pain in my chest matched his. For a moment my vision blackened, and I forgot to breathe.

"*Mamma,*" he whispered hoarsely, slowly, in Italian.

"*Muoio, mamma.*" I am dying, mamma.

With irreversible agony I realized he had called me "mother" for the first time in his life.

These were his last words.

~

I tried to remember afterwards if there had been any note of fear, of regret, of pain and horror in his voice. But there was only an expressionless certitude of the inevitability of his death. He knew well and accepted what was happening: as he knew—and I did not—that he had already been bitten too many times by vipers, and that another bite would be fatal.

His eyes clouded again and the body became rigid. Still holding his hand I lifted my eyes to Simon's. I read in them what I could not yet accept. Like all the rest he was waiting for a signal, an order about what to do next. My voice sounded unnaturally calm and far away. The other Kuki, "Simon, Mapengo.

Weka yeye kwa gari maramoja. Beba yeye pole pole. Sisi nakwenda saa hi." ("Carry him gently to the car immediately. Do not let him move. We go now.")

Of all the things I have ever done and will ever do in my life, the worst by far was having to drive my dying son to bring him to useless help. We carried him like a rigid log of wood and laid him on the back seat. Simon sat with Ema's head on his lap and Mapengo jumped in the boot. The noise of the engine drowned Sveva's screams. I would have to take care of her later. The gardeners and house-servants stood watching, mute, in a line, without waving.

I put my foot down on the accelerator and my hand on the horn. We took off, skidding in a cloud of dust and blaring noise I did not hear, wheels biting the road without mercy, careless of pot-holes and rocks . . . I kept switching my eyes from the road to the rear mirror which reflected Emanuele's grey face and staring eyes. There was nothing I wanted to do more than to hold him and kiss him and touch him, but I had to drive, I had to concentrate on the road.

Two giraffes crossed the track at the Kati Kati *boma* just in front of us, and the outraged trumpeting of a small herd of elephant I disturbed faded in the speed. Just before reaching the Centre I almost hit a donkey cart, and at that moment I felt a surge of pain in my limbs which came in waves, and my womb contracted as if giving birth. A voice, unrecognizable, was wailing loudly: who was it? I moved my head to look at Emanuele in the mirror and I stared at my face with an open mouth: I was screaming. Simon's hand had come forward and turned the mirror towards me so that I could not look.

I stopped on Colin's back lawn. The smell of burnt tyres hung in the air with the noise of the brakes when I erupted from the car. It seemed like a film in slow motion. Colin, Rocky, their children, the dogs . . . coming towards us, a question in their eyes.

I was past minding. I had gone to hell and died with him, and now the world could just crumple and swallow me for all I cared.

It is never so simple.

"He is dead," I just said. The voice, like my body no longer belonged to me. There was this disembodied numbness.

Colin was already opening the door, pulling him out, feeling his pulse, listening to his chest. "No. He is still alive. Just. Come on, Ema! Quick, Kuki! Mouth-to-mouth resuscitation. You. Now. I will do heart massage."

That other Kuki, with a face of stone, knelt on the grass over the young man's face. Numberless times she blew into his mouth while Simon held his head. It felt heavy on her bare legs. The lips were cold, like some resilient rubber. Air frothed back with saliva. Colin worked rhythmically on his chest. How long it went on I will never know, as time had ceased to matter. Nothing else existed but my boy's face and his mouth and my mouth and my wild hope, and my despair. I prayed to the unknown God who grants us life. I promised Him all I had, all I was, in exchange for that one life.

God did not hear me.

I concentrated on breathing my life back into Emanuele, pouring it out of me with all my love. I went on and on and on until I realized that a hand was heavy on my shoulder and a voice—Colin's voice—was saying: "Stop. He is gone, Kuki. Oh shit. Oh shit, Ema. He is gone, there is nothing you can do."

~

Slowly I lifted my head and looked up at the sky of Africa. The first to break the silence—it seemed to me—were the cicadas. Then the thousand hidden birds. Through the canopy of leaves above. I could see white clouds moving soundlessly. I waited quietly for the earth to crack open and swallow us all. The world went on as ever. The hills were as blue, the breeze as gentle.

From a great distance my voice said, "He was my son."

Colin's fingers dug deeper in my shoulder.

I looked up for my boy's smiling face soaring like a freed bird above the treetops.

"Where has he gone?"

Colin's voice had a broken edge when he answered quietly, "He is watching you, Kuki. He is right up there with Paolo. They are having a good laugh together."

Good, sane, dependable Colin. He knew these were only words, which could give me no comfort. I looked into Simon's antique eyes and in their mute depths I recognized my grief. I looked at Mapengo. He was crying without noise. *"Wapi yeye?"* ("Where has he gone?") I repeated, and did not need an answer. Time stood still.

A silent group of Africans had gathered around us in a circle. I had not seen them coming. Now I noticed their bare legs like a *boma* of wooden sticks, their patched trousers, old *shukas*, bare feet, rubber sandals, worn safari boots. I looked at their expressionless faces, one by one.

Emanuele's head was heavier on my lap.

I sat there, watching his young dead face, cradling it gently, not to hurt him more. A shadow of moustache on his upper lip. A tiny mole I had never noticed before on the cheekbone. A leather string around his strong neck with a Turkana charm which had not helped. The brown eyes were glazed and open, staring up and reflecting a sky he could no longer see. If I had to go on living, this was the turning-point, the pivot around which whatever happened to me after would revolve forever.

With Simon's apron, I wiped his mouth, his nose. A caress on his fore-head, to tidy his hair. A kiss, two kisses, to close his eyes forever.

The eyelids felt fragile, like petals of gardenia.

It had happened again. I, too had died. Another stage of my life had again ended. I, too, was now born new.

The other Kuki stood up and I heard her saying: "Let's bring him home, to bury him."

A ray of sun touched my cheeks, and it was a cool, lifeless sun, which bore no arrows.

~

From: *A Man in Full*

Tom Wolfe

AT SIXTY, CHARLIE COKER *is still a man's man, a heavily muscled specimen in love with his own machisimo, a former college football hero who is reminded of his days of gridiron glory with every gimpy step that he takes in a world that is suddenly closing in around him. He is a real estate developer, who escaped rural poverty by riding Atlanta's explosive growth to a position of fabulous wealth. His assets include Turpmtine, a 29,000-acre quail plantation with a "Big House" dating from the 1830s and a mile-long landing strip to handle Coker's Gulfstream Five. Coker also owns a wholesale food operation with a global reach—a solid business investment that he little values because it lacks the raw sex appeal of acquiring a landed empire and then building huge structures on it as granite monuments to his own towering will. The only problem is that he is a plunger more than an investor and his real pride and joy, the 40-story Coker Concourse, is just half occupied and hemorrhaging money because Coker became too greedy for cheap land and built the thing in a location not easily accessible from Atlanta.*

And so now he is nearly $100 million behind in his payments on a $515 million loan from PlannersBanc with an additional $285 million owed to other lenders. A "workout" session at the bank has gone badly for Coker, leaving him feeling humiliated in front of his own people.

Desperate at the prospect of being financially ruined, Coker goes straight from the bank to his Gulfstream to fly back to Turpmtine to steady his nerves. On the flight, Wismer Stroock—

"Wiz"—suggests that he consider selling the plantation. Coker counters by proposing a 15-percent payroll cut at Croker Global Foods. Wiz, his financial officer and a "technogeek," tells him that it's a bad idea. Meanwhile, the sight of Turpmtine appearing beneath the Gulfstream's wings is indeed a tonic. Charlie Croker, for the moment at least, can feel his manhood reviving.

~

It was breathtaking—*breath*taking! Charlie felt a catch in his throat.

The G-5 was now beyond the Big House. Lud was bringing it down close to Jookers Swamp before swinging about and heading into the glide path to the landing strip. Down this low, and with so little foliage on the trees, you could clearly see the stands of cypress and black tupelo maple rising out of the water . . . You could see their huge swollen knees just above the waterline . . . And there was the Jook House, a big white clapboard structure on stilts, cantilevered out over the water, which he had built as a twelve-bedroom guest house . . . Cost $2.4 million . . . Oh, how flush he had felt! . . . way back then . . .

The landing strip was an alley of asphalt cut through a pine forest. It was almost a mile long, so as to accommodate a jet this big. . . . What with the landing lights, the maintenance hangar and its asphalt apron, the fuel pumps, and the access roads that had to be built, the whole thing had cost him $3.6 million. He thought about that as the pines whizzed by in a blur on either side, and they glided in and touched down for the landing.

When they reached the hangar apron, Durwood was out there with the big Chevrolet Suburban, as promised, and Rufus Dotson, the black man who was in charge of the crew that maintained the runway and the hangar, was standing beside it. As soon as Charlie slid himself out from under his tupelo desk, he could tell his right knee had stiffened. He didn't want to be seen hobbling down the stairs, not even in front of Durwood and Rufus, but it couldn't be helped. His knee hurt so much he had to hold on to the cable that served as a railing. When he reached the bottom, Rufus was right there waiting. He was a short, squarely built man, in his fifties—or his sixties—with dark skin and gray hair that stuck out on either side of his head. He wore an old-fashioned cap, like a golfer's cap, that covered the top of his head, which was bald. He touched the cap's little visor, respectfully, with the thumb and forefinger of his right hand and said:

"How you doing, Cap'm Charlie? Lemme give you a hand." He reached out with his big, powerful right hand. He was wearing a long-sleeved gray work shirt of a sort you seldom saw anymore, buttoned at the wrist, and a pair of jeans.

"Aw, 'at's all right, Rufus," said Charlie, who would rather have died than be helped down those stairs, "it's jes'at damn knee a mine, from playin' football."

Rufus chuckled deep in his throat and said, "You don' have to tell me 'bout the rheumatiz, Cap'm Charlie."

Mine's not rheumatism, damn it, Charlie wanted to say, mine's from *football!*

All around were the deep cooling shadows of the pines, which reached up a hundred feet or more, but out here on the hangar apron it was painfully bright. Charlie squinted. Mirage slicks flared up in front of your eyes when you looked back down the runway, and caloric waves rose from the asphalt. It made him feel hot and tired and weak. Durwood was ambling over from the Suburban.

"Hey, Cap'm," said Durwood, "Mr. Stroock."

Every time Charlie saw this big man and heard his deep Baker County voice, he just knew that he was the archetype of what the overseers had been back when overseers rode herd on the field hands who were slashing pine out in that murderous heat ten or twelve hours a day, not only before the Civil War but for a good fifty years afterward. Slashing pine was as hellish as working in the pulp mills, the way Uncle Bud told it. It drove men so close to the ragged edge, the overseers used to sleep with loaded shotguns by their beds. That Durwood could have lived such a life Charlie had not the slightest doubt. He was stone-cold Georgia Cracker, top to bottom. He was one of those big men who are more intimidating in middle age than ever before, because their hide has gotten tougher and they've learned what it takes to be mean in a calculating way, which is the meanest way of all. He was about Charlie's height, a few inches over six feet. His head and neck were huge, and everything seemed to droop, his eyes, his cheeks, his nose, his mouth, which gave him a perpetual scowl. His beefy shoulders drooped, his huge chest drooped, and his belly drooped over his belt, and some sort of horrible and irresistible power seemed to be packed inside all that flesh. He wore a khaki-colored shirt with the sleeves rolled up over his immense forearms and khaki balloon-seat twill pants whose cuffs rested on top of a pair of old battered calf-high boots of the sort that anybody in Baker County who spent time in the fields wore as protection against the rattlesnakes, which usually went for the ankles. Riding on top of his big hips was a gunbelt and a holster with the handle of a huge .45-caliber revolver showing. The revolver was for shooting snakes.

"Hey, Durwood," said Charlie, "'zat First Draw's foal I saw ovair kickin' up his heels when we was comin' down?" He said it mainly to get some conversation going. To keep everybody thinking about something else while he step-*gimped*-step-*gimped*-step-*gimped*-step-*gimped*-step-*gimped*-step-*gimped* the twenty or thirty feet to the Suburban.

"S'peck hit was, Cap," said Durwood. "Tale you what. If you'n Mr. Stroock ain't too hungry yet, ahmoan swing on ovair fo' we git to the Gun House. 'At's the biggest, kickin'est dayum foal—I ain' never seed one 'at big, not fer no dayum two days old, anyhows."

So the three of them, Charlie, Durwood, and Wismer Stroock, got in the Suburban, and they swung on over there by the stables and the enclosure where First Draw's big foal was kicking up his heels. No sooner did they get out of the vehicle than they saw five or six of the black stablehands and the two little Australians, Johnny Groyner, the stud manager, and Melvin Bonnetbox, his steerer, standing in a semicircle out on a whitish sandy road where it emerged from the palmetto scrub and wire grass into the open space by the stable. They were so absorbed in whatever it was they were looking at, they barely even noticed that the Suburban had pulled up with their overseer, Durwood, and the master of Turpmtine, Cap'm Charlie Croker.

Durwood didn't take that too well, not with his boss having just arrived. "Hey!" he yelled out. "Cain chew boys think a nuthin' to do 'cep clusterfuckin' inna ballin' sun?" *Clusterfucking* was a term Durwood had picked up in Vietnam, where soldiers in the field weren't supposed to gather in clusters, lest all be wiped out by a single strike.

To Durwood's—and Charlie's—surprise, Johnny Groyner, a chesty elf with a close-cropped ginger-red beard, turned toward them and put his forefinger to his lips and motioned with his other hand as if to say, "Come on over and take a look at this."

So Durwood, the Wiz, and Charlie, limping worse than ever, walked on over, and right away they saw what all the fuss was about. On the edge of the road, next to a clump of palmetto scrub and wire grass, out in the boiling sun, was a diamondback rattlesnake, a huge one, six feet long if it was an inch, maybe seven . . . motionless . . . torpid . . .

A cold-blooded creature, it had found that toasty stretch of sandy road out in the sunshine of an April afternoon . . . and was soaking it up, oblivious to the growing audience. It was a monster, even for a part of Georgia notorious for big rattlers. It had such girth that you could see its skin's entire pattern of big and small brown diamonds outlined in black against a tan field. The stablehands stood a respectful distance to the rear. No one dared approach the head. Rattlers had no lids over their eerie vertical slits-for-eyes, and no one knew whether they actually slept or not.

One of the black stablehands, Sonny Colquitt, said, "Hey, Cap'm Charlie! What you want to do with that big sucker? Want me git a hoe?" He meant a hoe to chop the head off with.

Charlie stared at Sonny. Then he stared at the snake, which was a magnificent brute. And then he was aware that everybody else, including Durwood and the Wiz, was staring at him, Cap'm Charlie.

So he said to Sonny, "Go git me a croker sack."

He motioned toward the stable, and Sonny hightailed it toward the stable to get a croker sack, that being the local term for a burlap bag. While Sonny was gone, Charlie took off his jacket and loosened his necktie. He didn't care if they saw his saddlebags, because they wouldn't know what they came from, and nobody in Baker County was surprised to see a man sweating in the first place. Mainly he wanted to give them a proper eyeful of his huge chest, his broad back, his massive neck. Gimp or no gimp, he was still Cap'm Charlie Croker.

In no time Sonny was back with the croker sack. He handed it to Charlie. Charlie held the sack in his left hand and stepped through the semicircle of gawkers, right between the other Australian elf, Melvin Bonnetbox, and one of the new black employees, Kermit Hoyer, and advanced toward the snake. Step-*gimp*-step-*gimp*-step-*gimp*-step-*gimp* . . . he walked as slowly and softly as he could . . . pausing by the row of rattles . . . eight of them . . . still had the original button, or so it looked like . . . And now he crept on toward the head, and a strange and wondrous thing happened. The pain began to recede from his knee. He was now close enough to the beast's head to see its graceful heart shape and the sinister but beautiful mask of black that ran across its face and eyes. And now he stepped across its body, so that he was straddling the great somnolent brute.

He knew that what he was about to do was foolhardy—and he knew he would do it anyway. The only sane way to go about it would be to get a sapling branch and whittle it into a forked stick and pin the snake's head down first. But by the time he managed to get a forked stick made, the beast might come to and retreat into the underbrush, and everybody would just be staring at poor, feckless, gimped-up Cap'm Charlie. No, there was no other choice but the foolhardiest possible way.

He could no longer hear a thing from the outside world. A rushing sound, like steam, filled his skull. He was no longer aware of telling his sixty-year-old body what to do. He crouched, he leaned over at the waist, and—

—a flash of white filled his brain, and he thrust his right hand down and grabbed the rattlesnake around the neck at the base of its skull. With a single motion he straightened up and swept the reptile off the ground and held its head out in front of himself at arm's length.

He had done it! He had done it right! Right behind the jaws he had him! One inch off in either direction—one slip of the fingers—and the brute would have sunk its fangs into his forearm—but *he had done it!*

The snake was now six or seven feet of writhing bestial anger. Its huge mouth was wide open, and its two fangs, which were truly like hypodermic needles, were erect, and it bit at the air, and great gouts of yellowish venom spurted from the fangs, and its forked black tongue flicked in every direction, and a hissing sound burst from its throat. The beast was more than six feet of muscle, vertebrae, and ribs, literally hundreds of ribs, and it lashed about until Charlie wondered if he could maintain his grip much longer. A heavy musk, like a skunk's, spewed from the snake's body and choked the air, and to Charlie in that moment it was as rich as frankincense and myrrh. But above all, there was the sound of the rattles.

A chattering terror fills the place!

That was from a poem about rattlesnakes by somebody—Somebody Harte?—that Charlie had read in high school. It was one of the few poems he had ever willingly memorized.

The wild bird hears; smote with the sound,
As if by bullet brought to ground;
On broken wing, dips wheeling round!

Smote with the sound! Full-grown, one-ton horses would bolt on you when they heard the terrible castanet of the rattlesnake. That sound seemed to be a trigger of terror built into the nervous system of every creature possessing the sense of hearing, including, above all, man.

Charlie turned and held out the rattling beast toward everyone in the semicircle, and they all shrank back, even Durwood, as if the incredible Cap'm Charlie were about to march upon them and cram the venomous serpent down somebody's windpipe.

In fact, Charlie wondered how much longer he could hold the damned thing. Seldom did a rattler weigh more than five pounds, but this one did, and it was thrashing with tremendous jerks and spasms. On the other hand, as Charlie well knew, it couldn't thrash like a buggy whip, and it couldn't wrap itself around his arm. It could only thrash from side to side, in a later-al plane, and once its belly lost contact with the ground it was disoriented. The Wiz, he noted with grim satisfaction, had now drifted back a full twenty feet. He Who Would Live Forever had done an instantaneous back-of-the-envelope calculation and decided that the vicinity of the Chevrolet Suburban was a better strategic alternative than anyplace anywhere near that whitish sandy road above which a gigantic terror-chattering rattlesnake now thrashed in the grip of his boss gone berserk.

Charlie gave them all one more terrible look down the gaping, venom-spouting gullet, and then he flopped the mouth of the croker sack open with his left hand and thrust the head of the rattler down into the bottom of it. Then he released his grip on the snake and jerked his right hand and arm out of the sack and drew the drawstring tight and held the sack aloft by the strings. The sack was now a hive of primal anger. The burlap thrashed about furiously, the clattering terror filled the place, and you could see the beast's fangs knifing through the fabric's loose weave and squirting its seemingly inexhaustible supply of venom into the air.

"Awright, y'all," said Charlie in a tone of coldest command, "c'mon ov'ere."

He started walking toward the Snake House, which was about fifty yards beyond the stable. He held the croker sack far out from his shoulder, suspended by the drawstrings. He'd known of cases where men had got bitten by diamondbacks because they let the bag get too close to their bodies. The strain on his arm was fierce, but he was damned if he was going to ask anybody else to help him; not now he wasn't, not after having gone this far. Out of the corner of his eye he could see the others forming behind him in a straggling line . . . with the Wiz bringing up the rear. He could hear a couple of the stablehands going, "Unnnh-unnnhhh-*unnnnnhhhhhh.*" It was music to his ears.

Charlie's body was gimping on him a little bit, but he didn't feel a thing. He felt light on his feet. He felt as if he was floating. He had . . . *done it.* And he was about to . . . *do more.*

Inside, as well as outside, the Snake House was an absolute jewel of a little building; or that was the way Charlie saw it. Outside, its octagonal, almost circular, shape and its ancient red brick (meticulously hunted down by Ronald Vine) and its white wooden trim and its heavy slate roof made it look like one of those little buildings Charlie had seen when he was in Virginia and had visited Monticello and Colonial Williamsburg. Up on top, where the eight sides of the roof came to a point, instead of a weather vane or anything like that, there was the bronze sculpture of a coiled rattlesnake. Inside—and this had been Ronald Vine's true stroke of genius—the Snake

House's tiny interior was lined with what at first looked like some sort of lurid wallpaper. But then you realized the stripes were in fact rattlesnake skins, flattened out and stretched up vertically and touching, edge to edge, so that they created a vast field of rough, scaly diamonds. Around the lower part of the little eight-sided room ran an ornate white wainscoting, and at the top of the wainscoting was a wide white counter, and in the center of the counter on each of seven wall sections of the octagon—the eighth was devoted to the doorway—was a big glass aquarium, or, better said, terrarium, and in each terrarium were live snakes from the fields and swamps of Turpmtine: rattlers, copperheads, cottonmouths, and corals . . . all of them poisonous and all of them deadly.

There were plenty of Turpmtine employees, black and white, who didn't even like to go *inside* the Snake House. They had a sound instinct: you steer clear of snakes, and when you see them, you kill them. Some of the boys believed snakes were the Devil's agents. So the little band that followed Cap'm Charlie into the Snake House—they were quieter than they would have been if they were going into a Methodist church.

Charlie carried his croker sack over to the far wall, where there was a terrarium with six huge rattlesnakes, each one almost as big as the one in the sack, slithering around one another like the Devil making his appearance on earth in a slimy moving knot of coils bristling with fangs and swollen with pent-up venom. Sonny, Durwood, Kermit, Johnny, and Bonnie, as Melvin Bonnetbox was called—all of them hung back. The Wiz *truly* hung back; he made sure he was nearer the door than the terrarium.

Charlie shifted the croker sack from his left hand to his right hand, and then, without asking anybody's help or looking at a soul, he lifted up one end of the wire-mesh grille over the terrarium and laid the mouth of the croker sack on the lip of the glass. Then he lifted the bottom of the croker sack up to about a 60-degree angle. You could see the snakes in the bottom of the terrarium looking up at the croker sack and Charlie's bare left hand and wrist. Then you could see the head of the rattler in the croker sack beginning to protrude from the sack's mouth. That head and those fangs and that venom were no more than six inches from Charlie's left hand, which held up the lid. Now more and more of the snake's huge body began to slither out the mouth of the sack. Suddenly the serpent thrust its entire body, all six or seven feet of it, out of the croker sack and flopped down among its brethren in the bottom of the terrarium and joined the moving knot of slithering coils.

Ever so gingerly, Charlie lowered the lid and withdrew the croker sack. For a moment he just stood there and stared at the seven rattlesnakes inside the terrarium. The biggest of them all, the newcomer, the monster he had picked up with his bare hand, slithered about among all the deadly coils in a state of high agitation.

Then Charlie stepped back about two feet and stared some more. Out of the corners of his eyes he noticed that the boys, including even the Wiz, had now stepped forward to get a closer look. So he reached in his pants pocket, withdrew his car keys, concealing them in his fist. He stared at the serpents a few beats longer—then suddenly threw the keys against the side of the terrarium. The angry newcomer struck the spot first, his fangs smashing into the glass, but the other six hit the same spot, fangs bared, within the next fraction of a second. Everybody in the room, except for Charlie, jumped back, as if rocked by an explosion. Even Durwood; even Sonny; and the Wiz, He Who Would Live Forever, was almost out the door.

Charlie turned around and let his gaze run over the whole bunch of them, one by one, and then he said, in the calmest voice imaginable, "Boys, that's one damn fine snake."

~

Outside the snake house, as they dispersed, the others were conversing excitedly with one another. But not the Wiz; he was standing alone, his hands in his pockets. Charlie walked over to him, and he wasn't conscious of any gimp at all in his right leg. He put his arm around the young man's shoulders, and he said:

"Wiz, I been thinking it over. I've made up my mind. We're gonna do it. We're gonna lay off 15 percent of the food division."

The Wiz didn't look at his boss. He just nodded yes and looked straight ahead. Behind the titanium frames his bar-code-scanner eyes were open wide enough to take in the world.

Charlie Croker felt almost whole again.

~

The Cobra

Ogden Nash

This creature fills its mouth with venom
And walks upon its duodenum.
He who attempts to tease the cobra
Is soon a sadder he, and sobra.

~

Henry Aaron

PASSIVE COBRA

Ira Berkow

ATLANTA, AUGUST, 1973

First of all, Hank Aaron's swing is all wrong. He hits off his front foot. The great hitting textbook in the sky says you swing with the weight more on your back foot to get—the irony for Aaron—more power.

This is not so bad as when he first played in the Negro Leagues in 1952 and batted cross-handed. That's right, cross-handed; like your Aunt Fanny at the family picnic.

And Hank Aaron looks so passive at the plate, no trace of the cobra he is. Passive to a point, that is. If one has even the most cursory knowledge of those formidable serpents, it is understood that they are passive only when undisturbed. Roused, they are lethal. It is known widely that Hank Aaron looks less than fondly upon pitchers, who are to batters mortal enemies. And when a pitcher hurls a sphere toward one such as Aaron, it, to be sure, disturbs him. End of passivity.

"Henry Aaron is the only ballplayer I have ever seen who goes to sleep at the plate," said former big league pitcher Curt Simmons. "But trying to sneak a fast ball past him is like trying to sneak the sunrise past a rooster." Or, like a fat rat scurrying past a waiting cobra.

Aaron's nap is a ruse. He has become one of the greatest hitters in history, and is one, two, three or four in runs scored, hits, total bases, runs batted in, extra base hits, home runs and doubles among Ruth, Cobb, Speaker, Musial, Wagner, Mays . . .

Yet he has been buffeted with the faint praise of, of all things, bland consistency. He has been so uniformly outstanding in all areas of play for the last 20 years that, until two years ago when he began to seriously challenge the "legendary" career home-run record of 714 held by Babe Ruth, Aaron was playing in spectacular obscurity.

Aaron had always admired Joe DiMaggio's "cool perfection." But Aaron was cool in the shadows—like a coiled cobra laying in wait, while DiMaggio was in the glaring cynosure of fame. Aaron is reserved like DiMaggio, smooth like DiMaggio, talented like DiMaggio, versatile like DiMaggio.

But he did not play in New York like DiMaggio. And he is not white like DiMaggio.

Whenever he would hear talk of the greatest players, he was never included. "I'd hear Mays and Mantle and Killebrew and Clemente and Frank Robinson," he says. "I'd never hear me." The lack of recognition rankled.

When professional baseball celebrated its 100th anniversary with a gigantic banquet in a Washington hotel before the 1969 All-Star game, the All-Time team, as selected by writers and broadcasters, was announced. The All-Time "Living" outfield was Williams, DiMaggio and Mays.

"That wasn't so bad," said Aaron, who was on the National League All-Star team that year, "but I wasn't even invited to the dinner."

At the 1970 All-Star game in Cincinnati, Aaron came to the hotel where the baseball headquarters was and asked for a room. He had made a reservation. The clerk checked and checked and said, "Sorry, but we have nothing in your name, we've never heard of you." (This, says Aaron, did not peeve him so much. He has enough perspective of himself to say, "There are a lot of people walkin' the streets who nobody knows.")

"The thing about Hank," says Eddie Mathews, Aaron's one-time teammate with Milwaukee and Atlanta and later his manager, "is that he does everything so effortlessly, so expressionlessly.

"He runs as hard as he has to, for example. His hat doesn't fly off the way Mays' does. Clemente ran, and he looked like he was falling apart at the seams. Pete Rose runs hard everywhere, and he dives head first. Aaron runs with the shaft let out, but you'd never know it. Yet when the smoke clears, he's standing there in the same place as the others."

Aaron has wondered, though, why only recently has he been discovered by the nation. He believes that his blackness was the most important reason. There is a feeling that the white press wants to promote white players. And when one counters that he played in comparatively small towns like Milwaukee and Atlanta, he asks why Johnny Bench is so famous.

Even now he feels sensitive about the diminishment of his achievements. In Atlanta, Babe Ruth chase or no, the team is going poorly and attendance is only slightly more than 11,000 a game.

The letters of racial slurs against his run for the record also, of course, disturb him. And in a lesser way, so do the little slights. Bowie Kuhn, after "warning" pitchers not to groove pitches to Aaron, does not send Henry a congratulatory telegram on hitting No. 700. President Nixon does send a telegram, but sends it to the Milwaukee Booster Club, of all places. ("Maybe he didn't know my address," said Aaron. He also remembers that President Nixon sent him a Christmas card addressed to "Mr. Frank Aaron.")

An Atlanta paper runs a series on "The Truth about Ruth." One line reads: "While Braves' rightfielder Hank Aaron will probably break Ruth's home run record this year, no one has yet come close to matching the magnetism of the Babe."

Says Aaron, with a grimace: "No BLACK player has yet come close to matching the magnetism . . ."

Besides that, Aaron is now the Braves' "left fielder." He is thirty-nine years old. He has shifted this season from right field because, he admits, "my arm is not what it used to be."

He also knows he is no longer the player he was ten years ago, "or even five years ago," he said. "It used to be that before a season, I'd know I'd hit over .300, steal 25 bases, bat in 100 runs, score 100 runs and hit over 30 homers. Now I know I will hit over 30 home runs. That's all.

"I'd probably have retired by now if I wasn't going for the record. I'd probably be bored, what with the team 20 games out of first place, and me not able to do all that I once could. I wouldn't want to be an old man hanging on. But this record is so prodigious that I'm going to stay until I break it."

~

Aaron hit his 714th and 715th homers early in the 1974 season.

~

Exotic Encounters

In Winter in My Room

Emily Dickinson

In Winter in my Room
I came upon a Worm—
Pink, lank and warm—
But as he was a worm
And worms presume
Not quite with him at home—
Secured him by a string
To something neighboring
And went along.

A Trifle afterward
A thing occurred
I'd not believe it if I heard
But state with creeping blood—
A snake with mottles rare
Surveyed my chamber floor
In feature as the worm before
But ringed with power—

The very string with which
I tied him—too
When he was mean and new
That string was there—

I shrank—"How fair you are"!
Propitiation's claw—
"Afraid," he hissed
"Of me"?
"No cordiality"—
He fathomed me—
Then to a Rhythm Slim
Secreted in his Form
As Patterns swim
Projected him.

That time I flew
Both eyes his way
Lest he pursue
Nor ever ceased to run
Till in a distant town
Towns on from mine
I set me down
This was a dream.

The Man and the Snake

Ambrose Bierce

IT IS OF VERITABYLL *report, and attested of so many that there be nowe of wyse and learned none to gaynsaye it, that ye serpente hys eye hath a magnetick propertie that whosoe falleth into its svasion is drawn forwards in despyte of his wille, and perisheth miserabyll by ye creature hys byte.*

Stretched at ease upon a sofa, in gown and slippers, Harker Brayton smiled as he read the foregoing sentence in old Morryster's "Marvells of Science." "The only marvel in the matter," he said to himself, "is that the wise and learned in Morryster's day should have believed such nonsense as is rejected by most of even the ignorant in ours."

A train of reflections followed—for Brayton was a man of thought—and he unconsciously lowered his book without altering the direction of his eyes. As soon as the volume had gone below the line of sight, something in an obscure corner of the room recalled his attention to his surroundings. What he saw, in the shadow under his bed, were two small points of light, apparently about an inch apart. They might have been reflections of the gas jet above him, in metal nail heads; he gave them but little thought and resumed his reading. A moment later something—some impulse which it did not occur to him to analyze—impelled him to lower the book again and seek

for what he saw before. The points of light were still there. They seemed to
have become brighter than before, shining with a greenish luster which he
had not at first observed. He thought, too, that they might have moved a trifle—were somewhat nearer. They were still too much in the shadow, however, to reveal their nature and origin to an indolent attention, and he resumed
his reading. Suddenly something in the text suggested a thought which made
him start and drop the book for the third time to the side of the sofa,
whence, escaping from his hand, it fell sprawling to the floor, back upward.
Brayton, half-risen, was staring intently into the obscurity beneath the bed,
where the points of light shone with, it seemed to him, an added fire. His
attention was now fully aroused, his gaze eager and imperative. It disclosed,
almost directly beneath the foot rail of the bed, the coils of a large serpent—the points of light were its eyes! Its horrible head, thrust flatly forth
from the innermost coil and resting upon the outermost, was directed
straight toward him, the definition of the wide, brutal jaw and the idiotlike
forehead serving to show the direction of its malevolent gaze. The eyes were
no longer merely luminous points; they looked into his own with a meaning,
a malign significance.

II

A snake in a bedroom of a modern city dwelling of the better sort is, happily, not so common a phenomenon as to make explanation altogether needless. Harker Brayton, a bachelor of thirty-five, a scholar, idler, and something
of an athlete, rich, popular, and of sound health, had returned to San Francisco from all manner of remote and unfamiliar countries. His tastes, always
a trifle luxurious, had taken on an added exuberance from long privation;
and the resources of even the Castle Hotel being inadequate for their perfect
gratification, he had gladly accepted the hospitality of his friend, Dr. Druring, the distinguished scientist. Dr. Druring's house, a large, old-fashioned
one in what was now an obscure quarter of the city, had an outer and visible
aspect of reserve. It plainly would not associate with the contiguous elements
of its altered environment, and appeared to have developed some of the
eccentricities which come of isolation. One of these was a "wing," conspicu-
ously irrelevant in point of architecture, and no less rebellious in the matter
of purpose; for it was a combination of laboratory, menagerie, and museum.
It was here that the doctor indulged the scientific side of his nature in the
study of such forms of animal life as engaged his interest and comforted his
taste—which, it must be confessed, ran rather to the lower forms. For one of

the higher types nimbly and sweetly to recommend itself unto his gentle senses, it had at least to retain certain rudimentary characteristics allying it to such "dragons of the prime" as toads and snakes. His scientific sympathies were distinctly reptilian; he loved nature's vulgarians and described himself as the Zola of zoology. His wife and daughters, not having the advantage to share his enlightened curiosity regarding the works and ways of our ill-starred fellow-creatures, were, with needless austerity, excluded from what he called the Snakery, and doomed to companionship with their own kind; though, to soften the rigors of their lot, he had permitted them, out of his great wealth, to outdo the reptiles in the gorgeousness of their surroundings and to shine with a superior splendor.

Architecturally, and in point of "furnishing," the Snakery had a severe simplicity befitting the humble circumstances of its occupants, many of whom, indeed, could not safely have been intrusted with the liberty which is necessary to the full enjoyment of luxury, for they had the troublesome peculiarity of being alive. In their own apartments, however, they were under as little personal restraint as was compatible with their protection from the baneful habit of swallowing one another; and, as Brayton had thoughtfully been apprised, it was more than a tradition that some of them had at divers times been found in parts of the premises where it would have embarrassed them to explain their presence. Despite the Snakery and its uncanny associations—to which, indeed, he gave little attention—Brayton found life at the Druring mansion very much to his mind.

III

Beyond a smart shock of surprise and a shudder of mere loathing, Mr. Brayton was not greatly affected. His first thought was to ring the call bell and bring a servant; but, although the bell cord dangled within easy reach, he made no movement toward it; it had occurred to his mind that the act might subject him to the suspicion of fear, which he certainly did not feel. He was more keenly conscious of the incongruous nature of the situation than affected by its perils; it was revolting, but absurd.

The reptile was of a species with which Brayton was unfamiliar. Its length he could only conjecture; the body at the largest visible part seemed about as thick as his forearm. In what way was it dangerous, if in any way? Was it venomous? Was it a constrictor? His knowledge of nature's danger signals did not enable him to say; he had never deciphered the code.

If not dangerous, the creature was at least offensive. It was de trop—

"matter out of place"—an impertinence. The gem was unworthy of the set-ting. Even the barbarous taste of our time and country, which had loaded the walls of the room with pictures, the floor with furniture, and the furniture with bric-a-brac, had not quite fitted the place for this bit of the savage life of the jungle. Besides—insupportable thought!—the exhalations of its breath mingled with the atmosphere which he himself was breathing!

These thoughts shaped themselves with greater or less definition in Bray-ton's mind, and begot action. The process is what we call consideration and decision. It is thus that we are wise and unwise. It is thus that the withered leaf in an autumn breeze shows greater or less intelligence than its fellows, falling upon the land or upon the lake. The secret of human action is an open one—something contracts our muscles. Does it matter if we give to the preparatory molecular changes the name of will?

Brayton rose to his feet and prepared to back softly away from the snake, without disturbing it, if possible, and through the door. People retire so from the presence of the great, for greatness is power, and power is a menace. He knew that he could walk backward without obstruction, and find the door without error. Should the monster follow, the taste which had plastered the walls with paintings had consistently supplied a rack of murderous Ori-ental weapons from which he could snatch one to suit the occasion. In the meantime the snake's eyes burned with a more pitiless malevolence than ever.

Brayton lifted his right foot free of the floor to step backward. That moment he felt a strong aversion to doing so.

"I am accounted brave," he murmured; "is bravery, then, no more than pride? Because there are none to witness the shame shall I retreat?"

He was steadying himself with his right hand upon the back of a chair, his foot suspended.

"Nonsense!" he said aloud; "I am not so great a coward as to fear to seem to myself afraid."

He lifted the foot a little higher by slightly bending the knee, and thrust it sharply to the floor—an inch in front of the other! He could not think how that occurred. A trial with the left foot had the same result; it was again in advance of the right. The hand upon the chair back was grasping it; the arm was straight, reaching somewhat backward. One might have seen that he was reluctant to lose his hold. The snake's malignant head was still thrust forth from the inner coil as before, the neck level. It had not moved, but its eyes were now electric sparks, radiating an infinity of luminous needles.

The man had an ashy pallor. Again he took a step forward, and another, partly dragging the chair, which, when finally released, fell upon the floor with a crash. The man groaned; the snake made neither sound nor motion, but its eyes were two dazzling suns. The reptile itself was wholly concealed by them. They gave off enlarging rings of rich and vivid colors, which at their greatest expansion successively vanished like soap bubbles; they seemed to approach his very face, and anon were an immeasurable distance away. He heard, somewhere, the continual throbbing of a great drum, with desultory bursts of far music, inconceivably sweet, like the tones of an aeolian harp. He knew it for the sunrise melody of Memnon's statue, and thought he stood in the Nileside reeds, hearing, with exalted sense, that immortal anthem through the silence of the centuries.

The music ceased; rather, it became by insensible degrees the distant roll of a retreating thunderstorm. A landscape, glittering with sun and rain, stretched before him, arched with a vivid rainbow, framing in its giant curve a hundred visible cities. In the middle distance a vast serpent, wearing a crown, reared its head out of its voluminous convolutions and looked at him with his dead mother's eyes. Suddenly this enchanting landscape seemed to rise swiftly upward, like the drop scene at a theater, and vanished in a blank. Something struck him a hard blow upon the face and breast. He had fallen to the floor; the blood ran from his broken nose and his bruised lips. For a moment he was dazed and stunned, and lay with closed eyes, his face against the door. In a few moments he had recovered, and then realized that his fall, by withdrawing his eyes, had broken the spell which held him. He felt that now, by keeping his gaze averted, he would be able to retreat. But the thought of the serpent within a few feet of his head, yet unseen—perhaps in the very act of springing upon him and throwing its coils about his throat—was too horrible. He lifted his head, stared again into those baleful eyes, and was again in bondage.

The snake had not moved, and appeared somewhat to have lost its power upon the imagination; the gorgeous illusions of a few moments before were not repeated. Beneath that flat and brainless brow its black, beady eyes simply glittered, as at first, with an expression unspeakably malignant. It was as if the creature, knowing its triumph assured, had determined to practice no more alluring wiles.

Now ensued a fearful scene. The man, prone upon the floor, within a yard of his enemy, raised the upper part of his body upon his elbows, his head thrown back, his legs extended to their full length. His face was white between its gouts of blood; his eyes were strained open to their uttermost expansion. There was froth upon his lips; it dropped off in flakes. Strong convulsions ran through his body, making almost serpentine undulations. He bent himself at the waist, shifting his legs from side to side. And every movement left him a little nearer to the snake. He thrust his hands forward to brace himself back, yet constantly advanced upon his elbows.

IV

Dr. Druring and his wife sat in the library. The scientist was in rare good humor.

"I have just obtained, by exchange with another collector," he said, "a splendid specimen of the Ophiophagus."

"And what may that be?" the lady inquired with a somewhat languid interest.

"Why, bless my soul, what profound ignorance! My dear, a man who ascertains after marriage that his wife does not know Greek, is entitled to a divorce. The Ophiophagus is a snake which eats other snakes."

"I hope it will eat all yours," she said, absently shifting the lamp. "But how does it get the other snakes? By charming them, I suppose."

"That is just like you, dear," said the doctor, with an affectation of petulance. "You know how irritating to me is any allusion to that vulgar superstition about the snake's power of fascination."

The conversation was interrupted by a mighty cry which rang through the silent house like the voice of a demon shouting in a tomb. Again and yet again it sounded, with terrible distinctness. They sprang to their feet, the man confused, the lady pale and speechless with fright. Almost before the echoes of the last cry had died away the doctor was out of the room, springing up the staircase two steps at a time. In the corridor, in front of Brayton's chamber, he met some servants who had come from the upper floor. Together they rushed at the door without knocking. It was unfastened, and gave way. Brayton lay upon his stomach on the floor, dead. His head and arms were partly concealed under the foot rail of the bed. They pulled the body away, turning it upon the back. The face was daubed with blood and froth, the eyes were wide open, staring—a dreadful sight!

"Died in a fit," said the scientist, bending his knee and placing his hand upon the heart. While in that position he happened to glance under the bed. "Good God!" he added; "how did this thing get in here?"

He reached under the bed, pulled out the snake, and flung it, still coiled, to the center of the room, whence, with a harsh, shuffling sound, it slid across the polished floor till stopped by the wall, where it lay without motion. It was a stuffed snake; its eyes were two shoe buttons.

~

The Snakes

Mary Oliver

I once saw two snakes,
northern racers,
hurrying through the woods,
their bodies
like two black whips
lifting and dashing forward;
in perfect concert
they held their heads high
and swam forward
on their sleek bellies;
under the trees,
through vines, branches,
over stones,
through fields of flowers,
they traveled
like a matched team
like a dance
like a love affair.

The Crow and the Cobra

Finlay Lewis

His FEEBLE CHIRPING got my attention. I ran to the barn to grab a ladder, which I dragged to the neighboring woodlot. Wrestling it against the tree, I climbed up to reach the nest perched near the treetop where the little black fellow, barely alive, was shivering against the corpses of his siblings. Cupping him gingerly in my hands, I carried him into the kitchen where my mother revived him with a medicine dropper of lukewarm milk. Watching his tiny Adam's apple jiggle up and down as he sucked in the life-giving nourishment endeared him to both of us. I named him Crow Vadis. Mother thought that a clever name for a crow.

Her own inventiveness continually amazed me, particularly when it came to animals. Trained as a veterinarian, she always boasted that she could revive any animal—even ones that far more experienced vets figured were goners. It was something instinctual with her—she just seemed to understand a creature's psyche and how to bolster its will to live. My parents had bought an abandoned farm outside of town so mother could meet her patients in the barn. My father commuted from there to Minneapolis where he and his brother were detectives in the police department's narcotics division.

But the demands of her practice became such a problem—in a rural community a vet is on call at all hours—that she gave it up to raise my two older siblings and me. But then my father walked out on us when I was fourteen, by which time my brother and sister were on their own. I took his abandonment personally, which may explain why I felt such an attachment to Crow—his father had probably skipped out on him too.

At first, mother returned to normal animal medicine, but she found that too tame. For a while, she tried her hand at training German shepherds for the local sheriff's department. Getting them to attack was like their final examinations before being handed back to the cops, and she would get all dressed up in protective gear. Word got around about her ability to handle difficult creatures, and when emergencies would arise, she'd get the call. I once saw a local farmer's snarling, rabid dog become docile in her hands. Castrating bulls, dealing with marauding bears foraging too close to civilization for winter food, handling problem births involving farm animals—all in a day's work for her.

So, it seemed only natural that when a traveling circus came to the county fair grounds in Stillwater, Minnesota, her emergency phone rang with its customary urgency. The circus's prime attraction featured a series of poisonous snake acts. We don't have dangerous serpents in Minnesota—only garter snakes and some other harmless varmints. I had a garter as a pet, which probably was mother's only experience with snakes. So when the manager asked her if she could do something about an infection that was threatening his deadly reptiles, she was confronting a novel situation. But he pleaded with her—he had rattlers, vipers and a couple of cobras, and the snakes were the hit of the show. A handler would put one on his head, top it with a hat and then walk around the ring to the audience's amazement. Another act involved a guy swallowing a thin but deadly viper and then pulling him back out of his throat and wrapping it around his neck. There also was a glass enclosure filled with a tangle of deadly reptiles. A Hindu snake charmer who looked as though he had just arrived from the Punjab would walk through their midst playing a flute and soon have them swaying in time to a tune.

But now a couple of the circus's most prized snakes had died and the others were acting sickly, not even interested in devouring the rats that were their normal fare. People paid good money to see the act, and the manager was worried. Mother went to the fair grounds, studied the snakes for a while and then, talking to them in that soothing voice of hers, picked up a couple and studied their eyes. Then she told the guy to drape some mosquito netting over their cages and to call her in the morning. Snakes in Minnesota may not be much, but our mosquitoes are something else. (In fact, often the mosquito is referred to as teh Minnesota state bird.)

But that gave her an idea, and, before long, we were running a snake farm. That's what we called it. Only it was more like a zoo, with glassed-in, temperature-controlled cages lining the sides of the barn. By now, Crow was a mature and completely tame bird, who considered himself more human than fowl—eating with us at the table, sleeping on my head board, perching on our shoulders and uttering guttural sounds of mild approval and reproach as he watched the snake venture take shape on our property. Occasionally, if something happened that might strike a crow as unusual—like a snake giving birth—he would get our attention by flying back and forth between the barn and the house. He would flap his wings with great urgency on these occasions. There was never much doubt about what was on Crow's mind.

"He thinks they're his snakes," my mother said. "Everything they do, he examines."

Getting the reptile farm started was the hard part, and mother tapped into her veterinarian contacts to acquire the collection of rattlesnakes, boa constrictors, copperheads, and cobras that she hoped would entice paying customers to the barn for a viewing experience that could not be replicated anyplace else in Stillwater, Minnesota. She always had an eye out for exotic specimens, and so she was excited when one of her snake-broker contacts— they were mainly vets—told her that a guy in Miami would sell her a cobra at a discount on condition that she let an intermediary take possession of the snake before handing it over.

"He's what you might call a reptile biologist," my mother explained. "He wants to do some kind of experiment—research, you know—and then we can have it. The snake is twelve feet long—can you believe it?"

On the day the cobra was supposed to arrive, however, my mother got a frantic call from her Florida contact. The shipment had arrived at the Twin Cities airport, but something terrible had happened to the researcher the night before—some kind of random street-crime and he had ended up being shot to death. Could we hurry out to take delivery before the authorities destroyed the animal?

"We fed the snake a special chemical mixture contained in a plastic bag as part of the experiment," the dealer in Florida had said. "We expect that he'll excrete it sometime in the next 48 hours. The bag will weigh about 35 pounds. Call us immediately, and we'll send somebody around to pick it up right away, if you'll just hold it for us. My client will rebate your money and you can have the snake for free. This is for science, you know."

We rushed to the airport, where we found a huge, plastic-enclosed snake crate with air holes waiting to be picked up in the freight delivery section.

He was indeed a magnificent animal—long and sleek and lethal. The transaction had happened very quickly—the call from the Florida snake broker was unexpected and cloaked in secrecy—so the special cage my mother had in mind was still being built. For the time being, we put him in an open enclosure in the middle of the barn where Crow Vadis inspected him with what seemed more than his normal curiosity.

The next day, my uncle from the Minneapolis police department showed up to take me to baseball practice. Crow came swooping down to greet him and then curving back to the barn. It was his usual signal for us to follow.

His antics led us to the new cobra, which was coiled in a corner of the cage in apparent exhaustion. In the center was a slimy, smelly glistening plastic bag. My suspicious uncle tore open the bag. The contents were powdery white and he was immediately on the phone. Before long, police cars were surrounding the property and the feds were swarming all over the barn.

A couple of days later, when the local newspapers got wind of the drug story, one headline writer paid tribute to my friend. "Crow Vadis: Crocaine Hero," the headline read. But my mother said it was nothing to crow about—Vadis was just doing his duty.

~

The Snakes of Central Park

Karen Heuler

FIRST OFF, SHE wasn't very likeable. She had adjusted to that, she was an amputee of likeability, if you get it. She had lost it, it was gone, she learned to live without it, but it was there, itching sometimes, at the back of her mind, at the end of the stump.

As if that were a good analogy! What is losing your likeability to losing a limb? Think about it, which would you prefer? She was lucky, after all, she could still run away from her enemies.

And she had those, she had to acknowledge; she rubbed people wrong.

In her defense, let's say she was hypersensitive and you're born that way, not made. No one volunteers for it; it's a scourge, it's a bad way to live. She rarely had a good day; someone always said something that rattled her, or looked at her cross-eyed, or couldn't keep the contempt from their lips. Not everyone would have noticed it; she did; she had magnifying lenses for eyes; she had Geiger counters for ears.

So she quit her jobs often and always regretted it (storming out of one job only hastened the search for the next). But no more desk jobs! Desk jobs were out!

She could be a lab rat. In fact, she had always felt she was part of someone's experiment already. A worthless one—you know, the results fudged, the hypothesis clearly outlandish, but who reads it anyway? And certain side effects entirely ignored, not even to be mentioned. She would have a lovely personality if it was up to her, all things considered: life was obviously easier with friends, relatives, lovers, interested parties; who would deliberately forswear all that toothy smile and radiant eye and shiny hair stuff? Only a lab rat, never consulted and never informed. She wriggled her pink nose; her little pink paws quivered; that odd confusing discomfort must be a lump of something clinical growing underground.

But she wouldn't like anyone looking too closely! No indeed, not for her those probing eyes and prickling questions. Sooner or later they would figure out her abnormalities and dump her. And how did they dump lab rats? Gas, electricity, lethal injection or just a scientific incision on the way out?

No. Besides which, she'd tried one and they'd never gotten back to her.

Instead she decided to hand out flyers for a while. Actually, she wore a costume—she was a big brown cream-filled donut. She liked the anonymity of it. She looked out from the sprinkles and saw faces that couldn't see hers. Amazing how important seeing the face was. She was powerful because hers was hidden; they were naked and assailable. She shoved flyers in their faces; she loped after the refuseniks, the grumps (she would spit on flyers in civilian life; no matter), forcing flyers in their pockets, their bags, uttering unintelligible threats to squirt a bit of Creamy Crumpet up their noses or smear sugar frosting on their articulated, gym-loving butts.

"Calm down, calm down!" Ray whispered, shocked and delighted when he saw her grab a child by his backpack and shove a coupon in the pouch. "Your boss won't like it if they get complaints, you know. What if people get you mixed up with the product? Did you tell that child the sprinkles would hide under his bed and get him? Did you really?"

Ray had been the single sole solitary friend she'd had in the past year. Make it decade, make it life, it didn't matter. They'd once worked side by side in a record store before records became extinct and they'd kept in touch off and on, over the years. He had turned into an electrician for a school, she wasn't sure how, but now he had holidays and summer vacation. He was always interested in her and never got out of line and for years she'd assumed he was gay.

Say what you will about gays, they're not the ones to take a knife to your throat; she was glad he was gay.

Aside from all her other defects, she'd been born with this devastating flaw: she couldn't recognize predators, and she attracted them. She didn't know how other people did it, how they could survive unscathed—walk down dark streets, unlock their doors in the middle of the night, go out for milk, see a movie, ride the subway, unperturbed, undisturbed, still shrink-wrapped and shiny when they made it home. Some people lived in a safe city, around the corner or even one floor down from the city she lived in, where she'd become an improbable statistic, a stutter on the charts. Thank God the newspapers didn't know about her, they'd be gleeful, they'd track her down with an almost Creamy Crumpet determination ("How many times robbed? Really! And assaulted? Oh, my. And was that sexual assault as well? And tell me"—dropped voice, leaning in—"how about rape?")

How about it indeed? The last time she'd had to talk to cops, she'd seen them exchange glances. Maybe they knew her name, maybe she was part of the training lectures now. She'd have to move to another precinct just to escape that glance, that significant nod. Somehow they recognized her—not because she was a perp, but because she was marked, she was target, she was collateral prey. It almost made her stand up straight; she sensed a category. There must be others like her, and even if it was an association without walls, what a thrill to be a member of a team.

Like them, she couldn't tell, she honestly couldn't tell a wolf from a dog. Better to consider them all threats. So now she's on guard, no, she's armed, she looks at people's hands first, then their faces (if they're hiding their hands they may be hiding something else, a knife or a gun, a razor or who knows what they'll think of next; they're ahead of her, and not just one step either, they have time to run ahead and scout the area and get a nice neat alley all paced out, with a trap or two just for the likes of her).

She was born without the instinct; for years now she'd had to make do with rudeness, hostility, contempt, as if such things were sharp as knives, intimate as knives; sometimes she dreams of knives and wakes crying. That's the kind of intimacy she's known. Intimacy? Yes, intimacy makes you aware of the tang of life; knives do, too. So does a hand smacking you right and left as you plead, no, no. It concentrates the mind.

"Well," Ray said, and this was even after he'd told her his own secret (no, he wasn't gay, he was impotent, and her heart leapt up—well, at least she was safe from *that*, here at last one human being she could count on, instinct or not, a goldmine, what a find). "Well," he said, "I'm not sure, but if all you've told me is true, don't you wonder, you know: Why you? Do you ask for it in some weird psychological way, or are you God's goat?"

She jumped up in anger (ask for it? *ask* for it?). "Do I look like a goat? Do I look like a goat?"

Ray shrugged. "I don't know what a symbolic goat would look like. Maybe you do."

"Pssh," she said and sat down again, drumming her fingers against her coffee cup. "If I were a goat, then there'd have to be a plan, something the sacrifice is *for*. Can you think of any plan?"

He looked at her thoughtfully. "Sometimes they don't tell you. You could be a martyr for someone else's cause."

She snorted. "People like martyrs even before they're dead, don't they? That leaves me out."

That would have been a good place to say, "Don't be silly; I like you, don't I?" but he didn't. Not that she expected it, or missed it, but still. . . . Still.

They had stopped for coffee and she leapt up in agitation, wriggling her hand through her pockets, dropping bills on the table. "More than enough," Ray said. "You're putting down too much money."

"Paper and ink." She was abrupt, she was making a gesture (would a martyr do *this?*); she had thrown down a five for a one.

"The man without hands dismisses gloves," he answered smoothly, making her stop in her tracks. He liked to get Confucian, he liked to make her change her course. What was he saying: People without money don't value it?

Hardly. She grinned. "The man without gloves dismisses fingers." That would show him.

"And what would either of them do with a Creamy Crumpet?"

She winced. Back to daylight. "I'm thinking of dropping the donut thing."

"A vivid image."

"Maybe I'll be a dogwalker. I like dogs."

"I like dogs myself."

Dogs, she thought, how can you go wrong? And she pictured them, a goofy bunch of grinning, wagging, leaping goons, short-legged, long-legged, dauntless, and open-hearted. Dogs, she thought: what took me so long?

They were near the park—right on Columbus Circle. It looked like something was just starting to happen. They saw people slowly turning and moving, collecting like magnetized lint.

"What is it?" she murmured. She was magnetized lint, too; she bent forward. The crowd was new, just forming, a crystal thinking of becoming a snowflake. Suddenly it lost its indifferent air and became serious. The lint picked up speed, and so did they, momentum found and loved, there's nothing like a good surprise, say what you will, and if it's a bad surprise, at least it got someone else.

They rounded the entrance to a concrete bench in front of a short wall. A man was lying on the bench, partially swallowed by a tree trunk.

"What is it?" she said urgently, and everywhere around her people were saying, "What? What?"

Not a trunk, a snake. A python. The man on the bench wriggled desperately. "It's squeezing me!" he moaned. "Take it off me!"

A few big men grabbed the snake by the pinched waist where its swallowing of the man ended, and pulled. Other men grabbed on, it was a tug of war, it was a tractor pull, the benchman was drawn along with each tug of the snake, like a bobber on a fish line.

Some cops came running just as sirens broke through the background. The python inched up like an alimentary canal, rippling imperceptibly. "Oh, God!" the bench man cried. "I was sleeping it off, that's all, I just needed a nap, a little air, it's got my arm, my neck is next, it's like a great big tongue, kill it, kill it, save me please!" His face, all stubble mouth and eyes, beseeched them all. You could tell he was a drunk; you could smell the broken bottles. His eyes caught hers, she felt it like a stab, and then they moved on.

The cops rushed in and stopped like they'd hit a wall. Not covered at the academy, she thought: how do you whack a great big tongue? "Halt! Release that man!" they should have cried. "Halt or I'll shout!" For what could they shoot, after all?

It was a beautiful, sleek, speckled body, it went on longer than you'd expect, it had a pattern that could have been fashionable if anyone picked it up (and surely someone would use it, it would be all over town by next week), it coiled and looped and moved almost internally by inches, as if there were a giant centipede engine inside. But no head. She looked at it in utter interest, its mouth stretched out so taut now that it engulfed the shoulder, it looked like a band or belt where the snake met the man and you had to look close, to stare with parted, eager lips yourself to catch where the lips were, it was beautifully shocking the way it was so out of place and yet so there; and its pattern was so eye-catching and pleasing. It was the man himself who broke the spell, who spoilt the symmetry. Even if he'd been welldressed he'd look shabby next to that snake.

An ambulance shrieked to a stop, and the emergency people conferred until a cop took a knife and began to slit the snake open straight down the side, a horrible thing, the blood ran smooth and the snake would have screamed but they have no voice; you almost wanted to give it a voice. They leaned over it, working the knife and she thought again how those intimate hulking-over stances could be either murder or rape, how the sweeping down of the hands and torso could be death or sex, it was so close.

The snake moved even after its head was off and the man was free, his arm swollen and cut (or maybe it always looked like that, blistered and red, it was ugly), and the cops kept trying to coil it in a large, smooth circle like a water hose but it lost the shape time after time, sidling back and forth and left to right, like it might just be looking for its head after all.

"Let's go, let's go," she said urgently, "it's a terrible thing to watch."

"Well, it's all over now," he pointed out, "you've already watched it."

"It's one thing to watch when you don't know what you're seeing, and quite another when you do."

In a flagrantly mild voice he asked, "Which part didn't you know you were seeing?"

"You know," she said, grinding her teeth; "you know."

They walked on in silence for a few more blocks until Ray said, "It was the knife, wasn't it? The knife upset you."

"Don't be silly," she snapped. "It was the snake."

"Probably an escaped pet. You hear about that every so often, though I personally don't know how a snake could be a 'pet.' Do they recognize you? Are they pleased to see you? Do they wriggle into your lap and snuggle? Don't worry, you won't see another one."

She groaned. "I'm not afraid of pythons. I'm not afraid of snakes. In fact, I feel sorry for it, slit open like that."

"It was killing that man."

"That bum?"

He made a noise in his throat. "I'd have thought you'd feel for the guy, yes."

"I don't identify with victims," she snapped. "Is that what you think? Maybe I identify with predators. They weed out the sick or the old, don't they, cull the herd? Maybe the herd needs culling. Maybe they're good for us all."

"I want to see where you go with this."

"I'm not going anywhere. I'm just stating a fact."

"You've had a metamorphosis."

"I'm simply stating the theory of natural balance."

"But how do you feel about it?"

"Theories and feelings don't go together. They slit that snake open while it was alive. I keep wondering how that felt."

"It was the knife, after all," Ray said with satisfaction.

~

She quickly had four clients around Central Park: Biscuits, Joe-Boy, Scooter, and Fluke, listed in order of size. They always pulled head first, mouths open, stopping and starting, jerking and lifting legs or squatting. They were fools for squirrels; squirrels spurred their spirits (already risen) to extravagant heights. They would give up food to chase squirrels, to call them names and challenge them, they were elementally caught up. She praised them enormously; they slobbered all over her.

Quite soon into her new job Fluke, the dappled dachshund, stopped dead in her tracks and barked in a new way. The other dogs immediately tensed up. She did, too; her hands automatically gripped tighter and the back of her neck prickled. Hackles! She could see the dogs' hackles raised like bristles; she must have hackles too.

She was leaning backwards, trying to control the dogs. That meant she couldn't lean forward to see. Some people were passing by, and everyone looked her way, with all that yowling she was a public nuisance, and she begged someone to come and hold her dogs so she could see what was causing the racket after all. That got someone—curiosity always dragged them in, and just as some older guy came forward to grab all four so she could look, just then she saw the snake peering out, a gorgeous, gorgeous pale green with dark green scales in unfinished rings around its body. It had raised its head only slightly, but as the dogs retreated, it reared higher, as if they were connected (pull the dogs back and it raises the snake). It had an arrogant face, a painted face, a New York haute expression.

The dogs saw it and began to bark and leap, but with the snake standing up they were feinting, lunging, and stopping before being pulled back. Scooter began to shake. The man holding the dogs whistled in surprise. "That snake doesn't belong here. See that neck, the way it's pinched in? That snake's a biter. It ain't one of ours."

"It ain't one of mine, either," she muttered. She yanked the dogs, the overexcited bunch of them; beautiful or not, that snake wouldn't get them, not her dogs, no! And for a while she almost hated the dogs for their sheer tongue-lolling determination in finding, seeking out whatever moved, consequences be damned. The attraction was there, it was a fundamental thing, it wasn't personal at all. The dogs, their noses almost running on tracks along the ground, their ears up like radar seeking an invasion, those teeth! those claws! and snakes—what were they, heat-sensing? drawn to ultraviolet or something? Built-in detectors, dog and snake both, machines; they couldn't turn into lightbulbs or fennel, they were born to use their teeth.

All arranged in a chain, each mouth searching for the smaller mouth it could swallow, and careful of the bigger one behind it.

The sun was very nice, staying out later each day. The leaves were just turning from baby green to adult. The birds were shouting. The dogs had found a meaning to life.

~

"Ray," she said, "today I saw more snakes."

"They're phallic, I think," he answered, apparently thoughtfully. "They're universal. And when they're not phallic, I think they still have something to do with the birth of the world? Or medicine—healing—I'm not sure. A powerful symbol."

"I'm not talking about symbols. Symbols don't bite dogs."

"Maybe they do, somewhere," he said comfortably.

She looked at him; he annoyed her instantly. "And if it were phallic?" she whispered. "How do you feel about those phalluses popping up without you?" She was just annoyed, that was it; he wasn't listening to her, he was dismissing her.

His dark eyes shifted; they focused on her and then threw the focus elsewhere. His mouth tightened. If he were a snake, he would strike, she thought. If I were a dog I would charge.

"That was mean of me perhaps," she said sweetly.

"Perhaps?"

"Well, you raised the phallic thing." She gulped and swallowed a laugh. "That was unintentional. Oops."

"I have to get going."

She was stung. "No, don't! I'm sorry!" If nothing else, who would she tell about those snakes? "I'm in a bad mood. I don't understand what I'm seeing, and you dismissed it, you interpreted it."

He was still stiffly formal. "I was following my own thoughts. I'm allowed to have thoughts."

"Now don't get mad at me," she pleaded. "I didn't say anything that bad. And even if I did, it's not my fault, really; things just sort of slide out of my mouth like a rock down a hill, it's that unintentional."

"Intentions aren't the only issue here. You have an impact."

"Oh. Ah. Really sorry," she said in a way that was maybe just a little too quick, a little too darting. "The impact is entirely unintentional."

~

The story broke the next day. So far, there was an anaconda, a coral snake, an asp, two harmless beautiful snakes, and an explanation: a snake fancier with cancer had released all his pets before going in for surgery. He wanted to give them a chance, even if he didn't make it.

"What a sweet guy," she snorted. "What a charmer! What do you think he looks like?"

"Maybe a lot like you," Ray said, and she narrowed her eyes.

"What's up?" she asked.

"It's annoying, sometimes, how quick you are to judge."

"You didn't judge someone who released poisonous snakes into a large city park?"

"Well of course I did, but I didn't jump in about how he looks."

"No, you're right, I did. What was wrong with it?"

"There's no correlation between the way you look and the way you behave."

"Of course there is. The way you look is a signal."

"Only to a degree. But people aren't driven to a course of action by their appearances."

"Of course they are. Tall people get more responsibility, pretty people get more attention, white people get paid better, and women get screwed."

"I wasn't making a political statement," he said wearily. "You were about to imply that the snake guy was overweight, poorly dressed, and wore glasses."

She snickered. "You were," he insisted. "I know you well enough for that."

"I'm just getting on your nerves," she said serenely. "Your nerves will adjust. Besides, I just say the things you secretly long to hear. It's the role you want me to play. It's why you like me."

"And why do you like me?"

"You've got beautiful skin," she said, and he looked startled. "Isn't that what guys say about women no one else finds attractive? It's a joke. Someone told me that—a long time ago—and I didn't know it was ironic. I thought he thought it. They get me, they always get me."

"I think we're hiding out together," he said unhappily. "I don't put pressure on you, you don't expect anything from me."

She was getting suspicious. "We're a set."

"We're not a set. We just know each other."

~

The snakes got into the subway and settled there quite well. They ate mice and rats; the subway workers kept a list of sightings. They even formed clubs, like bird watchers.

There were curfews at the park for a few nights, but they were ineffective and the stories about snakes produced a kind of curfew of its own for those who were afraid of them. For others, it was like the Wild West had come to town. People got into costume—cowboy boots, Aussie hats, long poles with snoods. One guy caught an 8-foot grass snake, a harmless variety, and set up a photographer's stand. You could get your picture taken holding the reptile like a trophy or a belt. There was a bounty on snakes turned in and the snake fancier who started it all died on the operating table, so from his point of view, setting them free was a really good move.

And—it's the way they do things in New York—other people let other snakes go in Washington Square Park, Riverside Park, Van Cortlandt Park . . . unless you believe the stories that the snakes took cabs. The city was seized by articles inflating or belittling the danger (would they become indigenous like the parrots in New Jersey? Would they eat your pets or be eaten by them? Was this the end of city parks?).

Like a chariot pulled by variant horses, she took the dogs into the park (against the strict orders given by the dog owners). She listened for their snake-bark, for their calls of alarm or delight, she went home smelling of dog and woke up looking forward to work, even on rainy days when the dogs were reluctant or had to be toweled dry. She only had to see the owners for the first interview; after that they left money and she left notes: Joe-Boy had the runs, Fluke had a sneeze, Biscuits did a back-flip and landed quite surprised.

Of course the tourists were a problem: you couldn't tell who knew about the snakes and who would make the headlines. Sightings were getting rarer as spring grew old, and there were more articles about reptile mating habits and habitats. It wasn't long before you heard about people sneaking in and stealing snakes (they were excellent rat-catchers; they were better than cats—in fact, the cats were disappearing).

At first there was only one vendor of snake-on-a-stick, but then there were more, and it was never quite proven whether it was snake, or even local snakes (and were the snakes "local" now?).

And Ray had disappeared.

"Disappeared" could be the wrong word. He was avoiding her, he was returning her calls at the rate of one in four; he was agreeing to meet her and then canceling at the last minute. She'd been through this before; she could predict the stages; she was debating whether to make it easy on him, that bastard, the last of her friends, make it easy on him or demand an explanation, make him cringe (would he try to be diplomatic?), but after all, did she want to hear what had finally done it, what had turned the trick, what remark of hers had been the last straw? She knew she was impossible already, hateful even; how could it help to hear it again? And however hateful she was, he was worse, because he wasn't honest or kind or forgiving in any truly meaningful way. At least not to her, and let's face it that's where it mattered. How come she never met tolerant, indulgent people, people who could take her crabbiness as a sign of an ill-assigned life, a poor fit in fact; or were these indulgent people the ones she sneered at right from the start, because they were vacuous, limpid, lusterless, and dull? What a burden her unsympathetic mind was!

As if to prove it all, the horrors of her uncontrollable nerves, she sat down next to a woman on the subway who kept sucking her teeth. Just like that, hsst fssh, again and again. It was as regular as a piston, and a kind of steam from the sound enveloped her. She was being stifled by the sound. She glared at her, but the woman was impassive, concentrating on those teeth. It was incredible! How was it possible a person wouldn't know better than that—making noises as if it didn't matter, no one else mattered?

Her personality jerked in a spasm and she flounced up with a click of her own tongue and found a seat on the opposite side. Let others deal with it! Within minutes, however, she noticed the tooth-sucker's twitches and her heart shuddered almost to a halt. Tourette's; it must be Tourette's, and here she had done it, added to the suffering of a person who must go through life every day, helplessly bound to a treacherous body. She was ashamed; she was drenched in shame. She closed her eyes and when she opened them, the woman was gone.

She shuddered, still, as she got off the train. She was on her way to the dogs; that would help. The dogs loved to see her; maybe these, after all, were the tolerant, indulgent people she sought.

With each dog she felt a little better. Maybe she could fix things with Ray; maybe she could send him flowers. A funeral wreath? Would that be funny or annoying? She wasn't sure she could tell the difference; and wreaths were expensive. And, anyway, why bother about Ray, why should she lick the ground he walked on? Shouldn't that ground be a two-way street? No, no, she had to learn to be humble, it wasn't as if she didn't know she was flawed, it wasn't as if it didn't hurt to know, but as long as it was true, why dance around it? She owed Ray big, he had stuck by her till he could take it no more, why shouldn't she be tolerant, indulgent, and kind for a change? She could do it, she remembered being able to, before one day her intentions had snapped like a twig and that was the end of it.

It was a cool spring evening and the dogs were alert, sniffing and preening and prancing. Dusk was developing, thickening; it smelled sweet. There was a couple up ahead, under the overpass, quarreling. She could tell that by the way the woman's elbow jerked back when his arm came towards her. They were partly shadowed by a bush and a bench. And then he leaned over her, pushing her back, shifting his hips around her, and it looked for a moment like he would embrace her, and then the woman screamed.

For a microsecond, a filament of time, the picture flashed: the man hulking over her, the woman crumbling, and had it been a scream and was it from her? The image of him over her provoked an internal conspiracy on her part—was it sex? was it death?—and she took off without even knowing it, gone in an instant, her own dust storm, until she heard it again and stopped, her eyes lashing back and forth, and she fought to regain herself.

It was hard to deny now, it was a scream and the sound provoked in her a desire to scream again too as if she were a, what was it, coyote, answering a fellow's call? A scream like that is a kind of life, it is insurmountable instinct, it is the embryo itself calling loud for life, the fish, the reptile inside us, the chain itself begging, voices combined. If you scream like that you can't feel anything else, can't think anything else, a whole new structure is triggered, an empire of fear finding sound; if you were asked, What was it like when you screamed? you would be baffled, a scream like that inhabits you; there's nothing left.

It's not like a yell of rage or the harsh despairing call of sorrow; it's not the clap of frustration or the clamor of outrage, nor yet the child's beseeching wail of fear; it's terror; it's the loss of wit; it's the sudden, personal slam of fatality bellowing out your lungs.

And, for her, it hit her legs as well. When she could think again—when she noticed she was thinking again—she was near the edge of the park. Her heart was smashing so hard she could hardly breathe; she bent over, hands on her knees, gasping. It had gotten suddenly still; surely she wasn't the only one listening, certainly there were other things out there with ears, noting the vacuum without the scream, wondering uneasily, wondering why it was so still, what it meant for a certain figure whose mouth now was most notice-ably closed. Was she alive?

She looked down; she had the dogs panting and prancing. Fluke looked ragged; had Fluke been dragged?

She had the dogs—surely the dogs would have been effective? No one knew they were wimps; no one knew they fled the snakes if the snakes reared up.

She felt herself melting with dread and regret and self-loathing. How could she have run? Now time was clicking insanely fast, so fast she couldn't keep up with it, couldn't work with it, she was trying to run in deep water—she wanted to be back there, back where that woman screamed; she wanted to see, to help, she wanted to reverse her flight because that had been an aid to crime, hadn't it? She had abetted it, whatever it was, and she couldn't believe it of herself—she had abandoned someone who cried out for help. One of her own; one of her kind.

Her mouth was dragged down at the sides in the effort to get there, get back there before it was too late, whatever "too late" meant. The dogs caught her urgency, they were lunging but sometimes in different directions, all whimpers and growls, but they had heart, they had guts, no wonder everyone despised her because here it was, she knew what that cry meant, it had twist-ed her heart in midstroke, but she had run. Now nothing was as important as finding that woman, restoring her, getting forgiveness no matter what it took, let it take her own blood, her own throat.

She was back, finally, her knees faltering as though badly made, the street-lights coming on strong now.

Back to the underpass. There the bench, the bushes. She held her dogs and leaned forward. Joe-Boy sniffed the air. She could see a small spatter of dark spots and a paper bag. She held the dogs and moved closer, looking all around, looking paranoid and disappointed. The place was empty. She was sure it was here, though, she was sure of it.

She picked up the paper bag, which held a container of milk. A man walked by and she shouted, "Did you see anything? Did you hear anything?"

and he moved a little faster past her, a little startled quickstep when she spoke.

She looked around, behind the trees. It was getting dark now, but there seemed to be more people and her voice was getting too urgent; she could hear it herself and the wrong sound of it made it get even worse because she couldn't help herself. She tried to make it more normal and instead it came out false, like the world's worst self-conscious actress shouting on a small stage. "Did you see a woman? Was she hurt? Did anyone get hurt?"

And then she gave it up. Whatever had happened had stopped happening there at least, and it was pointless, mindless; she had to pull it all together and begin to think or she would lose it somehow in a way she hadn't already—a new and it could only be assumed even more appalling way.

She gritted her teeth, her eyes almost rolling back, she still had to know if that woman had made it, but in New York, in a city like New York, where people go missing without being missed, where someone disappears by moving across town, where some deaths matter and others don't—how would she ever find out if she had allowed someone to die out of cowardice, out of instinct (that hit her hard: her instinct then had chosen that); she hoped it wasn't that bad but never again in an idle moment could she imagine herself as brave, or heroic, or even decent because she didn't know, she simply didn't know what had happened and how could she get through this day and the next, looking out for a headline, a mention, a remark, and wondering, Did that happen because of me? Was that one lost because of me?

~

Snake

D. H. Lawrence

A snake came to my water-trough
On a hot, hot day, and I in pyjamas for the heat,
To drink there.

~

In the deep, strange-scented shade of the great dark carob tree
I came down the steps with my pitcher
And must wait, must stand and wait, for there he was at the trough
   before me.

~

He reached down from a fissure in the earth-wall in the gloom
And trailed his yellow-brown slackness soft-bellied down, over the edge
   of the stone trough
And rested his throat upon the stone bottom,
And where the water had dripped from the tap, in a small clearness,
He sipped with his straight mouth,
Softly drank through his straight gums, into his slack long body,
Silently.

~

Someone was before me at my water-trough,
And I, like a second-comer, waiting.

~

He lifted his head from his drinking, as cattle do,
And looked at me vaguely, as drinking cattle do,
And flickered his two-forked tongue from his lips, and mused a
   moment,
And stooped and drank a little more,
Being earth-brown, earth-golden from the burning bowels of the earth
On the day of Sicilian July, with Etna smoking.

~

The voice of my education said to me
He must be killed,
For in Sicily the black, black snakes are innocent, the gold are
      venomous.

~

And voices in me said, If you were a man
You would take a stick and break him now, and finish him off.

~

But must I confess how I liked him,
How glad I was he had come like a guest in quiet, to drink at my water-
      trough
And depart peaceful, pacified, and thankless,
Into the burning bowels of this earth?

~

Was it cowardice, that I dared not kill him?
Was it perversity, that I longed to talk to him?
Was it humility, to feel so honoured?
I felt so honoured.

~

And yet those voices:
If you were not afraid, you would kill him!

~

And truly I was afraid, I was most afraid,
But even so, honoured still more
That he should seek my hospitality
From out the dark door of the secret earth.

~

He drank enough
And lifted his head, dreamily, as one who has drunken,
And flickered his tongue like a forked night on the air, so black,
Seeming to lick his lips,
And looked around like a god, unseeing, into the air,
And slowly turned his head,
And slowly, very slowly, as if thrice adream,
Proceeded to draw his slow length curving round
And climb again the broken bank of my wall-face.

~

And as he put his head into that dreadful hole,
And as he slowly drew up, snake-easing his shoulders, and entered
            farther,
A sort of horror, a sort of protest against his withdrawing into that
            horrid black hole,
Deliberately going into the blackness, and slowly drawing himself after,
Overcame me now his back was turned.

~

I looked round, I put down my pitcher,
I picked up a clumsy log
And threw it at the water-trough with a clatter.

~

I think it did not hit him,
But suddenly that part of him that was left behind convulsed in
            undignified haste,
Writhed like lightning, and was gone
Into the black hole, the earth-lipped fissure in the wall-front,
At which, in the intense still noon, I stared with fascination.

~

And immediately I regretted it.
I thought how paltry, how vulgar, what a mean act!
I despised myself and the voices of my accursed human education.

~

And I thought of the albatross,
And I wished he would come back, my snake.

~

For he seemed to me again like a king,
Like a king in exile, uncrowned in the underworld,
Now due to be crowned again.

~

And so, I missed my chance with one of the lords
Of life.
And I have something to expiate:
A pettiness.

~

Rattlesnake Roundup

THE LYNDON OLSEN STORY

Willee Lewis

LYNDON OLSON JR. clambered onto a flatbed truck with no apparent difficulty and surveyed the 400 farmers, ranchers, women and children waiting for the show to begin. As he gazed out at the upturned faces, he knew that this was a unique opportunity. For weeks, Olson had been campaigning across Texas's 11th Congressional District—a piece of political real estate anchored by Waco but sprawling across nineteen different counties. During much of that time, he had been taking flak—from Marvin Leath on his right and Lane Denton on his left. But today they were nowhere in sight. It was springtime in Lometa, Texas—at one of the year's premier political-social events, the Rattlesnake Roundup. Mayor Clyde McAnnelly had not only endorsed Olson, but assured him that he would be the only congressional candidate invited to speak at the roundup. It would be the perfect arena for a politician to pitch his platform.

By the time Olson grasped the mike, snake handlers had been entertaining the spectators for some time. They were actually tough, ornery cowpokes, who knew when—and how—to smoke out and scoop up a den of hibernating diamondbacks at no peril to themselves. For weeks before the roundup, they had been doing just that and about a hundred of the critters had been dumped into a large, fenced-off pit on a concrete slab, about thirty feet by thirty feet with two gates facing each other—one to enter; the other to exit, hastily. The crowd had ooohed and aaaaahhhed as these rough rascals/handlers, while reciting a prayer or two, snatched up snakes, put them in their ten-gallon hats and then clapped the hats on their heads. One fellow slid into a sleeping bag that he chose to share with a rattler. Others did rope tricks—only the ropes were not rawhide . . . but real snakes! All in all, a rather amazing sideshow extravaganza, even better than a rodeo roundup.

Lyndon Olson himself had had a fair amount of experience with a particular species of snake—the two-legged kind who slink through the corridors of the Texas State Capitol where he had spent three terms in the State Legislature. They called themselves politicians, but some were simply snakes in the grass, slippery experts at lining their own pockets while conniving with their jackal friends, the lobbyists.

As for the creepy-crawly kind of serpent on display at the Lometa Rattlesnake Roundup, Olson intended to keep them at a safe distance—until he spied his opponents, Leath and Denton. It was an unwelcome surprise: they were both leading Olson in the polls and here they were—working the fringes of the crowd, shaking hands and slowing worming their way toward the flatbed and the mike that Olson was now so jealously guarding.

He quickly sized up the situation, but, before he had even thought it all out, Olson heard himself bellowing into the mike, "Now here come my two opponents. And let me say to them that if you think you're man enough to get elected to that pit of vipers in Washington, DEE CEE, you ought to be willing to walk with me across this pit of vipers right here in Lometa, Texas."

With that, he climbed down from the flatbed and made his way to the rattlesnake pit—all the while he could hear a voice or two in the crowd whispering, "Is he insane?" One woman muttered to her neighbor, "Does he realize what he's about to do? Just to go to Congress?"

But Olson didn't stop. Swinging open one of the gates to the rattlesnake pit to the astonished murmuring of the crowd, he tried to plot a path to the other side that would be the least unsettling to the writhing, hissing snakes coiled between him and safety. He felt as though he was entering the mighty Texas House of Representatives. About midway across, one snake hit him halfway up his right shin and then another took similar aim at his other leg. This is a lot like politicking, he thought. A silent prayer crossed his mind:

Oh, Lord, I hope these suckers are really as lethargic as they seem, so maybe they won't strike any higher.

Olson could hear gasps from the astonished crowd, which by now was pressing close to the fence surrounding the pit. Just like Romans at the Coliseum, and I'm the Christian, he worried.

"Go, go," a couple of onlookers shouted.

After what seemed like an eternity, but with great confidence in his stride, Olson grabbed the opposite gate and quickly escaped the pit—with an inaudible sigh of relief. Only then did he permit himself a close look at the crowd. Leath and Denton were nowhere to be found. Apparently they had hightailed it out of there before he even had finished spitting out his challenge. Surely they had fled to the next county . . .perhaps for a more pressing engagement. The flabbergasted bystanders were aghast at the display of such bravery—or foolhardiness.

Before long, Olson's pit stop was the talk of central Texas. Unfortunately, it did him little good. For on primary day, he ran a strong third to his two more prudent opponents.

"Makes sense," his father said. "Folks thought you were mighty courageous but just too darn crazy to be trusted with taxpayers' money."

What Leath and Denton, and most of the district's voters didn't know, was that Olson, born club footed and the victim of a botched childhood surgery, made that fateful walk with a hidden advantage. The real story is that Lyndon Olson has two wooden legs.

AFTERTHOUGHT: The moral of this story is that what often appears to be stupidity may end up being blind good luck. In the crowd that day were Sen. Lloyd Bentsen and Gov. Dolph Briscoe.

A year later, the governor, impressed by the young man's grit and savvy, named Lyndon L. Olson Jr. as the state insurance commissioner. Incidentally, about that time, Olson married the daughter of the surgeon from his childhood medical travails. Later, he became a cattle rancher, a banker and CEO of the Travelers Insurance Company. In addition, President William Clinton, a comrade from the 1972 McGovern campaign in Texas, named him ambassador to Sweden. He served in that post under Clinton for four years and stayed on another year at the request of President George W. Bush.

The Snake

John Steinbeck

IT WAS ALMOST DARK when young Dr. Phillips swung his sack to his shoulder and left the tide pool. He climbed up over the rocks and squashed along the street in his rubber boots. The street lights were on by the time he arrived at his little commercial laboratory on the cannery street of Monterey. It was a tight little building, standing partly on piers over the bay water and partly on the land. On both sides the big corrugated-iron sardine canneries crowded in on it.

Dr. Phillips climbed the wooden steps and opened the door. The white rats in their cages scampered up and down the wire, and the captive cats in their pens mewed for milk. Dr. Phillips turned on the glaring light over the dissection table and dumped his clammy sack on the floor. He walked to the glass cages by the window where the rattlesnakes lived, leaned over and looked in.

The snakes were bunched and resting in the corners of the cage, but every head was clear; the dusty eyes seemed to look at nothing, but as the young man leaned over the cage the forked tongues, black on the ends and pink behind, twittered out and waved slowly up and down. Then the snakes recognized the man and pulled in their tongues.

Dr. Phillips threw off his leather coat and built a fire in the tin stove; he set a kettle of water on the stove and dropped a can of beans into the water. Then he stood staring down at the sack on the floor. He was a slight young man with the mild, preoccupied eyes of one who looks through a microscope a great deal. He wore a short blond beard.

The draft ran breathily up the chimney and a glow of warmth came from the stove. The little waves washed quietly about the piles under the building. Arranged on shelves about the room were tier above tier of museum jars containing the mounted marine specimens the laboratory dealt in.

Dr. Phillips opened a side door and went into his bedroom, a book-lined cell containing an army cot, a reading light and an uncomfortable wooden chair. He pulled off his rubber boots and put on a pair of sheepskin slippers. When he went back to the other room the water in the kettle was already beginning to hum.

He lifted his sack to the table under the white light and emptied out two dozen common starfish. These he laid out side by side on the table. His preoccupied eyes turned to the busy rats in the wire cages. Taking grain from a paper sack, he poured it into the feeding troughs. Instantly the rats scrambled down from the wire and fell upon the food. A bottle of milk stood on a glass shelf between a small mounted octopus and a jellyfish. Dr. Phillips lifted down the milk and walked to the cat cage, but before he filled the containers he reached in the cage and gently picked out a big rangy alley tabby. He stroked her for a moment and then dropped her in a small black painted box, closed the lid and bolted it and then turned on a petcock which admitted gas into the killing chamber. While the short soft struggle went on in the black box he filled the saucers with milk. One of the cats arched against his hand and he smiled and petted her neck.

The box was quiet now. He turned off the petcock, for the airtight box would be full of gas.

On the stove the pan of water was bubbling furiously about the can of beans. Dr. Phillips lifted out the can with a big pair of forceps, opened it, and emptied the beans into a glass dish. While he ate he watched the starfish on the table. From between the rays little drops of milky fluid were exuding. He bolted his beans and when they were gone he put the dish in the sink and stepped to the equipment cupboard. From this he took a microscope and a pile of little glass dishes. He filled the dishes one by one with sea water from a tap and arranged them in a line beside the starfish. He took out his watch and laid it on the table under the pouring white light. The waves washed with little sighs against the piles under the floor. He took an eyedropper from a drawer and bent over the starfish.

At that moment there were quick soft steps on the wooden stairs and a strong knocking at the door. A slight grimace of annoyance crossed the young man's face as he went to open. A tall, lean woman stood in the doorway. She was dressed in a severe dark suit—her straight black hair, growing low on a flat forehead, was mussed as though the wind had been blowing it. Her black eyes glittered in the strong light.

She spoke in a soft throaty voice, "May I come in? I want to talk to you."

"I'm very busy just now," he said half-heartedly. "I have to do things at times." But he stood away from the door. The tall woman slipped in.

"I'll be quiet until you can talk to me."

He closed the door and brought the uncomfortable chair from the bedroom. "You see," he apologized, "the process is started and I must get to it." So many people wandered in and asked questions. He had little routines of explanations for the commoner processes. He could say them without thinking. "Sit here. In a few minutes I'll be able to listen to you."

The tall woman leaned over the table. With the eyedropper the young man gathered fluid from between the rays of the starfish and squirted it into a bowl of water, and then he drew some milky fluid and squirted it in the same bowl and stirred the water gently with the eyedropper. He began his little patter of explanation.

"When starfish are sexually mature they release sperm and ova when they are exposed at low tide. By choosing mature specimens and taking them out of the water, I give them a condition of low tide. Now I've mixed the sperm and eggs. Now I put some of the mixture in each one of these ten watch glasses. In ten minutes I will kill those in the first glass with menthol, twenty minutes later I will kill the second group and then a new group every twenty minutes. Then I will have arrested the process in stages, and I will mount the series on microscope slides for biologic study." He paused. "Would you like to look at this first group under the microscope?"

"No, thank you."

He turned quickly to her. People always wanted to look through the glass. She was not looking at the table at all, but at him. Her black eyes were on him, but they did not seem to see him. He realized why—the irises were as dark as the pupils, there was no color line between the two. Dr. Phillips was piqued at her answer. Although answering questions bored him, a lack of interest in what he was doing irritated him. A desire to arouse her grew in him.

"While I'm waiting the first ten minutes I have something to do. Some people don't like to see it. Maybe you'd better step into that room until I finish."

"No," she said in her soft flat tone. "Do what you wish. I will wait until you can talk to me." Her hands rested side by side on her lap. She was completely at rest. Her eyes were bright but the rest of her was almost in a state of suspended animation. He thought, "Low metabolic rate, almost as low as a frog's, from the looks." The desire to shock her out of her inanition possessed him again.

He brought a little wooden cradle to the table, laid out scalpels and scissors and rigged a big hollow needle to a pressure tube. Then from the killing chamber he brought the limp dead cat and laid it in the cradle and tied its legs to hooks in the sides. He glanced sidewise at the woman. She had not moved. She was still at rest.

The cat grinned up into the light, its pink tongue stuck out between its needle teeth. Dr. Phillips deftly snipped open the skin at the throat; with a scalpel he slit through and found an artery. With flawless technique he put the needle in the vessel and tied it in with gut. "Embalming fluid," he explained. "Later I'll inject yellow mass into the veinous system and red mass into the arterial system—for bloodstream dissection—biology classes."

He looked around at her again. Her dark eyes seemed veiled with dust. She looked without expression at the cat's open throat. Not a drop of blood had escaped. The incision was clean. Dr. Phillips looked at his watch. "Time for the first group." He shook a few crystals of menthol into the first watch glass.

The woman made him nervous. The rats climbed about on the wire of their cage again and squeaked softly. The waves under the building beat with little shocks on the piles.

The young man shivered. He put a few lumps of coal in the stove and sat down. "Now," he said. "I haven't anything to do for twenty minutes." He noticed how short her chin was between lower lip and point. She seemed to awaken slowly, to come up out of some deep pool of consciousness. Her head raised and her dark dusty eyes moved about the room and then came back on him.

"I was waiting," she said. Her hands remained side by side on her lap. "You have snakes?"

"Why, yes," he said rather loudly. "I have about two dozen rattlesnakes. I milk out the venom and send it to the antivenom laboratories."

She continued to look at him but her eyes did not center on him, rather they covered him and seemed to see in a big circle all around him. "Have you a male snake, a male rattlesnake?"

"Well, it just happens I know I have. I came in one morning and found a big snake in—in coition with a smaller one. That's very rare in captivity. You see, I do know I have a male snake."

"Where is he?"

"Why, right in the glass cage by the window there."

Her head swung slowly around but her two quiet hands did not move. She turned back toward him. "May I see?"

He got up and walked to the case by the window. On the sand bottom the knot of rattlesnakes lay entwined, but their heads were clear. Their tongues came out and flickered a moment and then waved up and down feeling the air for vibrations. Dr. Phillips nervously turned his head. The woman was standing beside him. He had not heard her get up from the chair. He had heard only the splash of water among the piles and the scampering of the rats on the wire screen.

She said softly, "Which is the male you spoke of?"

He pointed to a thick, dusty grey snake lying by itself in one corner of the cage. "That one. He's nearly five feet long. He comes from Texas. Our Pacific coast snakes are usually smaller. He's been taking all the rats, too. When I want the others to eat I have to take him out."

The woman stared down at the blunt dry head. The forked tongue slipped out and hung quivering for a long moment. "And you're sure he's a male."

"Rattlesnakes are funny," he said glibly. "Nearly every generalization proves wrong. I don't like to say anything definite about rattlesnakes, but—yes—I can assure you he's a male."

Her eyes did not move from the flat head. "Will you sell him to me?"

"Sell him?" he cried. "Sell him to you?"

"You do sell specimens, don't you?"

"Oh—yes. Of course I do. Of course I do."

"How much? Five dollars? Ten?"

"Oh! Not more than five. But—do you know anything about rattlesnakes? You might be bitten."

She looked at him for a moment. "I don't intend to take him. I want to leave him here, but—I want him to be mine. I want to come here and look at him and feed him and to know he's mine." She opened a little purse and took out a five-dollar bill. "Here! Now he is mine."

Dr. Phillips began to be afraid. "You could come to look at him without owning him."

"I want him to be mine."

"Oh, Lord!" he cried. "I've forgotten the time." He ran to the table. "Three minutes over. It won't matter much." He shook menthol crystals into the second watch glass. And then he was drawn back to the cage where the woman still stared at the snake.

She asked, "What does he eat?"

"I feed them white rats, rats from the cage over there."

"Will you put him in the other cage? I want to feed him."

"But he doesn't need food. He's had a rat already this week. Sometimes they don't eat for three or four months. I had one that didn't eat for over a year."

In her low monotone she asked, "Will you sell me a rat?"

He shrugged his shoulders. "I see. You want to watch how rattlesnakes eat. All right. I'll show you. The rat will cost twenty-five cents. It's better than a bullfight if you look at it one way, and it's simply a snake eating his dinner if you look at it another." His tone had become acid. He hated people who made sport of natural processes. He was not a sportsman but a biologist. He could kill a thousand animals for knowledge, but not an insect for pleasure. He'd been over this in his mind before.

She turned her head slowly toward him and the beginning of a smile formed on her thin lips. "I want to feed my snake," she said. "I'll put him in the other cage." She had opened the top of the cage and dipped her hand in before he knew what she was doing. He leaped forward and pulled her back. The lid banged shut.

"Haven't you any sense," he asked fiercely. "Maybe he wouldn't kill you, but he'd make you damned sick in spite of what I could do for you."

"You put him in the other cage then," she said quietly.

Dr. Phillips was shaken. He found that he was avoiding the dark eyes that didn't seem to look at anything. He felt that it was profoundly wrong to put a rat into the cage, deeply sinful; and he didn't know why. Often he had put rats in the cage when someone or other had wanted to see it, but this desire tonight sickened him. He tried to explain himself out of it.

"It's a good thing to see," he said. "It shows you how a snake can work. It makes you have a respect for a rattlesnake. Then, too, lots of people have dreams about the terror of snakes making the kill. I think because it is a subjective rat. The person is the rat. Once you see it the whole matter is objective. The rat is only a rat and the terror is removed."

He took a long stick equipped with a leather noose from the wall. Opening the trap he dropped the noose over the big snake's head and tightened the thong. A piercing dry rattle filled the room. The thick body writhed and slashed about the handle of the stick as he lifted the snake out and dropped it in the feeding cage. It stood ready to strike for a time, but the buzzing gradually ceased. The snake crawled into a corner, made a big figure eight with its body and lay still.

"You see," the young man explained, "these snakes are quite tame. I've had them a long time. I suppose I could handle them if I wanted to, but everyone who does handle rattlesnakes gets bitten sooner or later. I just don't want to take the chance." He glanced at the woman. He hated to put in the rat. She had moved over in front of the new cage; her black eyes were on the stony head of the snake again.

She said, " Put in a rat."

Reluctantly he went to the rat cage. For some reason he was sorry for the rat, and such a feeling had never come to him before. His eyes went over the mass of swarming white bodies climbing up the screen toward him. "Which one?" he thought. "Which one shall it be?" Suddenly he turned angrily to the woman. "Wouldn't you rather I put in a cat? Then you'd see a real fight. The cat might even win, but if it did it might kill the snake. I'll sell you a cat if you like."

She didn't look at him. "Put in a rat," she said. "I want him to eat."

He opened the rat cage and thrust his had in. His fingers found a tail and he lifted a plump, red-eyed rat out of the cage. It struggled up to try to bite his fingers and, failing, hung spread out and motionless from its tail. He walked quickly across the room, opened the feeding cage and dropped the rat in on the sand floor. "Now, watch it," he cried.

The woman did not answer him. Her eyes were on the snake where it lay still. Its tongue, flicking in and out rapidly, tasted the air of the cage.

The rat landed on its feet, turned around and sniffed at its pink naked tail and then unconcernedly trotted across the sand, smelling as it went. The room was silent. Dr. Phillips did not know whether the water sighed among the piles or whether the woman sighed. Out of the corner of his eyes he saw her body crouch and stiffen.

The snake moved out smoothly, slowly. The tongue flicked in and out. The motion was so gradual, so smooth that it didn't seem to be motion at all. In the other end of the cage the rat perked up in a sitting position and began to lick down the fine white hair on its chest. The snake moved on, keeping always a deep S curve in its neck.

The silence beat on the young man. He felt the blood drifting up in his body. He said loudly, "See! He keeps the striking curve ready. Rattlesnakes are cautious, almost cowardly animals. The mechanism is so delicate. The snake's dinner is to be got by an operation as deft as a surgeon's job. He takes no chance with his instruments."

The snake had flowed to the middle of the cage by now. The rat looked up, saw the snake and then unconcernedly went back to licking its chest.

"It's the most beautiful thing in the world," the young man said. His veins were throbbing. "It's the most terrible thing in the world."

The snake was close now. Its head lifted a few inches from the sand. The head weaved slowly back and forth, aiming, getting distance, aiming. Dr. Phillips glanced at the woman. He turned sick. She was weaving too, not much, just a suggestion.

The rat looked up and saw the snake. It dropped to four feet and back up, and then—the stroke. It was impossible to see, simply a flash. The rat jarred as though under an invisible blow. The snake backed hurriedly into the corner from which it had come, and settled down, its tongue working constantly.

"Perfect!" Dr. Phillips cried. "Right between the shoulder blades. The fangs must have almost reached the heart."

The rat stood still, breathing like a little white bellows. Suddenly it leaped in the air and landed on its side. Its legs kicked spasmodically for a second and it was dead.

The woman relaxed, relaxed sleepily.

"Well," the young man demanded, "it was an emotional bath, wasn't it?"

She turned her misty eyes to him. "Will he eat it now?" she asked.

"Of course he'll eat it. He didn't kill it for a thrill. He killed it because he was hungry."

The corners of the woman's mouth turned up a trifle again. She looked back at the snake. "I want to see him eat it."

Now the snake came out of its corner again. There was no striking curve in its neck, but it approached the rat gingerly, ready to jump back in case it attacked. It nudged the body gently with its blunt nose, and drew away. Satisfied that it was dead, the snake touched the body all over with its chin, from head to tail. It seemed to measure the body and to kiss it. Finally it opened its mouth and unhinged its jaws at the corners.

Dr. Phillips put his will against his head to keep it from turning toward the woman. He thought, "If she's opening her mouth, I'll be sick. I'll be afraid." He succeeded in keeping his eyes away.

The snake fitted its jaws over the rat's head and then with a slow peristaltic pulsing, began to engulf the rat. The jaws gripped again.

Dr. Phillips turned away and went to his work table. "You've made me miss one of the series," he said bitterly. "The set won't be complete." He put one of the watch glasses under a low-power microscope and looked at it, and then angrily he poured the content of all the dishes into the sink. The waves had fallen so that only a wet whisper came up through the floor. The young man lifted a trapdoor at his feet and dropped the starfish down into the black water. He paused at the cat, crucified in the cradle and grinning comically into the light. Its body was puffed with embalming fluid. He shut off the pressure, withdrew the needle and tied the vein.

"Would you like some coffee?" he asked.

"No, thank you. I shall be going pretty soon."

He walked to her where she stood in front of the snake's cage. The rat was swallowed, all except an inch of pink tail stuck out of the snake's mouth like a sardonic tongue. The throat heaved again and the tail disappeared. The jaws snapped back into their sockets, and the big snake crawled heavily to the corner, made a big eight and dropped its head on the sand.

"He's asleep now," the woman said. "I'm going now. But I'll come back and feed my snake every little while. I'll pay for the rats. I want him to have plenty. And sometime—I'll take him away with me." Her eyes came out of their dusty dream for a moment. "Remember, he's mine. Don't take his poison. I want him to have it. Good-night." She walked swiftly to the door and went out. He heard her footsteps on the stairs, but could not hear her walk away on the pavement.

Dr. Phillips turned a chair around and sat down in front of the snake cage. He tried to comb out his thought as he looked at the torpid snake. "I've read so much about psychological sex symbols," he thought. "It doesn't seem to explain. Maybe I'm too much alone. Maybe I should kill the snake. If I knew—no, I can't pray to anything."

For weeks he expected her to return. "I will go out and leave her alone here when she comes," he decided. "I won't see the damned thing again."

She never came again. For months he looked for her when he walked about in the town. Several times he ran after some tall woman thinking it might be she. But never saw her again—ever.

~

Gold Snake

Rose Styron

November. still
our isle reels gold.
Maple leaves that catch the wind
shake
tree and lawn
its wide green cloth, its
gold-rimmed floral china strewn
from merrie England
under the bard's globed sky.

Sunrise out the abandoned window
(how I star-tired dimmed to sleep)
wakes the Sound—
stray swan, pale sand grass
dahlias nodding by the wall—
and spotlights:
Snake.

(what dreams unfold
luring me down
the gates of day to keep).

Gold snake atop my garden wall
just as dawn in Vineyard Haven
haloes East Chop, I
in thrall to sunrise always
plunging waveward
racing shorebirds in crescendo,
free,
shiver, stock-still, shadowed
watch your tongue flick, savoring air
watch you, shadowed, snaking inland
gone from sea.

Golden moment that still slithers
snake, you slither under ivy
through some creek I have not found
yet though I follow

golden snakeskin now.

~

Snake in a Rug

Winston Groom

SOME PEOPLE LIKE SNAKES; some probably even love them. Not me. I am one of those "unenlightend" people with fear and loathing for those things that will bite and hurt me. Most recent case in point:

Pat Oliphant, the famed political cartoonist, was stopping through to see me in the mountains of North Carolina en route from his home in Santa Fe to his residence in Washington, D.C. The morning before he was to arrive a call came from his wife, Susan, saying they'd be late.

"We're in Memphis," she explained, "and Pat's been bitten by a rattlesnake."

"Jesus!"

"He never felt it at first," she went on. "He was loading some Najavo rugs from the garage into the back of our SUV and one of them must have been in it. As we drove across the country his arm began to itch and then swell and there were two little bitty fang marks in it. By the time we got to Memphis we knew we'd better stop."

The first hospital they saw was Elvis Presley Memorial and by luck and coincidence there was a woman doctor there who was Memphis's resident expert in snakebites. They gave him antivenom and did other things and sent him on his way. When they arrived at my place Oliphant was in fine fettle, proudly showing off the fang bites in his badly disclored wrist.

"And you never saw the snake or felt it bite?" I asked incredulously.

"Nope. Must have been a little one, hiding in one of the rugs." He pointed to the back of the SUV.

"You think it's still in there?" I inquired.

"Don't know. Might be. Well, Susan," he said jovially, "I might as well bring in our suitcases." He started to open the car door.

"Wait!" I said. "What if the snake's still in there?"

"Good point," says Oliphant. "Well, what do we do now?"

"Er, I guess you've got to have your luggage, right?" I said.

"Right."

"Is it where the rugs are—the rug with the snake in it?" For some reason I suddenly thought about Cleopatra and her asp. It had been an answer to a clue in the *Times* crossword puzzle that day.

"No," he said, "its closer up front."

"Good." I told him. "So here's what you do. Open the door quick. Snatch out the luggage. Lock the door and give me the keys."

"You want my keys?"

"I will give them back to you tomorrow. When you leave."

~

Snakes are sneaky, like the one in the Garden of Eden, which is another reason I don't like them. Most of the time you don't know if the snake is there until it jumps up and bites you or slithers away under your feet. But not always.

When I was in college I spent a lot of summertime up at an old duck hunting and fishing camp in the huge swampy delta north of Mobile, Alabama. The only way you could get to the place was by motorboat, about an hour and a half. It was a great old place, but primitive. We had WWII surplus bunk beds, an iron railroad caboose stove and propane gas mantle lights that had to be turned on by twisting a handle in a wooden box located on the wharf outside.

One time a friend and I had been up there fishing all day and around dusk were cleaning the fish out on the wharf and throwing the offal into the water. Soon we began to notice the water churning.

"What's that?" I asked.

"Probably mullet going after the fish guts," my friend said. Then:

"Jesus!"

"What?"

"Look!"

It wasn't mullet. It was snakes. Big fat water moccasins; dozens of them. They had sensed the blood and fish entrails and had come out of the big cyprus swamp to eat. It was revolting.

"Uggg," I said, "Let's go inside and have a drink."

I don't think either of us thought much more about it until a few weeks later.

Summer was nearly over and we'd gone back up to the camp for one last weekend of fishing. I tied the boat up to the rickety dock and my friend walked along the wharf to the propane gas tank to turn it on. I was unloading gear when I heard him scream.

"Jesus!"

He came suddenly tearing past me and leaped into the shallow, murky water. Before I could ask what in hell was going on, I found out. Hornets. They had built a big nest inside the propane box and when my friend had reached in to turn on the propane, he disturbed them. (By the way, that's another thing I don't like—hornets or, for that matter, cockroaches, mosquitoes, rats, etc.)

The hornets, in hot pursuit of my friend, discovered me, too, and I took two or three quick hits before joining him in the water, which was about waist deep and mucky on the bottom. We'd squat down and hold our breath long as we could, surface and get another gasp and submerge again. We'd been doing that for a couple of minutes when we both surfaced at the same time.

"Jesus!"

"What?"

"The snakes!"

We both had the same recollected thought simultaneously. We looked at each other. The hornets, though not as many as before, were still zipping and diving around us in the darkening sky.

We looked at each other again, then, like a pair of Siamese Twins, each took a deep breath and slowly submerged beneath the brackish tepid waters.

Jesus.

~

Snakes Alive

Dave Barry

IT'S A CHILLING QUESTION that all of us—even veteran airline passengers—ask ourselves every time we get on an airplane: "Is this going to be the one? Is this the flight where I get eaten by a python?"

This question takes on an even greater urgency than usual in light of a recent lawsuit filed by a Texas couple against Continental Airlines. According to an Associated Press article sent in by many alert readers, the suit alleges that the couple and their 5-year-old daughter boarded a Continental flight from Houston to La Guardia last October, unaware that "the passenger seated in front of them had brought a python aboard in a gym bag, tucked under the seat."

As a frequent flier, I find this ironic. I mean, when I fly, I have to go through a checkpoint staffed by beady-eyed security personnel who act deeply suspicious about my laptop computer, as though I'm going to leap up in the middle of the flight and yell, "Take this plane to Cuba, or I'm going to REFORMAT MY HARD DRIVE!" And yet these same personnel just let this guy waltz through carrying a MAJOR snake.

Anyway, after the plane took off, the python, as you have no doubt already guessed, decided to get out of the gym bag and stretch its legs. The couple's lawsuit states that when the mother saw the snake, it was crawling toward the daughter "in preparation for attack."

The article does not state what happened next, although apparently nobody was physically harmed. Perhaps an alert passenger thrust his airline dinner entrée at the python, causing it to flee in terror back into its gym bag. (On a recent flight I was handed a piece of alleged chicken that was much scarier than anything Sigourney Weaver ever fought with a flamethrower.) But the point is that, unless you like the idea of becoming Purina Brand Viper Chow at 35,000 feet, you should write to your congressman and demand passage of a federal law requiring that any snake traveling on a commercial flight must be (1) securely locked inside an escape-proof container, and (2) dead.

Perhaps you don't think this issue concerns you. Perhaps you're thinking, "I rarely fly, so what do I care about snakes in airplanes? It's not as though . . . mmm . . . snakes are showing up in kitchen-appliance cartons!"

Try telling that to the woman in Roanoke, Texas, whose chilling ordeal was reported in an October 5 *Fort Worth Star-Telegram* story sent in by several alert readers. The woman brought home a brand-new Proctor-Silex Ovenmaster toaster oven, and when she opened the box, guess what she found, writhing around on its scaly belly, flicking out its evil forked tongue? You guessed it: O. J. Simpson.

No, that was a cheap shot, and I am instructing you to disregard it. What this woman found was an eighteen-inch snake. Needless to say she screamed, because the Ovenmaster is supposed to come with a Gila monster.

No, seriously, she screamed because she was expecting a 100 percent reptile-free appliance. Her husband killed the snake (the story does not say how; perhaps he struck it with an airline omelet), and the woman took it, in a plastic bag, back to the Target store where she purchased the Ovenmaster. There, the story states, "a store clerk with some reptile knowledge" identified it as a harmless corn snake. The store's merchandise manager assured consumers that this type of incident is very rare. "It's not something I've heard about happening in my lifetime," he stated.

Perhaps not. But just in case, we all should be more aware of basic reptile-safety procedures, which is why I am so grateful that an alert reader who lives in Thailand sent in an article that appeared in the *Bangkok Post* following the escape of an estimated 100 crocodiles from what are described as "reptile farms" along the Chao Phrays River. This article begins, I swear:

"People should not fear being eaten by hungry crocodiles that escape from reptile farms because they can be easily caught using a piece of rope and some food as bait, according to a secretary to Prime Minister and Interior Minister Banharn Silpa-archa."

(Don't you wish OUR politicians told us useful stuff like this, instead of yammering about Medicare?)

The article quotes an official named Veerakorn Kharnprakob as saying that all you have to do is put out some food, wait until the crocodile approaches, then "simply tiptoe close to it and gently place a noose around its head." The article states that "the chance of the crocodile eating you instead of the bait is apparently very remote and hardly worth worrying about."

That is certainly reassuring, and I hope you'll bear Mr. Veerakorn's easy capture technique in mind the next time you're in a potentially crocodile-intensive environment, such as Thailand, or a Continental Airlines plane. You can make a noose from your audio headset cord; for bait, you can use the drunk in seat 23F who keeps calling the flight attendant "babe."

Lucca's Big Do

Thomas Caplan

LUCCA ARRIVED in the United States aboard the B.O.A.C. afternoon flight from Bermuda not too long after John F. Kennedy was elected president. As usual, he said not a word—didn't make a sound, really—during the trip. The long, narrow cabin of the VC-10 channeled dozens of conversations into a single lulling vibration that seemed, at least to others, to harmonize with the rhythmic shiver of the fuselage itself. Yet all Lucca cared about was the pleasant sensation—a rapid repetition of tingles—transmitted to the bones of his skull. He had been asleep for far too many hours now, but he craved more. In fact, the nearer the calendar brought him to the end of his curse, the more passionately and single-mindedly he desired his sleep. For sleep, to him, meant relinquishing not only observation but the subsequent analysis and judgment that observation, once exercised, necessitated.

Strictly speaking, Lucca was not yet his name. Having slipped through (yet again) both Immigration and Customs under cover of his new protector, he remained, as ever, a nameless, stateless fellow—practically shapeless, too, although that hardly needed pointing out. Lucca, as everyone who had known him in his youth knew, could rise or, if required, shrink to any occasion. His christening was accidental, the inadvertent gift of a boy—an American scion, blond and not quite five—who lived in the Georgetown house where he would be staying and whose tongue-tied enunciation of "Look at" one Saturday morning all of a sudden yielded up "Lucca." Not that Lucca minded! By then he had been everywhere, met everyone, known just about everything there was to know. And he liked Italians—the very idea of them, sleek in profile, low, ready and imperturbable on the spur of any adventure, in their blood orange Ferraris. He could have fared much worse; he could have been someone who breathed, yet was afraid of pleasure—a defensive being, more complicated than was likely to be salutary in the end. Over the centuries, the epochs, he had observed several such among God's creations.

At the end of the day, he preferred simplicity to sophistication. He could help neither his own incomparable longevity, which was the result of an ancient and intricate curse most of whose exact clauses had been forgotten, nor the unusual perspective with which it had burdened him: an admixture of humor and fatigue. Anyway, time was growing short. There was very little left of it for him to bear.

Not quite a yard in length, flourishing, after a recent shedding, a bright new coat of protectively colored scales, Lucca had been petrified in a moment of undulating forward movement. His head, plated in fine silver, remained fierce, but cocked at a jaunty angle that would have seemed wholly unthreatening were he not a serpent. His forked tongue had been replaced by a narrow gauge, fire-breathing rope wick to which one or another shaman had imparted the magical property of self-regeneration. All in all, not a bad idea, Lucca decided when he first realized he had been fashioned into a cigarette lighter by that elfin jeweler in Constantinople. He was on the way back from Shanghai at that point, an adder-commuter on the Silk Road for what felt like forever now. He had known other incarnations—bookend, doorstop, *objet d'art*—but the more he considered the matter, the more satisfied he was with this one. It was still a golden, if, by the time he decamped to Washington, a waning age of tobacco and, keen of sight but hard of hearing (like all snakes), he preferred the close-to-the-action view afforded from coffee and occasional side tables.

One afternoon the boy of the house, alone in the care of a uniformed maid while his mother took tea at an embassy, put aside his reader and soon fell asleep on the reupholstered French provincial sofa. This proved convenient as, until the expiration of his curse, Lucca could communicate only by telepathic means and, even then, exclusively to sleeping children.

"All alone?" Lucca finally asked the dreaming boy, whose name was Oliver.

"Yes. I didn't know you could talk," Oliver replied. "I didn't realize you could move your eyes. That's really cool."

"Where's your mother?"

"Out. At another big do. That's what she told me. She'll be back by five-thirty, '*at the latest*.'"

"I have a 'big do' coming up myself soon," the viper said. He had a high voice.

"You do?"

"Um-huh," Lucca said. "Want me to tell you a secret? I'm going to break free."

"You are?"

"At last. At *long* last!"

Oliver furrowed his young brow, which was smooth but querying.

So Lucca continued to hold forth. "Well then, since there appears to be time, would you like to hear a story?"

"About what?" Oliver's tone, despite his best intentions, sounded peevish. Lucca hesitated.

"Is it a story about you?"

Lucca nodded shyly, by instinct; he smiled a gentleman's smile of embarrassment. Then he went on—quickly, almost brusquely—to reprise for Oliver the story of his peripatetic, glamorous, though misfortune-filled life. Before any of today's religions were born a sorcerer in possession of mystical powers had enchanted him into a petrified state within which he had remained utterly conscious, but from which he could never—well, very seldom—make his consciousness known. In this form he had been bought, bartered and sold for several millennia and on every continent save Antarctica. It was, he was certain Oliver could understand, very frustrating. Nevertheless, though long lasting, that curse, like everything in life, was ultimately temporary. In fact, according to the schedule that had accompanied the curse and which he had at once burned into his memory, it should be coming to an end "imminently."

"What will happen to you then?"

"That depends."

"On what?" the boy inquired.

"Time and circumstance," Lucca declared. "What else?"

"What is 'circumstance'?"

"The when, where and why of a thing."

"I don't understand."

"Depending upon," Lucca explained hurriedly, "the balance of things at the precise instant my curse expires. As I understand it."

"What?" Oliver looked even more profoundly confused.

"You know," Lucca prodded, "the presence or absence of love. That sort of thing." He paused, then, dissembling, abruptly added, "In the world—the world at large." He didn't mean this exactly. For by "love" he meant the love of innocents, that pure and credulous generosity that falls upon its object without expectation or qualification and without which the world seemed, if not unjustified then irredeemable. Given time, of course, love was bound to mutate into desire. Such was human nature—the inevitable way of things—but, oh my, before that happened, before selflessness and selfishness embraced . . . He dared not elaborate for the very concept was both too complex and too subtle to articulate, especially to an innocent.

Oliver mulled the idea, which struck chords both familiar and foreign. Bangs covered his closed eyelids. Then a sound—larger creaks succeeding smaller ones, the regular transit of tumblers in the front door's lock—startled him. His father was arriving home early from the Senate. Coming awake, Oliver saw two men beside his father. One, the taller, he knew immediately, had all his life. The other he had never seen. Practiced in the art of self-presentation, Oliver grabbed his reader in his fist and stood up smartly.

"*Ollie! There's* my boy," his father exclaimed as he bounded across the fraying Persian carpet, then lifted the child high in his strong, right, serving arm.

Both visitors smiled at him warmly, but, cradled at his father's biceps, Oliver determined that they had short attention spans.

"So there are missiles in Cuba, and we've got *proof*," one of the men proclaimed eventually in a world-weary, "I could have told you so" way. "And this from the president, no less, not some pettifog."

Oliver, having not yet dispatched his dream, not only listened and watched; he observed Lucca listening and watching.

"I'd like to know what in hell we're going to do about it," the same man pressed on.

"Go up in smoke!" warned the other.

"Take it easy," his father told them. His father was wonderful. His manner was so assured, just right for a man in control of things, a father with a promising son. Even a boy halfway through kindergarten could comprehend that much.

Without letting go of Oliver, indeed without ever releasing his focus upon him, his father lifted the invisibly sensate lighter from the tabletop and, not too cavalierly, handed it to his colleague, who was already tugging a Camel from its tight new pack. "Here," his father offered, "I believe you just might find this helpful."

~

From: *My India*

Jim Corbett

BACHELORS AND THEIR SERVANTS, as a rule, get into more or less set habits and my servants and I were no exception to the rule. Except when work was heavy I invariably returned to my house at 8 P.M. and when my house servant, waiting in the veranda, saw me coming he called to the water-man to lay my bath, for whether it was summer or winter I always had a hot bath. There were three rooms at the front of the house opening onto the veranda: a dining room, a sitting room, and a bedroom. Attached to the bed-room was a small bathroom, ten feet long and six wide. This bathroom had two doors and one small window. One of the doors opened on the veranda, and the other led to the bedroom. The window was opposite the bedroom door, and set high up in the outer wall of the house. The furniture of the bathroom consisted of an egg-shaped wooden bath, long enough to sit in, a wooden bath mat with holes in it, and two earthen vessels containing cold water. After the waterman had laid the bath my servant would bolt the outer door of the bathroom and on his way through the bedroom pick up the shoes I had discarded and take them to the kitchen to clean. There he would remain until I called for dinner.

One night after my servant had gone to the kitchen I took a small hand-lamp off the dressing table, went into the bathroom, and there placed it on a low wall, six inches high and nine inches wide, which ran halfway across the width of the room. Then I turned and bolted the door, which like most doors in India sagged on its hinges and would not remain shut unless bolted. Since I had spent most of that day on the coal platform I did not spare the soap, and with a lather on my head and face that did credit to the manufacturers I opened my eyes to replace the soap on the bath mat when, to my horror, I saw the head of a snake projecting over the end of the bath and within a few inches of my toes. My movements while soaping my head and splashing the water about had evidently annoyed the snake, a big cobra, for its hood was expanded and its long forked tongue was flicking in and out of its wicked-looking mouth. The right thing for me to have done would have been to keep my hands moving, draw my feet away from the snake, and moving very slowly stand up and step backwards to the door behind me, keeping my eyes on the snake all the time. But what I very foolishly did was to grab the sides of the bath and stand up and step backwards, all in one movement, onto the low wall. On this cemented wall my foot slipped, and while trying to regain my balance a stream of water ran off my elbow onto the wick of the lamp and extinguished it, plunging the room into pitch darkness. There I was, shut in a small dark room with one of the most deadly snakes in India. One step to the left or one step to the rear would have taken me to either of the two doors, but not knowing where the snake was I was afraid to move for fear of putting my bare foot on it. Moreover, both doors were bolted at the bottom, and even if I avoided stepping on the snake I should have to feel about for the bolts where the snake, in his efforts to get out of the room, was most likely to be.

The servants' quarters were in a corner of the compound some fifty yards on the dining-room side of the house, so shouting to them would be of no avail and my only hope of rescue was that my servant would get tired of waiting for me to call for dinner, or that a friend would come to see me, and I devoutly hoped this would happen before the cobra bit me. The fact that the cobra was as much trapped as I was in no way comforted me, for only a few days previously one of my men had a similar experience. He had gone into his house in the early afternoon in order to put away the wages I had just paid him. While he was opening his box he heard a hiss behind him, and turning round saw a cobra advancing towards him from the direction of the open door. Racked against the wall behind him, for there was only one door to the room, the unfortunate man had tried to fend off the cobra with his hands, and while doing so was bitten twelve times on his hands and legs. Neighbors heard his cries and came to his rescue, but he died a few minutes later.

I learned that night that small things can be more nerve-racking and terrifying than big happenings. Every drop of water that trickled down my legs was converted in my imagination into the long forked tongue of the cobra licking my bare skin, preparatory to burying his fangs in my flesh.

How long I remained in the room with cobra, I cannot say. My servant said later it was only half an hour, and no sound has ever been more welcome to me than the sounds I heard as he came to lay the table for dinner. I called him to the bathroom door, told him of my predicament, and instructed him to fetch a lantern and a ladder. After another long wait I heard a babel of voices, followed by the scraping of the ladder against the outer wall of the house. Even when the lantern had been lifted to the window, ten feet above ground, it did not illuminate the room, so I told the man who was holding it to break a pane of glass and pass the lantern through the opening. The opening was too small for the lantern to be passed in upright. However, after it had been relit three times it was finally inserted in the room. Feeling that the cobra was behind me, I turned my head and, by the light of the lantern, saw it lying at the bottom of the bedroom door two feet away. Leaning forward very slowly, I picked up the heavy bath mat, raised it high and let it fall as the cobra was sliding over the floor towards me. Fortunately I judged my aim accurately and the bath mat crashed down on the cobra's neck six inches from its head. As it bit at the wood and lashed about with its tail I took a hasty stride to the veranda door and in a moment was outside among a crowd of men, armed with sticks and carrying lanterns, for word had got round to the railway quarters that I was having a life-and-death struggle with a big snake in a locked room.

The pinned-down snake was soon dispatched and it was not until the last of the men had gone, leaving their congratulations, that I realized I had no clothes on and that my eyes were full of soap. How the snake came to be in the bathroom I never knew. It may have entered by one of the doors, or it may have fallen from the roof which was made of thatch and full of rats and squirrels, and tunneled with sparrow's nests. Anyway, the servants who had laid my bath and I had a reason to be thankful, for that night we had approached very near the gate of the Happy Hunting Grounds.

Folklore and Mythology

The Serpent-Symbol

Anonymous

I.

Raise the silver-crusted goblet
    Pour the golden champagne wine;
Drinking deep a flowing bumper
    To the cause of truth divine,
For the serpent-Symbol crawling
    In his murk and slimy bed,
Now lies crushed to earth and bleeding
    With our heel upon his head.

II.

Through the blinding seething tempest,
    Through the rocking, raging sea;
To its glorious destination
    Sailed the armies of the free,
Sailed the fleet of white-singed specters
    An inevitable fate,
Towards the recreant rebel brother,
    Towards the Serpent-Symbol State.

III.

We had nursed him in our bosom
    Through long years of peace and strife,
Warmed and quickened through our pulses

He had struck our very life.
Robbed, insulted and dishonored
    With our heads bowed down in shame
Now, like death, the blow unerring,
    Sped to win us back our name.

IV.

Hark! The shells that burst and shattered,
    Hurling death on every side,
Rings the death-peal of Rebellion—
    Hear it echo far and wide!
In their heart the thorn is rankling,
    Traitors—they shall traitors find,
Till in death their eyes shall open
    Seeing then that they were blind.

V.

In the glorious God of battles,
    We can place our earnest trust,
Till we see the Serpent-Symbol
    Writhing, dying, bite the dust,
Nerved like steel and strong as iron,
    Let us forward to the last;
Till a peace, in glory conquered,
    With a future like the past.

Metamorphoses

BOOK THREE

Ovid

Deep in the dreary den, conceal'd from day,
Sacred to Mars, a mighty dragon lay,
Bloated with poison to a monstrous size;
Fire broke in flashes when he glanc'd his eyes:
His tow'ring crest was glorious to behold,
His shoulders and his sides were scal'd with gold;
Three tongues he brandish'd when he charg'd his foes;
His teeth stood jaggy in three dreadful rowes.
The Tyrians in the den for water sought,
And with their urns explor'd the hollow vault:
From side to side their empty urns rebound,
And rowse the sleeping serpent with the sound.
Strait he bestirs him, and is seen to rise;
And now with dreadful hissings fills the skies,
And darts his forky tongues, and rowles his glaring eyes.
The Tyrians drop their vessels in the fright,
All pale and trembling at the hideous sight.
Spire above spire uprear'd in air he stood,

And gazing round him over-look'd the wood:
Then floating on the ground in circles rowl'd;
Then leap'd upon them in a mighty fold.
Of such a bulk, and such a monstrous size
The serpent in the polar circle lyes,
That stretches over half the northern skies.
In vain the Tyrians on their arms rely,
In vain attempt to fight, in vain to fly:
All their endeavours and their hopes are vain;
Some die entangled in the winding train;
Some are devour'd, or feel a loathsom death,
Swoln up with blasts of pestilential breath.

And now the scorching sun was mounted high,
In all its lustre, to the noon-day sky;
When, anxious for his friends, and fill'd with cares,
To search the woods th' impatient chief prepares.
A lion's hide around his loins he wore,
The well poiz'd javelin to the field he bore,
Inur'd to blood; the far-destroying dart;
And, the best weapon, an undaunted heart.

Soon as the youth approach'd the fatal place,
He saw his servants breathless on the grass;
The scaly foe amid their corps he view'd,
Basking at ease, and feasting in their blood.
"Such friends," he cries, "deserv'd a longer date;
But Cadmus will revenge or share their fate."
Then heav'd a stone, and rising to the throw,
He sent it in a whirlwind at the foe:
A tow'r, assaulted by so rude a stroke,
With all its lofty battlements had shook;
But nothing here th' unwieldy rock avails,
Rebounding harmless from the plaited scales,
That, firmly join'd, preserv'd him from a wound,
With native armour crusted all around.
With more success, the dart unerring flew,
Which at his back the raging warrior threw;
Amid the plaited scales it took its course,

And in the spinal marrow spent its force.
The monster hiss'd aloud, and rag'd in vain,
And writh'd his body to and fro with pain;
He bit the dart, and wrench'd the wood away;
The point still buried in the marrow lay.
And now his rage, increasing with his pain,
Reddens his eyes, and beats in ev'ry vein;
Churn'd in his teeth the foamy venom rose,
Whilst from his mouth a blast of vapours flows,
Such as th' infernal Stygian waters cast.
The plants around him wither in the blast.
Now in a maze of rings he lies enrowl'd,
Now all unravel'd, and without a fold;
Now, like a torrent, with a mighty force
Bears down the forest in his boist'rous course.
Cadmus gave back, and on the lion's spoil
Sustain'd the shock, then forc'd him to recoil;
The pointed jav'lin warded off his rage:
Mad with his pains, and furious to engage,
The serpent champs the steel, and bites the spear,
'Till blood and venom all the point besmear.
But still the hurt he yet receiv'd was slight;
For, whilst the champion with redoubled might
Strikes home the jav'lin, his retiring foe
Shrinks from the wound, and disappoints the blow.

The dauntless heroe still pursues his stroke,
And presses forward, 'till a knotty oak
Retards his foe, and stops him in the rear;
Full in his throat he plung'd the fatal spear,
That in th' extended neck a passage found,
And pierc'd the solid timber through the wound.
Fix'd to the reeling trunk, with many a stroke
Of his huge tail he lash'd the sturdy oak;
'Till spent with toil, and lab'ring hard for breath,
He now lay twisting in the pangs of death.

The Serpent in Mythology

Sophia van Matre

A CERTAIN REPULSIVENESS belongs forever to the race of serpents. There is enmity between us and them—enmity deep and lasting, and ever ready of manifestation. We wander some sunny day in such a place as gentle Edmund Spenser loved, "Where joyous birds, shrouded in cheerful shade, Their notes unto the voice attemper sweet," when suddenly amid this loveliness a loathly, creeping serpent emerges from the depths of some hollow tree to writhe away in the Summer sunshine. Or down in some deep, stony ravine, where overhanging trees keep out the day's full light, we come upon a little ribbed snake that leaves the warm blood curdling in our veins as it crawls away. The dull yet fascinated feeling of disgust lingers long after, while a hundred tales that thrilled us once in childhood renew their strange and horrible charm. We dream once more of great boa-constrictors crushing man and horse with one dread contraction, of cobra capellos winding stealthily around the victim's arm and waiting the instant to dart their fangs into the swollen vein, or of rattlesnakes shaking their calendar tails and threatening the bare feet of some heated haymaker. We remember the day when innocent Eve sat beneath the forbidden tree and listened to those hateful arguments which wrought her woe. Was this beguiling creature, in whom, although animated by the

Prince of Art, there could still have been no repulsiveness, the serpent that we know? Shall we not rather adopt the theory of certain geologists, who consider that it was then not only the wisest but the noblest in form and carriage of all the brute tenants of the garden, and that the fall from its early beauty and majesty was no less than that of unhappy Eve herself? "Upon thy belly shalt thou go," was his curse, just as Adam's obligation to earn his bread by the sweat of his brow implied a previous exemption from such a necessity. How well has that triple and fearful curse been fulfilled! Enmity most deadly is between the race of man and the race of the serpent. The child, the maiden, and the woman shrink from it in terror; the man and the boy seek instruments of death to their degraded foe, and then cry,

"Io triumphe!"

Art, however, has given to the serpent a certain position and dignity which our natural repugnance denies it in nature. The ancients did not disdain to invest the countenances of their sculptured gods with the traits of those animals which most resembled them in character. Thus to the countenance of the Olympian Jove was added the arrangement of hair and expression of the lion, greatly enhancing the dignity and majesty of his aspect. Upon the face of a Triton were placed, in such a manner as to form the eyebrows, small fins, in order to signify its aquatic nature. So is the swift, gliding motion of the serpent not without a certain beauty, and it may without difficulty recall our fancies of the movements of the gods.

One who has critically discussed the subject of ancient art says: "Pherycides, one of the oldest Greek poets, seems to have intended to express this light and gliding movement in the snake form which he gave to the deities. The step of the Vatican Apollo floats, as it were, in the air; he touches not the earth with the sole of his foot."

The mythologists, who used fables and symbols to illustrate Divine truth by employing two of the less prominent qualities of the serpent, have made it the emblem of youth and of immortality; of youth, since, by casting its skin, it reappears clothed in all its early smoothness and freshness, and of immortality, since it retains life even after being divided, and what seems certain death is only adding another life. I have seen this emblem in a German Roman Catholic church, to which all the time-worn and time-honored customs of the mother country had been transported. The brown dress, and cape, and cord of the Franciscan monk, the bright, ill-tinted paintings, and rough engravings, and flaxen-haired madonnas made it seem like a church of

those old, old cities on the Rhine. Beneath a wooden crucifix of the Savior
nailed to the wall, with mimic blood streaming from imaginary veins, was a
bracket upon which lay an empty skull with the skeleton serpent coiled
around it, representing, no doubt, the emblems of mortality and of immortality. So have the old mythologic fables permeated all the distant rills of
society, and a thousand years after their mystic glory has departed teach the
sober-fancied Dutchman no less than they once taught the poetic Greek. In
this character of emblem to youth and immortality the serpent was
employed as an accessory symbol to almost every heathen deity. It is the constant attendant of Hygeia. There is an engraving of a fine statue of this goddess in which a large serpent falls from her left shoulder down the arm and
drinks from a small vase which she holds in the other hand. Asculapius was
worshiped either under the form of a serpent or else, like the goddess of
health, caressing it or coiling its folds around him. Serpents are always found
on the egis of Minerva as they' form the hair of Medusa. It may be that in
this instance they symbolize that wisdom or caution which would afford
surer protection than even the breast-plate itself. A statue of Minerva found
at Ostia in 1797, a companion to the previous-mentioned one of Hygeia, has
small snakes for the fringe of the ægis she wears. This excellent work of art
is supposed to be a copy of that statue wrought by Phidias for the temple in
the Acropolis. It is of the heroic size. The goddess stands leaning lightly
upon the long spear in her left hand, while in her right she bears a small
image. The helmet, ornamented with a gryphon between two sphinxes, is
upon her head, and her aspect is earnest and serene. The Greeks employed
the serpent as a sign of consecration when deifying the images of departed
heroes. The Tartar bears a coiled snake into battle placed on the top of his
standard, and Macha Allo, his god of life and death, is represented with serpents twining around him to express the first of these attributes, and a string
of skulls hanging at his side to express the second.

But to make it the emblem of life, and youth, and immortality was not
the only use to which mythology applied the serpent. It was assigned also its
natural position as the symbol and accessory of all vile and horrible person-
ification. Envy wore them hissing in her hair—and circling her waist in place
of a girdle.

"Mad Discord there her snaky tresses tore," says Virgil. The Furies are
generally represented with snakes upon their heads and torches and whips of
scorpions in their hands. "The Furies, in common with the other inferior
goddesses, graces, houris, nymphs, etc., are represented as beautiful young

virgins." "Virgins ever young," they are called by Sophocles, though why these dread sisters—Dirae as the Greeks expressly named them—should ever have been imagined in other forms than those of such beings as Macbeth met on the wild heath,

> "So withered and so wild in their attire
> That look not like the inhabitants of earth,
> And yet are on't,"

appears somewhat mysterious to us. But to the ancients the gods were ever young because immortal, and art refused to array them in any other robe than that of grace and beauty. More than one inheritance from the past represents even Medusa as beautiful. There is a famous intaglio by Solon now in the Florentine Museum, an engraving of which may be seen in Winckleman's History of Ancient Art. The sculpture is small and very beautiful, as even the engraving will show, the small serpents twining in the tresses of her hair adding unexpectedly to its beauty. The fable concerning Medusa, one of the three Gorgon sisters, is that she was the daughter of Phorcus, and that after his death she assumed the government and the command of the army. She attacked the army of Perseus, who had been sent to make war with her by Minerva, and was slain. He thought her so beautiful that he cut off her head to show to the Greeks, and afterward presented it to Minerva, who wore it upon her breastplate.

Poetry and sculpture have combined to render the fable of Laocoon immortal. The magnificent sculpture in the Vatican selects the fearful moment when Laocoon and his sons writhe within the coils of the ministers of Neptune's wrath. The marvelous anatomy of the bodies, the fearful grace and strength of those serpentine coils, the agony which every muscle bespeaks, makes this statue the wonder of the world. It is a living image of agony wrought from the dull and soulless stone. Not less grand than the sculpture is Virgil's description of that previous moment when the dread monsters of the deep advance over the smooth and calm sea. Greek and Trojan suspend each hostile demonstration to behold them. The spiral coils of their long bodies lash the soft waves into white foam behind them as they swim. Their heads rise above the water, their glaring eyes are spotted with fire and blood, their tongues lick their hissing mouths. What fearful fascination in this picture!

These are the dreams of an age long since gone by, an age of dreams, which we scruple not to scorn as fanciful and puerile. And yet perhaps the practical extreme to which we have gone is not better. We are eminently utilitarians, and live in an age of the world when events of the grandest character transpire with astonishing rapidity. We have penetrated so many secrets and discovered the practical cause of so many wonders that we forget there is still a region—a region of signs and wonders—into which we may not as yet enter. We forget that all things are now to us but emblems and symbols. The old Greeks and Egyptians fabled and dreamed too much, but we too little. The meteor of a starry November night may shine a moment, and when the bright track is darkened we do not say with them of old, "the gods have spoken," "it is a sign," "some great event will happen;" but "it is an aerolite," "a meteoric stone," "what loss?" " who loses?" Not so the ancients, and especially the ancient Greeks. Had a meteor like that of 1860 shone in their sky, would they not have looked up and lifted up their heads and thought that the time of their redemption drew nigh? In these latter days, amid these stupendous and marching events, imagination has no season of rest for her quiet, contemplative dreams. Reality is too wonderful to need the aid of fancy for her embellishment. We draw no horoscopes from the angles of the stars, we have no image of our God upon which to exercise combining or creative art. Least of all, do we continue the study of symbols down to the low type of animal life belonging to the serpent. And yet this study of the use which mythology, and poetry, and art have continually made of it reveals a certain quality of mind which it were well to perceive more frequently in these latter days. See how these priests, and poets, and artists often in that early day combined in one person, pass by the prominent characteristics of the serpent—its glassy eye and slimy skin, its horrid head and poisonous fang—to make it the chosen emblem of lovely youth and infinite immortality. They twine it round the lovely and perfect form of Hygeia, or place the hand of Aesculapius caressingly upon its hooded head; they write the sacred epitaph upon its sculptured form; they wreathe its coils on the standard of victory; they make it the companion of the glorious god of day, and place it as a foil or contrast around the dread emblem of mortality—the skeleton head. Say not that these are childish fancies, fables transmitted to us from that past time when the world was young.

But, youth is pleasant, and there is something of its joyous and happy faculty in this strange elevation of the despised and hated serpent, something of that sublimation of spirit which aids the patriot in the dread hour of battle, looking away from the hideous and visible realities of war to see the angelic form of Liberty floating in the ambient air, forever young and forever immortal.

14 Rue Serpentine

Nicholas Christopher

1.

The snake charmer's daughter
enfant clairvoyant born in a carnival tent
with a crescent of stars on her brow
has opened a storefront studio at the corner
She wears a gold headdress and calls herself
The Serpent Priestess her bracelets jangling
when she arranges Tarot cards on a zodiac wheel
She says it is not for its windingness
that this street was named but for the snakes
Napoleon's soldiers brought back from Egypt
which infest the neighborhood
though you yourself have only seen one:
the cobra coiled in a basket at her feet

2.

The next time you visit the Serpent Priestess
she examines a single snake scale with a magnifying glass
and divines your fortune in the crisscrossing lines

insisting that this was the preferred method
of Cleopatra and Antiope the Amazon queen
and Clytymnestra when she plotted her husband's murder
From ragged clouds the first snow spins down
onto the river path beaten centuries ago
by foxes and their prey
You stroll there at twilight mulling over
the priestess' reading of the snake scale
information that might have been useful to you
back when you cared about the future
a long time ago

From: *Mules and Men*

Chapter Six

Zora Neale Hurston

"WELL, ANYHOW, MR. JIM, please tell us how come de snakes got poison."

Well, when God made de snake he put him in de bushes to ornament de ground. But things didn't suit de snake so one day he got on de ladder and went up to see God.

"Good mawnin', God."

"How do you do, Snake?"

"Ah ain't so many, God, you put me down there on my belly in de dust and everything trods upon me and kills off my generations. Ah ain't got no kind of protection at all."

God looked off towards immensity and thought about de subject for awhile, then he said, "Ah didn't mean for nothing to be stompin' you snakes lak dat. You got to have some kind of a protection. Here, take dis poison and put it in yo' mouf and when they tromps on you, protect yo' self."

So de snake took de poison in his mouf and went on back.

So after awhile all de other varmints went up to God.

"Good evenin', God."

"How you makin' it, varmints?"

"God, please do somethin' bout dat snake. He' layin' in de bushes there wid poisin in his mouf and he's strikin' everything dat shakes de bush. He's killin' up our generations. Wese skeered to walk de earth."

So God sent for de snake and tole him:

"Snake, when Ah give you dat poison, Ah didn't mean for you to be hittin' and killin' everything dat shake de bush. I give you dat poison and tole you to protect yo'self when they tromples on you. But you killin' everything dat moves. Ah didn't mean for you to do dat."

De snake say, "Lawd, you know Ah'm down here in de dust. Ah ain't got no claws to fight wid, and Ah ain't got no feets to git me out de way. All Ah kin see is feets comin' to tromple me. Ah can't tell who my enemy is and who is my friend. You gimme dis protection in my mouf and Ah uses it."

God thought it over for a while then he says:

"Well, snake, I don't want yo' generations all stomped out and I don't want you killin' everything else dat moves. Here take dis bell and tie it to yo' tail. When you hear feets comin' you ring yo' bell and if it's yo' friend, he'll be keerful. If it's yo' enemy, it's you and him."

So dat's how de snake got his poison and dat's how come he got rattles.

Biddy, biddy, bend my story is end.

Turn loose de rooster and hold de hen.

"Don't tell me no mo' 'bout no snakes—specially when we walkin' in all dis tall grass," pleaded Presley. "Ah speck Ah'm gointer be seein' 'em in my sleep tonight. Lawd, Ah'm skeered of snakes."

~

From: *The Adventures of Huckleberry Finn*

(CHAPTER TEN)

Mark Twain

AFTER BREAKFAST I WANTED to talk about the dead man and guess out how he come to be killed, but Jim didn't want to. He said it would fetch bad luck; and besides, he said, he might come and ha'nt us; he said a man that warn't buried was more likely to go a-ha'nting around than one that was planted and comfortable. That sounded pretty reasonable, so I didn't say no more; but I couldn't keep from studying over it and wishing I knowed who shot the man, and what they done it for.

We rummaged the clothes we'd got, and found eight dollars in silver sewed up in the lining of an old blanket overcoat. Jim said he reckoned the people in that house stole the coat, because if they'd a knowed the money was there they wouldn't a left it. I said I reckoned they killed him, too; but Jim didn't want to talk about that. I says:

"Now you think it's bad luck; but what did you say when I fetched in the snake-skin that was found on the top of the ridge day before yesterday? You said it was the worst bad luck in the world to touch a snake-skin with my hands. Well, here's your bad luck! We've raked in all this truck and eight dollars besides. I wish we could have some bad luck like this every day, Jim."

"Never you mind, honey, never you mind. Don't you git too peart. It's a-comin'. Mind I tell you, it's a-comin'."

It did come, too. It was a Tuesday that we had that talk. Well, after dinner Friday we was laying around in the grass at the upper end of the ridge, and got out of tobacco. I went to the cavern to get some, and found a rattlesnake in there. I killed him, and curled him up on the foot of Jim's blanket, ever so natural, thinking there'd be some fun when Jim found him there. Well, by night I forgot all about the snake, and when Jim flung himself down on the blanket while I struck a light the snake's mate was there, and bit him.

He jumped up yelling, and the first thing the light showed was the varmint curled up and ready for another spring. I laid him out in a second with a stick, and Jim grabbed pap's whisky-jug and begun to pour it down.

He was barefooted, and the snake bit him right on the heel. That all comes of my being such a fool as to not remember that wherever you leave a dead snake its mate always comes there and curls around it. Jim told me to chop off the snake's head and throw it away, and then skin the body and roast a piece of it. I done it, and he eat it and said it would help cure him. He made me take off the rattles and tie them around his wrist, too. He said that that would help. Then I slid out quiet and throwed the snakes clear away amongst the bushes; for I warn't going to let Jim find out it was all my fault, not if I could help it.

Jim sucked and sucked at the jug, and now and then he got out of his head and pitched around and yelled; but every time he come to himself he went to sucking at the jug again. His foot swelled up pretty big, and so did his leg; but by-and-by the drunk begun to come, and so I judged he was all right; but I'd druther been bit with a snake than pap's whisky.

Jim was laid up for four days and nights. Then the swelling was all gone and he was around again. I made up my mind I wouldn't ever take aholt of a snake-skin again with my hands, now that I see what had come of it. Jim said he reckoned I would believe him next time. And he said that handling a snake-skin was such awful bad luck that maybe we hadn't got to the end of it yet. He said he druther see the new moon over his left shoulder as much as a thousand times than take up a snake-skin in his hand.

~

Simple Wisdom

Virginia Hamilton Adair

What does it mean, this tale you tell me
of the python and the boa constrictor?

They too have a little room with bars,
daily bread, frozen food,
a pan of water for the python,
a life sentence for both.
The consolation is food,
a sort of joyless safety,
companionship without privacy or fruitfulness.
They relax together in trusting coils,
twining and reclining on the plastic floor.
No grass, no hiding place of leaves or stones,
the freedom of earth is forbidden them.

The python, it turns out, was a female.
Some stoppage took place in her fertility.
Her eggs were imprisoned behind her secret bars,
the handsome pattern of her skin.

What simple wisdom: to let go of life,
sealing the next generation pure in her long body,
ending her long incarceration in a five-foot cage.

The boa constrictor coils in his solitude
while surviving with his daily bread.
A spot of light touches him now and then
with a secret intelligence from the sun.
But he cannot tell us what it says,
and the message from the energy of God
hovers just beyond us, untranslatable.

~

Snake Pet Owners

Chuck Goldstone

WITH THE ASSORTMENT of pets available to us, I do not understand the appeal of an animal that is not furry, cuddly or capable of performing tricks. But some people are perfectly willing to adopt a small non-venomous snake as a pet. They find the animals intriguing and beautiful and treat them no differently than they would cats, gerbils or ferrets. "We just see snakes," a committed owner might say, "As slender, legless dogs."

Most of these people are rational and responsible. They have no more incidence of madness than the rest of us. It's just that squirming and crawling creatures can get past their visual or tactile receptors without setting off any alarms.

I do not personally see the appeal of an animal that most people find disturbing. Nor do I understand how parents could voluntarily expose the children they presumably love to an animal that might cause a fear-induced stroke in a six-year-old.

These otherwise responsible mothers and fathers—who might also be members of the PTA, good citizens, and people who voluntarily recycle—will select a pet snake that is small, docile, and neither aggressive nor poisonous. Enlightened parents, who are not fearful of snakes themselves and want to propagate the trait of non-sniveling in their progeny, might invest in one of the popular breeds known to make acceptable pets: milk snakes, green snakes, garter snakes or corn snakes, all of which have names that are snuggly and non-threatening and all considered small because they grow no more than 5 or 6 feet. These joyful snakes transport no poison. Their eyes sparkle. Tiny cute faces smile and flicking tongues seem to be their way of saying hello. These are the kind of snakes parents feel comfortable leaving alone with their children.

Benefits of Snakes

Objectively, a snake as a pet does offer some benefits over more conventional animal buddies. First, snakes are inexpensive. You can go to a pet store and buy all but the huge ones for short money, because snakes are easy to procure and the demand for them is not high. Where you may have to pay upward of $400–1000 for a pedigreed dog with good bloodlines, you may not have to pay more than $4 or 5 for a little snake. If you prefer to save even more money, just journey out in the woods for an afternoon and lift a few rocks and logs.

Once brought home, snakes are easy to maintain. They are happy to reside in very Spartan quarters, sometimes just an old converted aquarium that can no longer hold fish because of a hairline crack, which causes all the water to leak onto the den carpet overnight and leaves a few puddles of water on the sandy aquarium floor the following morning, with bewildered fish flopping on their sides remembering the place as a lot more moist. This aquarium can be reborn as a terrarium, until the crack becomes big enough for whatever is inside to escape.

You'll spend nothing on snake playthings. Since there are no official "snake toys," you can save money just grabbing a downed tree branch, a paint can, or any other garbage which the snake can form-fit in or around. As long as a snake can move, it is amused.

Of course, food will not be a major expense for an animal that is happy to eat just once during the vernal and autumnal equinoxes, making it perfect for pet owners who travel a lot or are forgetful and irresponsible.

"Is your snake hungry?" a curious visitor might ask, scrunching down to look through the terrarium glass.

"I don't think so," you might answer, "I remember feeding him in March."

If a snake dies, the fact can be easily hidden from the children. You can explain an immobile snake for up to a few months just by saying it is hibernating, giving you enough time to find an identical snake to replace it. Since a snake cannot be trained to do specific tricks or anything else that might distinguish it from other generic versions of its species, your kids will never be the wiser.

Compromises

Snakes are incapable of supplying the same benefits that accrue to owners of traditional pets. Should you decide to adopt a snake, be prepared to compromise.

How can I say this without offending snake fans? Snakes are, frankly, stupid. I am not being judgmental. Snakes cannot help it. They have tiny heads, some no bigger than a human thumb, and once you subtract out the space needed for a skull, eyes, fangs and the like, there is not much space left for a brain. They are low on the neurological development scale and it takes a lot of effort on their part to get their synapses to fire with any consistency. Snakes have dismal memories, no powers of reason and no recognition of causal relationships. If you are ever trying to train a snake, you will find yourself explaining the same thing over and over. In short, do not expect much from a snake intellectually.

While they will surprise you by eating the occasional rodent, they cannot be trained for this or any other useful purpose. Though farmers have long respected snakes for eating vermin and insects that might otherwise destroy crops and clog combines, reptiles perform these tasks by happenstance, that is, one will eat a rodent only if the rodent happens to be nearby. In theory, a reptile could keep your condominium free of mice, chipmunks, and squirrels, but you might have to invest in many of them for complete coverage. From my perspective, if my home were overrun by rats, I would consider snakes freely moving from room to room to be just one more inconvenience.

Likewise, you cannot rely on a snake for protection from home invasion as you would with say, Dobermans. Though reptiles could conceivably function as a deterrent to crime, especially when decals warning THIS PROPERTY PROTECTED BY SNAKES are prominently displayed on doors and windows, snakes are less discriminating in their ability to distinguish whom to protect. In response to breaking and entering, a snake is just as likely to panic and attack you and your fleeing children as it is to find and pin down the burglar.

Unlike the cerebrally versatile pets, snakes cannot be taught a repertoire of even the simplest household tasks, so you will have to get your newspaper and slippers yourself, just making sure the snake isn't already curled up inside of either. You will not find them necessarily entertaining as you would with a mammal-based pet. You cannot teach a snake to sit, catch a Frisbee or speak on command. Based on their simplistic external physiology, essentially a long, thin organic cylinder, "roll over" may be as close as you will get to a trick. Then the problem here is, once they get rolling and gathering momentum, it is hard for them to learn how to stop.

You will sadly realize that even "fetch the ball," where you gently roll the ball a few feet across the yard, will be painstakingly difficult for a snake to comprehend, and you will eventually discard the project when you see a snake slither back ten or so minutes later with a huge round bulge a few inches down its neck.

Finally, and this may ultimately be the single biggest failing, snakes are not warm and fuzzy. Being cold blooded, your snake will be the same temperature as the room, the tabletop, and your stemware. While snakes lovers have convinced us that snakes are not slimy and wet as fear-lore has suggested—and we will gladly just take their word for it rather than actually touching one ourselves to find out—even the most steadfast of herpephiles cannot look us straight in the face and tell us that reptiles are cuddly, and to snuggle up next to one would not be too different from curling up with a piece of vinyl.

Snakes are, frankly, not puppies, and nothing that even the most devout herpetic animal lover can say to the contrary will change any of our minds. While snake owners are absolutely convinced that their snakes love them, empirical data do not support this. Snakes are not doting in the same way conventional pets are. In fact, it may be advantageous to actively discourage your snake from showing affection. Owners of huge reticulated pythons learn very quickly that when returning home after a long day to a snake they missed, it is not a good idea to say, "How about a big hug?"

The Wrong Kind of Pet Snake Owner

There are people who, for whatever reason, are not content to own reasonably safe, non-threatening snakes, and seek out peculiar, exotic and often more dangerous specimens.

They may be adventuresome or risk takers, the same kind of people who drive fast cars and climb rocks with their fingertips. They may be people who take delight in shocking others. For them, a milk snake or a cute little hog-nose is not enough and they are drawn to massive and muscular constrictors or even poisonous specimens.

Granted, some people will be convinced that exotic snakes are fine pets, and as far as I am concerned, this is a "free country," and, while our founding fathers did not mention snakes specifically, our Freedom of Pets should include the right to own pretty much whatever we want, so long as we can keep it from killing and eating others.

I live in Massachusetts, a state that has spawned freedom, birthed some of the most noteworthy advancements in science and technology, and helped to ignite the information revolution. Entrepreneurs here, armed only with vision and a few dollars, have built giant computer firms, and have sired the biotech, genetic engineering and pharmaceutical industries. Harvard and MIT are in rock throwing distance of each other, and the state is home to some of the nation's top publishers, universities and consulting firms. Physicians conduct lifesaving medical research in the shadows of Beacon Hill. The state's think tanks have influenced government leaders and the captains of industry for many decades. Frankly, we have a lot of really smart people here.

Yet, there is an incontestable law in nature that says for every really smart person, there must be an equally moronic person as a counterbalance. A few years ago I read about a man who apparently had been assigned to this area, perhaps to cancel out the genius of someone doing cancer research. He lived a few miles north of Boston and decided that it would be really "neat" to raise a deadly Egyptian banded cobra in his suburban home.

Remember, a cobra is a snake that can grow to be eighteen feet long, has one of the world's most astonishing venoms housed in its mouth, does not really want to be a house pet, and cannot be trusted to refrain from striking a loved one because honestly, it loves no one.

While a warning of the cobra's inherent dangers may not be written on the side of the snake, it is information that is readily accessible. No one has ever purchased a cobra "by accident," and a thinking person would know better than to have one in striking distance.

Yet this man in suburban Boston did just that.

It is not legal to own a poisonous snake in Massachusetts. There is a law on the books. It was written in arcane legislative language, but its meaning was unambiguous: If you are a moron and bring a snake filled to the brim with venom into Massachusetts, we will arrest you and drive you directly to one of our prisons. Then we will put you in one of its cages and kill the snake. Or vice versa.

Bucking the laws of Massachusetts and to a degree the very laws of nature and common sense that have kept our species alive for the past 100,000 years, the man went ahead and acquired a huge length of cobra, venom intact, as a pet. A single cobra comparable to his could produce enough venom to wipe out the entire Massachusetts legislature in an afternoon, and still have enough juice left over to put the judiciary and their appointed staffs in intensive care.

The irresponsibility of the owner would be story enough, but it seemed he saw no reason to keep the snake indoors in its secure snake house, and routinely took it into his front yard to let it relax and sun itself, within shimmying distance of parks, school grounds and a nursing home where the elderly on walkers would have no chance to outrun even the slowest of snakes. Still, no one would have known he even had the cobra, had it not wandered off one afternoon, and in doing so, no longer endangered just its owner, but everyone from Portland, Maine, to Cape Cod as well.

The snake was lounging one afternoon, when the owner apparently left momentarily, forgetting he was leaving the third deadliest thing on the planet unchaperoned in his front yard. Never knowing such freedom, the cobra saw a hitherto unavailable opportunity to explore the Bay State, and swiftly slithered past the patio door, across the driveway, and past the guy's set of lawn darts, which incidentally is thought to be the fourth deadliest thing on the planet. It wandered off, looking for a between-meal snack or maybe because it missed Egypt.

I cannot fathom the amplitude of panic when the guy returned to find his unleashed snake gone. It may be like coming back to a parking lot and discovering your car has been stolen. You continue looking at the empty space, looking away, then back again, hoping you had just missed seeing it the first time. Perhaps his first thought was that he had walked over to the wrong part of the yard, and the snake was where he left it, some feet away, patiently waiting its owner's return. Maybe he thought the snake was tired and went back inside on its own to take a nap in its comfy snake quarters. Maybe a neighbor borrowed him.

After running in panic throughout the yard looking for anything that was (1) up to eighteen feet long and (2) moving, the owner concluded that the cobra was missing, leaving without a clue, and was probably now bellying past children playing in the street, past housewives carrying in bags of groceries through kitchen doorway, they left invitingly open, over bicycles and toys, finally taking temporary refuge in landscape shrubbery.

The snake had bolted, leaving the frightened owner with the undeniable conclusion that, aside from misplacing an expensive animal investment, he would have to explain to local officials that there was an illicit cobra loose and he might need their help finding it, now painfully aware that putting up a lost snake poster would not be sufficient. The owner also knew his hope that the snake would return in an hour scratching on the back door was unrealistic.

So for the weeks to follow, terrified families in this Boston suburb hid their children indoors, cancelled Little League games, sealed their garage doors shut, and moved the patio furniture inside. Dogs, no longer taken on daily walks or even given access to the backyard, were allowed to squat freely in the kitchen and dining room, and homeowners put on hold all outdoor projects and barbecues. Home vegetable gardens went to seed, lawns weeded over, and previously well coiffed hedges turned haggard and unkempt. Married couples slept in shifts.

The snake that had previously been one man's pet was now everyone's problem, receding without a trace into the suburban landscape. It could be hiding, coiled, ready to strike anywhere. Some calculated that statistically they were no more likely to be killed by the snake than win the state Big Game Lottery, not frightening until you remember that there is usually at least one lottery winner every week. Neither the police nor reptile experts could comfort a frightened community by confirming the snake's whereabouts. At any given moment, they could only provide inadequate assurance, telling the concerned residents where the snake wasn't.

Herpetologists speculated that a cobra that had gotten used to a cushy life inside a posh carpeted terrarium—with branches for it to crawl about and its own fluorescent light under which to bask, all to simulate life in India and Northern Africa—could not survive long on its own. News stories hoping to quell panic reminded residents that, with each passing day, the probability of the snake dying of hunger, thirst, or being flattened by an oil delivery truck increased measurably. The fact that a snake cannot cover a lot of ground quickly was also reassuring, especially to homeowners west of Bloomington, Indiana, who were confident that a cobra starting in New England, even a very fit one, could probably make it no farther than Ohio.

Officials continued to assure quaking residents, now holed up in their split-level homes, that a cobra turning up in a silverware drawer or inside a

clothing hamper was statistically improbable. Still, I doubt a single townsper-
son was able to slide a foot into a sneaker or reach into a dishwasher without
at least a moment of hesitation. Trying to stem panic, zoologists reminded
everyone that the snake, if still alive, would probably not appear in public
because, "It is probably more afraid of us than we are of it." They failed to
acknowledge, however, a more important fact that snakes are poisonous and
we are not.

The escaped cobra story remained newsworthy for about three weeks, but
then life gradually reverted to normal. Surely the authorities were correct: the
snake had to be dead. Draperies were reopened; sun-deprived children, pupils
constricted and skin pallid, returned cautiously to the streets, able to finally
curb their daily hypodermic injections of vitamin D.

But a few months later the snake story re-emerged. Truth, as it always
turns out, is much more bizarre than even the most brilliant literary irony.
The snake turned up, not dead in some sewage culvert, not flattened and a
bit longer and wider on Interstate 95, but inside a local elementary school,
peacefully curled up asleep on a library shelf. Instantly, it was back on the
front pages again. I read the *Boston Globe* article about the discovery and the
subsequent rescue while on a flight out of the area. I sighed in relief, certainly because the dangerous snake was finally apprehended and no one got hurt,
but more importantly because I was at least 40,000 feet away from the cobra
at that moment.

The snake had somehow survived, still healthy, a little hungry and fully
lethal. No one, including the cobra, was injured in the capture.

The public was relieved that the school administration did not stumble
onto a trail leading to the card catalog littered with the convulsing little bodies of children thrashing wildly on the ground, or worse yet, did not discover
a snake sitting content in some dark corner of the gym with the unmistakable
bulge a third of the way down its back in the shape of a fourth grader.

Turn on Owners/Done in by Snakes

Not to belabor the point about snake intelligence, but the only reason they
do not bite or eat us is because we are not threatening or hurting them at
that very moment.

With its rudimentary just-barely-more-than-a-brain-stem brain, a snake
is a live-for-the-moment kind of animal. A snake does not know loyalty or
love. It is not good with faces and does not remember how well you treated it

yesterday. A snake does not see you as the caring pet owner, but just another animal who is not, at this moment, a threat or a meal. It forges no emotional attachments as you do with it. It might forget all about the kind stroking and the playful intertwining you've provided in the past. Your ongoing safety is at the pleasure of the snake. If your snake has not crushed you to death in the past, that is no guarantee that it will not do so in the future, and a good day with a dangerous snake is defined as one where it does not actively attempt to take your life

Case in point: A New York man was done in a few years ago by his own crushing python, bringing to a tragic close a man-pet relationship of many years' duration. You would have thought that after a certain point the man would have figured out how to survive in such a household. But the pet owner's death, as tragic as it was, should serve as a reminder that those with dangerous snakes are just asking for trouble.

Apparently this guy was making his own dinner, and while cutting up chicken, splattered a little pullet juice on his T-shirt. While waiting for the meal to roast, he decided to play with his snake, forgetting that he was drenched in appetizing chicken fluids. Although the constrictor was not scheduled to eat for many weeks, it was aroused by the aroma, and thought that eating a month ahead of schedule wasn't such a bad idea and perhaps was the snake version of an "Early Bird Special." Momentarily convinced that a meal was at hand, and with the smell of fowl in the air, it decided to wring out a little from its owner's T-shirt.

Imagine how the man struggled with his own pet, as the python grabbed him and wrapped its massive muscular trunk about his chest, squeezing tighter and cutting off blood and oxygen flow, strangling him like a garrote. Imagine how disappointing it must have been knowing he would be unsuccessful convincing the snake he was not a chicken, and was in fact, Larry.

In any event, the man was crushed to death, sad for him because he died at the hands of a beloved pet, and sad for the snake, which killed its dutiful owner and still did not get any chicken out of it. Lucky for the snake, it could continue to go some period longer without food, and was able to hold out until the police came a few weeks later, after the neighbors complained of the smell.

So, let these accounts be a strong warning. Avoid poisonous snakes at all costs. If you decide on a constricting pet against my advice, just don't let it sleep on the bed, for fear you will wake up at about three in the morning, look toward the foot of the mattress and find that your snake has already swallowed you up to your thighs.

First-Class Snake Stories

Brooklyn Eagle

"Do you want some items about snakes?" asked an agriculturally-rural-looking gentleman of the *Eagle*'s city editor the other day.

"If they are fresh and true," responded the city editor.

"Exactly," replied the farmer. "These items are both. Nobody knows 'em but me. I got a farm down on the island a piece, and there's lots of snakes on it. Near the house is a pond, about six feet deep. A week ago my little girl jumped into the pond, and would have drowned if it hadn't been for a snake. The snake seen her, went for her, and brought her ashore. The particular point about this item is the way he did it."

"How was it?" asked the city editor.

"It was a black snake, about thirty feet long, and he just coiled the middle of himself around her neck so she couldn't swallow any water, and swam ashore with his head and tail. Is that a good item?"

"First-class."

"You can spread it out, you know. After they got ashore the girl patted the snake on the head and it went off pleased as Punch. Ever since then he comes to the house regular at meal-times, and she feeds him on pie. Think you can make anything out of that item?"

"Certainly. Know any more?"

"Yes. I got a baby six months old. He's a boy. We generally sit him out on the grass of a morning, and he hollers like a bull all day; at least he used to, but he don't any more. One morning we noticed he wasn't hollering, and wondered what was up. When we looked, there was a rattlesnake coiled up in front of him scanning his features. The boy was grinning and the snake was grinning. Bimeby the snake turned his tail to the baby and backed his rattle right into the baby's fist."

"What did the baby do?"

"Why, he just rattled that tail so you could hear it three-quarters of a mile, and the snake lay there and grinned. Every morning we found the snake there, until one day a bigger snake came, and the baby played with his rattle just the same till the first snake came back. He looked thin, and I reckon he had been sick and sent the other to take his place. Will that do for an item?"

"Immensely," replied the city editor.

"You can fill in about the confidence of childhood and all that, and you might say something about the blue-eyed cherub. His name is Isaac. Put that in to please my wife."

"I'll do it. Any more snake items?"

"Lemme see. You've heard of hoop-snakes?"

"Yes, often."

"Just so. Not long ago we heard a fearful row in our cellar one night. It sounded like a rock-blast, and then there was a hiss and things was quiet. When I looked in the morning the cider barrel had busted. But we didn't lose much cider.

"How did you save it?"

"It seems that the staves had busted out, but before they could get away, four hoop-snakes coiled around the barrel and tightened it up and held it together until we drew the cider off in bottles. That's the way we found 'em, and we've kept 'em around the house ever since. We're training 'em for shawl-straps now. Does that strike you favorably for an item?"

"Enormously!" responded the city editor.

"You can fix it up so as to show how quick they was to get there before the staves were blown off. You can work in the details."

"Of course. I'll attend to that. Do you think of any more?"

"Ain't you got enough? Lemme think. O yes! One Sunday me and my wife was going to church, and she dropped her garter somewhere. She told me about it, and I noticed a little striped snake running alongside and listening to her. Bimeby he made a spring and just wound himself around her stocking, or tried to, but he didn't fetch it."

"Why not?"

"He wasn't quite long enough. He jumped down and shook his head and started off. We hadn't gone more'n a quarter of a mile, when we see him coming out of the woods just ahead of us. He was awful hot and tired, and he had another snake with him twice as big as he was. They looked at my wife a minute and said something to each other, and then the big snake went right to the place where the garter belonged. He wrapped right around it, put his tail in his mouth and went to sleep. We got him yet. We use him to hold the stovepipe together when we put the stove up. Is that any use as an item?"

"Certainly," said the city editor.

"You can say something about the first snake's eye for distances and intellectuality, when he found he wouldn't go 'round. You know how to do that better than me."

"I'll give him the credit he deserves. Can you tell us any more?"

"I don't call any to mind just at present. My wife knows a lot of snake items, but I forget 'em. By the way, though, I've got a regular living curiosity down at my place. One day my oldest boy was sitting on the back stoop doing his sums, and he couldn't get 'em right. He felt something against his face, and there was a little snake coiled up on his shoulder and looking at the slate. In four minutes he had done all them sums. We've tamed him so he keeps all our accounts, and he is the lighteningest cuss at figures you ever seen. He'll run up a column eight feet long in three seconds. I wouldn't take a reaper for him."

"What kind of a snake is he?" inquired the editor curiously.

"The neighbors call him an adder."

"O, yes, yes!" said the city editor, a little disconcerted. "I've heard of the species. When did all these things happen?"

"Along in the fore part of the spring, but I didn't say anything about 'em, 'cause it wasn't the season for snake items. This is about the time for that sort of thing, isn't it?"

"Yes," chipped in the exchange editor, "you couldn't have picked out a better time for snake stories."

Biographies

John Milton (1608-1674) wrote his epic poem, *Paradise Lost*, over a dozen years after losing his sight in 1652. Milton won renown as a historian, scholar, pamphleteer and civil servant for Parliament and the Puritan Commonwealth. Milton served in the Cromwell government and then was briefly arrested during the restoration. He published *Paradise Regained* and *Samson Agonistes* in 1671.

Philip Bobbitt, a law professor at the University of Texas, is the author of several books, including *Shield of Achilles: War, Peace and the Course of History*. At different times, he has served in all three branches of the United States government during administrations of both parties. During one of those tours, he was senior director for strategic planning at the National Security Council under President Bill Clinton.

Virginia Hamilton Adair was born in 1913 in New York City. Educated at Kimberly, Mt. Holyoke, Radcliffe, and the University of Wisconsin, she taught briefly at Wisconsin, William & Mary, and Pomona College, and for many years at California Polytechnic University at Pomona. She lives in Claremont, California. Her first book of poetry, *Ants on the Melon*, was published when she was eighty-three. By that time, she had suffered the death of her husband by suicide and the onset of her own blindness.

Paul Bowles (1910–1999) was a composer before he was a writer. An early disciple of Aaron Copland, Bowles as a young man visited Gertrude Stein in Paris and agreed with her judgment that he was not a poet. In the 1940s, he composed scores for movies, musicals and ballets. Bowles and his wife, the playwright and novelist Jane Auer, settled in Tangiers in 1947 and two years later he published his masterpiece, *The Sheltering Sky*, a novel set in North Africa.

Margaret Atwood was born in Ottawa in 1939 and has degrees from the University of Toronto and Radcliffe College, and has been a full-time writer since 1972—fiction, screenplays, poetry, non-fiction—with short interludes of guest teaching here and there. Along the way she has won numerous awards, including the Booker Prize in 2000 for her novel, *The Blind Assassin*. She was chair of The Writers' Union in 1981–82, and president of PEN Canada in 1985 and 1986.

George Plimpton founded the *Paris Review* in 1953 and has edited it ever since. A writer of astonishing range, Plimpton almost single-handedly created the genre of participatory journalism in which he covered himself as a quarterback for a professional football team, a sparring partner for a champion boxer and a musician in a major symphony orchestra, among his many roles. He also once fought in a bullfight staged by Ernest Hemingway, and even worked as a trapeze artist, lion-tamer and clown for the Clyde Beatty–Cole Brothers Circus. In addition to sports, his writings have ranged a broad landscape, including children's fiction, history, literary criticism, sports, memoir, biography and satire.

Arthur Conan Doyle (1859–1930) graduated from the University of Edinburgh and practiced medicine for a number of years. By the mid 1880s, Conan Doyle had created the characters who would establish his place in literature—the detective Sherlock Holmes and his straight-man sidekick, Dr. Watson. Conan Doyle was knighted in 1902 for his medical contributions to the English war effort during the Boer War.

Peter Sacks is the author of five books of poetry, including *Necessity* (W. W. Norton, 2002), and of *The English Elegy: Studies in the Genre from Spenser to Yeats*. He has taught at The Johns Hopkins University, and currently is the John P. Marquand Professor of English and American Literature and Language at Harvard. He teaches literature and creative writing.

Richard Wiley is the author of five novels and a winner of the PEN/Faulkner Award for *Soldiers in Hiding*. A Peace Corps volunteer in South Korea, Wiley has lived and worked as well in Japan, Nigeria and Kenya, enabling him to set a novel in all four of those locales. He recently won a grant from the NEA/Japan–United States Friendship Commission and the Japanese Foundation for work on a forthcoming novel, *Commodore Perry's Ministrel Show*. A graduate of the University of Puget Sound, Sofia University in Tokyo and the University of Iowa Writers Workshop, Wiley now teaches creative writing at the University of Nevada, Las Vegas.

Kate Lehrer writes novels, short stories, essays and book reviews and participates in the monthly Book Club on the Diane Rehm Show on National Public Radio. Her most recent novel, *Out of Eden*, won the Western Heritage Award. She grew up in Texas and now resides in Washington, D.C.

Theodore Roethke (1908–1963) developed an artistic affinity for the natural world as a boy growing up in Saginaw, Michigan, where his father and uncle owned a greenhouse. Impressions formed during those years helped to shape his development as a poet. Roethke won the Pulitzer Prize in 1954 for his collection of poems entitled *The Waking*. He taught at various colleges and universities, including Lafayette, Pennsylvania State, Bennington and the University of Washington.

Randall Kenan was the John and Renee Grisham Writer-in-Residence at the University of Mississippi, Oxford, and has also taught at the University of Memphis. His first novel, *A Visitation of Spirits*, was published by Grove Press in 1989. A collection of short stories, *Let the Dead Bury Their Dead*, Harcourt Brace, 1992, was nominated for the *Los Angeles Times* Book Award for fiction, was a finalist for the National Book Critics Circle Award, and was among *The New York Times* Notable Books of 1992.

Susan Kinsolving's new book *The White Eyelash* will be published by Grove/Atlantic in autumn, 2003. Her previous book, *Dailies & Rushes*, was a finalist for the National Book Critics Circle Award. Kinsolving has taught poetry at the University of Connecticut and the California Institute of the Arts.

Joanne Leedom-Ackerman is a novelist, short story writer and journalist, whose works of fiction include *No Marble Angels* and *The Dark Path to the River*. A former reporter for *The Christian Science Monitor*, Ms. Leedom-Ackerman has won awards for her writing and has published in anthologies, magazines and newspapers. She is vice president of international PEN and also of the PEN/Faulkner Foundation.

Willie Morris (1934–1999) made an early mark as a crusading journalist when he blasted censorship and segregation as editor of the student newspaper at the University of Texas in the mid 1950s. After studying at Oxford University as a Rhodes Scholar, Morris became editor of the antiestablishment *Texas Observer* from 1960 to 1962. By 1963, he moved to New York to become associate editor of *Harper's* magazine and, later, editor in chief. He wrote about his experiences at *Harper's* in *North Toward Home* and *New York Days*. A long list of books followed, including his 1995 best-seller, *My Dog Skip.*

Emily Dickinson (1830–1886) published only seven of her poems during her lifetime, which was largely spent unmarried in the family homestead in Amherst, Massachusetts. She began writing about 1850, but the volume of her output only began to intensify later in the decade. Under the mounting pressures and anxieties of the Civil War, Emily Dickinson devoted herself to her art, producing about 800 poems. Friends, family members and admirers urged her to share her genius with the public, but that desire had to await her death. It was only then that her sister Lavinia and others arranged the publication in 1890 of *Poems by Emily Dickinson.*

Antoine De Saint-Exupéry (1900–1944) was born in Lyons, France, and became a pilot at 26, flying routes linking France and Africa. The German occupation sent him to the United States, where he wrote several novels, including *The Little Prince.* Returning to France after the outbreak of World War II, he joined the battle against Nazism. He was lost when his plane was shot down over the Mediterranean on July 31, 1944.

Ogden Nash (1902–1974) was a Harvard College dropout who tried his hand at several different jobs until 1930 when *The New Yorker* published his poem, "Spring Comes to Murray Hill." A prolific writer, he published *Hard Lines*, a collection of his poetry, a year later. In 1932 he joined *The New Yorker's* staff. The author of three screenplays for MGM, Nash collaborated with S. J. Perelman in 1943 in writing *One Touch of Venus*, a Broadway hit. He was born in Rye, New York, although an ancestor lent his name to Nashville, Tennessee.

J. D. McClatchey, editor of *The Yale Review*, has written five books of poetry, published two collections of essays and edited a number of books. McClatchy has also written four opera libretti. Among his honors, he has won the Witter Bynner Award for Poetry of the American Academy of Arts and Letters, and been awarded fellowships from the Guggenheim Foundation and the National Endowment for the Arts.

Gail Godwin graduated in 1959 from the University of North Carolina with a degree in journalism. That led to a job on the *Miami Herald*. At twenty-nine, she entered the graduate writing program at the University of Iowa, and her thesis became her first novel, *The Perfectionists.* Nine other novels followed, as well as two collections of stories. She and her longtime companion, the composer Robert Starer, have live since 1976 in Woodstock, New York. Together, they written ten musical works.

MaryOliver, author of ten books and three prose works, won the Pulitzer Prize for *American Primitive*, published in 1983. *New and Selected Poems*, published nine years later, was recognized with the National Book Award. Born in 1935 in Maple Heights, Ohio, she has also written *A Poetry Handbook*, now considered a classic guide to the poet's art, and *Blue Pastures*, a book of essays. Her many honors and awards include fellowships from the Guggenheim Foundation and the National Endowment for the Arts.

Marie Ridder has spent much of her life moving among the worlds of journalism, government, and environmental activism. Her newspaper affiliations have included the *Philadeliphia Evening Bulletin*, the *Boston Globe*, the *Washington Post* and the *Philadelphia Inqirer*. Her late husband, Walter, was a columnist, correspondent, and Washington bureau chief for the Ridder papers and later Knight Ridder chain.

Susan Eisenhower is president of the Eisenhower Institute, a nonprofit policy forum with a mandate to provide timely analysis of a range of domestic and foreign policy issues. She is herself a Russian expert, who wrote widely on the Soviet Union before its collapse. Her book titles also include an account of her grandmother, *Mrs. Ike: Memories and Reflections on the Life of Mamie Eisenhower.*

Stanley Kunitz was named United States poet laureate in 2000. A founder of the Fine Arts Work Center in Provincetown, Massachusetts, and Poets House in New York City, Kunitz is also chancellor emeritus of the Academy of American Poets. Among his many other honors, he has won the Pulitzer Prize and the National Book Award.

Mary Lynn Kotz is the author of *Upstairs at the White House*, a best-selling social history of the executive mansion from 1941 until 1969; *Marvella: A Personal Journey;* and *Rauschenberg/Art and Life.* In collaboration with her journalist husband, Nick Kotz, she wrote *A Passion for Equality: George Wiley and the Movement* and has contributed to a long list of publications such as *ARTnews*, *Vogue* and *Museum and Arts Washington*. A lecturer, she has taught writing and journalism at the University of Iowa, the University of North Carolina and the University of Mississippi.

Michael Collier, the Poet Laureate of Maryland, was born in Phoenix, Arizona, May 25, 1953. He is associate professor of English at the University of Maryland, College Park, and director of the Breadloaf Writers' Conference. He is the author of *The Clasp and Other Poems* (1986), *The Folded Heart* (1989), and *The Neighbor* (1995). He is also the editor of *The Wesleyan Tradition: Four Decades of American Poetry (1993).*

Jim Lehrer, a onetime Marine infantry officer, is best known to millions of Americans as the host of *The NewsHour with Jim Lehrer* on PBS and as the evenhanded moderator of presidential debates. In 1972, after spending a decade on Dallas newspapers and a stint as the host of a local experimental news program on public television, he headed for Washington to begin his PBS career. He has also found time to write 13 novels, two memoirs and three plays. He is married to the novelist Kate Lehrer.

Carlos Fuentes, son of a Mexican diplomat, has made his mark both as a Mexican public servant—he was ambassador to France in the mid 1970s—and as an acclaimed man of letters. During a career marked by many accolades, Fuentes has won among numerous other awards the prestigious Miguel Cervantes Prize, the highest honor available for a Spanish language writer. The author of more than a dozen books, Fuentes has won international acclaim for such titles as *A Change of Skin*, *The Hydra Head*, and *The Old Gringo*—a novel based on Ambrose Bierce's presumed death during the Mexican Revolution.

Rudyard Kipling was born in 1865 in Bombay, India, where servants raised him until he was sent to the United Services College in England. His education complete, Kipling returned to India at seventeen and began working for the *Civil and Military Gazette*. Later he wrote for the *Allahabad Pioneer*. His first important book, *Plain Tales from the Hills*, is comprised of the sketches, stories and poems that flowed from his pen as a newspaperman. *Plain Tales* was published in 1888, along with *Soldiers Three*. The following year Kipling returned to England where *The Light that Failed* was published in 1890. In 1892, he married Caroline Balestier, an American. The couple settled in Vermont, where they began a family. By 1896, they had returned to England, with Kipling on the threshold of his most productive years. *Kim* was published in 1901. The family finally settled in Sussex, the setting for *Puck of Pook's Hill*, published in 1906. In 1907, Kipling became the first Englishman to win the Nobel Prize for Literature. He died in 1936 and was buried in Westminster Abbey.

Roald Dahl , born in Wales in 1916, worked in East Africa for the Shell Company and then joined the RAF in 1939 in Nairobi. Soon thereafter he was badly hurt when his plane crashed in the Libyan desert. After a lengthy recuperation, he resumed flying in Greece and compiled a distinguished war record before a flareup of his old injuries grounded him. He then was assigned to Washington as assistant air attaché where he began his writing career with stories about his RAF adventures.

Kuki Gallmann developed a childhood fascination with Africa. Born near Venice and trained in political science at the University of Padua, Gallmann settled in Kenya in 1972 with her husband and son. She lost both there—her husband losing his life in a car crash and the son dying at seventeen from an attack by a puff adder. She founded The Gallmann Memorial Foundation in their memory and has devoted it to the cause of conservation.

Tom Wolfe, a former reporter for *The Washington Post* and the *New York Herald Tribune*, has produced a series of penetrating portraits of America over the course of writing more than a dozen books, both fiction and nonfiction. He made a flamboyant publishing debut in 1965 with a collection of pieces about that decade entitled, *The Kandy-Kolored Tangerine-Flake Streamline Baby*. It was a pioneering venture in the new journalism movement, which adapted the techniques of fiction to nonfiction storytelling. Three years later, he published *The Pump House Gang*, made up of more articles about the sixties, and *The Electric Kool-Aid Acid Test*, a nonfiction story of the hippie era. Other literary accomplishments followed, including the publication in 1979 of *The Right Stuff*, a best-selling and award-winning study of the American space program. His 1987 best-seller, *The Bonfire of the Vanities*, described the money greed that gripped New York during the Reagan era. His two most recent books are *A Man in Full* and *Hooking Up*.

Ira Berkow has been a sports columnist and feature writer for *The New York Times* since 1981. In 2001 he shared the Pulitzer Prize for National Reporting. He is the author of more than a dozen books, including, most recently, a collection of his *Times* pieces, *The Minority Quarterback, and Other Lives in Sports*. The column on Hank Aaron was written when Mr. Berkow was with the Newspaper Enterprise Association.

Ambrose Bierce disappeared in 1914 during the Mexican Revolution, bringing to an end a career as a newspaper columnist, satirist, essayist, short-story writer and novelist. Born in

Ohio in 1842, Bierce fought in the Civil War as a Union officer, sustaining a wound at Kene-saw Mountain. After the war, he settled in San Francisco where he began his writing career.

Finlay Lewis, a veteran political reporter and White House correspondent for the Copley News Service, is author of *Mondale: Portrait of an American Politician.*

Karen Heuler's stories have appeared in *Prize Stories 1998: The O. Henry Awards, Tri-Quarterly, Alaska Quarterly Review, Ms.* magazine and many other publications. The University of Missouri published her first collection of short stories, *The Other Door* in 1995. She lives in New York with her dog, Booker Prize, and the cats, Nobel and Pulitzer.

D. H. Lawrence (1885–1930) was the son of a coal miner and teacher-poet. After his university studies, Lawrence began a turbulent and nomadic life as a writer profoundly at odds with the social norms of his place and time. His major works include *The Rainbow* and *Women in Love* and, of course, his final novel, *Lady Chatterley's Lover.*

John Steinbeck, (1902–1968), a Nobel laureate, is the author of *The Grapes of Wrath* and numerous other works written during an illustrious career that ended with his death in 1968. Steinbeck's story, "The Snake," was published in *The Long Valley* in 1938.

Rose Styron has published three volumes of poetry (*From Summer to Summer*—Viking, 1965; *Thieves' Afternoon*—Viking, 1973; *By Vineyard Light*—Rizzoli, 1995) and collaborated in translations from Russian (*Modern Russian Poetry*—Viking, 1972). Her work has appeared in numerous periodicals (*Harper's*, the *Yale Review*, the *American Scholar*, etc.) and anthologies, the most recent entitled *A Map of Hope* (Rutgers University Press, 1999). She has contributed articles to such publications as the *New York Review of Books, The Nation, The American Poetry Review, The New Republic, MS, Vogue* and *The Paris Review.* A board member of the Academy of American Poets, Rose Styron lives with her novel-ist-husband, William Styron, in Roxbury, Connecticut and Martha's Vineyard.

Winston Groom served as an officer in the Fourth Infantry Division in Vietnam in 1966–67 after graduating from the University of Alabama. Following a stint at the *Washington Star*, Groom moved to New York and drew on his Vietnam experiences in his first novel, *Better Times than These.* In 1984, Groom and Duncan Spencer coauthored *Conversations with the Enemy*, a nonfiction work that garnered a Pulitzer Prize nomination. Returning to Alabama in 1986, Groom gave literary birth to a memorable character when he completed his novel *Forrest Gump.* In 1994, the book was made into an enor-mously successful film starring Tom Hanks who won an Oscar for best actor.

Dave Barry has been at *The Miami Herald* since 1983. His humor column appears in more than 500 newspapers in the United States and abroad. He won the Pulitzer Prize for commentary in 1988, and has written two novels, and long list of nonfiction books, including *Dave Barry Hits Below the Beltway* and *Dave Barry Is Not Taking This Sitting Down.*

Thomas Caplan is the author of three novels; *Line of Chance, Parallelogram* and *Grace and Favor.* His fourth novel will be published next year.

Ovid (43 BC–AD 17) was a Roman poet whose reputation lives on in part for his *Ars Amatoria* (Art of Love) and *Metamorphoses.* His early poems dealt with themes of love, and one of them, a meditation on seduction and intrigue, placed Ovid at odds with the emperor Augustus and his program of moral reform. Years later, he was arraigned on charges of high treason. While authorities used the poem against him, the real case against Ovid remains veiled in mystery. He died in exile.

Sophia van Matre is credited with the authorship of the essay on "The Serpent in Mythology," which was published in the November 1865 issue of *The Ladies Repository.*

Nicholas Christopher is the author of seven volumes of poetry, four novels and a nonfiction book. He is the recipient of numerous awards and fellowships, most recently from the Guggenheim Foundation, the Academy of American Poets, the Poetry Society of America, and the National Endowment for the Arts and is a professor and member of the permanent faculty of the graduate Writing Division of the School of the Arts at Columbia University.

Zora Neale Hurston died in penniless obscurity in 1960—and her seven books were out of print—but she has subsequently gained recognition as a major writer and a pioneer of African-American ethnography. Born in 1891, Hurston studied anthropology at Howard University and, as a writer, devoted herself to preserving the black folk heritage. In 1936, she published *Their Eyes Were Watching God*, a work that is generally considered her masterpiece. Six years later, she wrote an autobiography, *Dust Tracks on a Road.*

Mark Twain (1835–1910) grew up in Hannibal, Missouri., on the west bank of the Mississippi with the name Samuel Langhorne Clemens. His adventures as a river pilot inspired his nom de plume—"Mark Twain" being a riverman's call in taking soundings on a steamship. His childhood memories of the river inspired his best remembered works, especially the classic *The Adventures of Huckleberry Finn.*

Chuck Goldstone began his career in radio as a disk jockey in Pittsburgh and now provides commentary for Public Radio International's "Marketplace" program. His company, "!deaworks," specializes in advising companies on how to improve their corporate communications. His latest work, This Book is Not a Toy, will be published by St. Martin's Press.

Jim Corbett (1875–1955) was an ardent conservationist as well as famous big game hunter who made his name killing nearly a dozen man-eating tigers and leapards in the jungles of India, where he lived most of his life. Corbett stalked and killed these animals not for sport but because they had taken the lives of about 1,500 Indians over about a thirty year period beginning in 1907. His book, *The Man-Eaters of Kumaon*, became an almost instant international best seller after it was published in 1946. *My India*, published in 1952, describes his years living and working among the Indians. It is dedicated to "My Friends—The poor of India."

Willee Lewis has taught high school English in Chicago and Minneapolis and at the Washington International School in Washington, D.C., where she has lived since 1972.

Acknowledgments

There are fifty contributors in this collection, and I am indebted to the 33 thirty-three writers and seventeen poets for their creativity. Their stories and verses are obviously the essential ingredient. From the beginning, George Plimpton was a constant source of encouragement. Without his incomparable skills as a storyteller, there would be no book. George's amusing account of his faux cobra bite planted the idea for this anthology.

Nobody was more enthusiastic than the late Willie Morris, and his support convinced me I was on the right track. His premature death denied American literature the future fruits of his creative muse. It also deprived readers of this volume of an original Willie Morris story, but I hope the inclusion of a segment from his book, *My Dog Skip*, will help to fill that void.

But there is more to preparing a book than just having a good idea. It took the patience, experience, and judgment of my agent, Timothy Seldes, to bring my project to fruition. Timothy guided me to my publisher, M. Evans and Co., where the manuscript found its way into the skillful hands of the late George de Kay. As a rookie in the world of publishing, I am grateful for their sympathetic guidance, great goodwill and agreeable attitudes.

One of the most rewarding results of this project was the opportunity to enlist the creative talents of my childhood friend, Paul Bruner. A graphic artist and professor at Rutgers, Paul responded with insights, information and illustrations, producing a series of brilliant snake drawings. In addition Robin Hill and Edith Kuhnle, both talented artists, generously contributed sketches that complement the book's themes.

Susan Eisenhower offered advice, reassurance and subtle prodding from the outset. Susan Kinsolving was a faithful consultant, lending her wisdom and familiarity with the world of poets. Berta Ledecky, Luciano Rebay, George Herrick and Brooks Rogers helped me immensely by pointing to literary works that I might have otherwise overlooked.

A host of friends also offered suggestions. On that and so many other scores, I am indebted to LaSalle Lefall, Susan Shreve, Molly Ivins, Mary Rooney, and Kay Kendell. In addition, Michael Beschloss, Madzy Beveridge, Jack Bray, Ann Brown, Prudence Squire, Stewart Blue, Susan Rappaport, Myra Moffett, Strobe Talbott, John Harbert, VV Harrison, Elizabeth Pedersen, Jane Hughes, John Kuhnle, Nicki Sant, Mary Weinmann, Christopher Buckley, Joanna Sturm, Jim Conaway, Janice Delaney, Lou Stovall, Lolo Sarnoff, Virginia Bruner, Carol Butler, John Peterson, Faith Lewis, Ellie Trowbridge, Kathy Stephen, Amy Tan, Bill Dunlap, Baba Groom, Neil Folger, Nick Folger, Wendy Gimball, Tricia Saul, Sherrye Henry, and Melody Crawford.

Finally, I want to acknowledge my supportive family in Indiana (who know me as Wilda Eskew), and to thank my son, Finlay Ingersoll Lewis, for his constructive criticism. Moreover, there is no way to measure the help and humor, direction and devotion of my husband, Finlay.